Chaise 1

Language and Solitude

Wittgenstein, Malinowski and the Habsburg Dilemma

Ernest Gellner (1925–1995) has been described as 'one of the last great Central European polymath intellectuals. His last book throws new light on two of the most written-about thinkers of their time, Wittgenstein and Malinowski. Wittgenstein, arguably the most influential and the most cited philosopher of the twentieth century, is famous for having propounded two radically different philosophical positions. Malinowski was the founder of modern British social anthropology and is usually credited with being the inventor of ethnographic fieldwork, a fundamental research method throughout the social sciences. This book shows, in a highly original way, how the thought of both men, and both of Wittgenstein's two philosophies, grew from a common background of assumptions – widely shared in the Habsburg Empire of their youth – about human nature, society and language. It is also a swingeing critique of Wittgenstein, and implicitly therefore of conventional philosophy as well, for failing to be aware of these assumptions. Tying together themes which preoccupied him throughout his working life, Gellner's final word epitomises his belief that philosophy – far from 'leaving everything as it is' – is about important historical, social and personal issues.

ERNEST GELLNER was born in Paris in 1925, raised in Prague, and came to England from Czechoslovakia in 1939. He studied at Balliol College, Oxford, and taught philosophy in Edinburgh, before joining the Sociology Department of the London School of Economics and Political Science in 1949. He was Professor of Philosophy with special reference to Sociology from 1962 to 1984, when he became William Wyse Professor of Social Anthropology in Cambridge. After retirement from the University of Cambridge, he joined the Central European University in Prague where he established and headed a Centre for the Study of Nationalism. He died in 1995. He was the author of many books, including *Words and Things* (1959), *Thought and Change* (1964), *Saints of the Atlas* (1969), *Muslim Society* (1981), *Nations and Nationalism* (1983), *The Psychoanalytical Movement* (1985), *Plough, Sword and Book* (1988), *Postmodernism, Reason and Religion* (1992), *Conditions of Liberty* (1994), and *Nationalism* (1997).

Ernest Gellner, 1925–1995

Language and Solitude

*Wittgenstein, Malinowski and
the Habsburg Dilemma*

Ernest Gellner

CAMBRIDGE
UNIVERSITY PRESS

PUBLISHED BY THE PRESS SYNDICATE OF THE UNIVERSITY OF CAMBRIDGE
The Pitt Building, Trumpington Street, Cambridge CB2 1RP, United Kingdom

CAMBRIDGE UNIVERSITY PRESS
The Edinburgh Building, Cambridge, CB2 2RU, United Kingdom
http://www.cup.cam.ac.uk
40 West 20th Street, New York, NY 10011–4211, USA
http://www.cup.org
10 Stamford Road, Oakleigh, Melbourne 3166, Australia

First published 1998

Printed in the United Kingdom at the University Press, Cambridge

Typeset in Plantin 10/12 pt [CE]

A catalogue record for this book is available from the British Library

Library of Congress Cataloguing in Publication data

Gellner, Ernest.
Language and solitude: Wittgenstein, Malinowski, and the
Habsburg dilemma / Ernest Gellner.
    p. cm.
Includes bibliographical references.
ISBN 0 521 63002 9 (hardback). – ISBN 0 521 63997 2 (pbk.)
1. Wittgenstein, Ludwig, 1889–1951.
2. Malinowski, Bornislaw, 1884–1942.
3. Austria – Intellectual life – 20th century.   I. Title.
B3376.W564G44   1998
192 – dc21   97–50568   CIP

ISBN 0 521 63002 9 hardback
ISBN 0 521 63997 2 paperback

Contents

Preface David N. Gellner   *page* vii
Foreword Steven Lukes   xiii

Part I: The Habsburg dilemma   1

1 Swing alone or swing together   3

2 The rivals   7

3 Genesis of the individualist vision   14

4 The metaphysics of romanticism   17

5 Romanticism and the basis of nationalism   21

6 Individualism and holism in society   26

7 Crisis in Kakania   30

8 Pariah liberalism   35

9 Recapitulation   37

Part II: Wittgenstein   41

10 The loneliness of the long-distance empiricist   43

11 The poem to solitude, or: confessions of a transcendental
    ego who is also a Viennese Jew   46

12 Ego and language   59

13 The world as solitary vice   62

14 The mystical   65

15 The central proposition of the *Tractatus*: world without
    culture   68

16 Wittgenstein mark 2   71

17   *Tertium non datur*   74

18   Joint escape   79

19   Janik and Toulmin: a critique   85

20   The case of the disappearing self   96

21   Pariah communalism   100

22   Iron cage Kafka-style   107

Part III: Malinowski   **111**

23   The birth of modern social anthropology   113

24   The Malinowskian revolution   120

25   How did Malinowski get there?   123

26   Whither anthropology? Or: whither Bronislaw?   127

27   The difference between Cracow and Vienna   138

28   Malinowski's achievement and politics   140

29   Malinowski's theory of language   145

30   Malinowski's later mistake   151

31   The (un)originality of Malinowski and Wittgenstein   155

Part IV: Influences   **157**

32   The impact and diffusion of Wittgenstein's ideas   159

33   The first wave of Wittgenstein's influence   164

34   A belated convergence of philosophy and anthropology   174

Part V: Conclusions   **179**

35   The truth of the matter   181

36   Our present condition   189

General bibliography   192
Bibliographies of Ernest Gellner's writings on Wittgenstein,
   Malinowski, and nationalism   195
Index   205

Preface

My father left two unpublished book-length manuscripts when, on 5 November 1995, he died in his flat at the Central European University, Prague. One manuscript required relatively little work and was published by Weidenfeld in 1997 as *Nationalism*. This is the other.

This book is in many ways a fitting – almost autobiographical – last work. In the first place, it brings together themes that he worked on throughout his academic career, from *Words and Things*, the attack on Wittgensteinianism that made his name in 1959, through *Nations and Nationalism* (1983) and *Nationalism* (1997), to studies of the development of his adopted discipline, social anthropology, and in particular the canonical place of Bronislaw Malinowski within it (published in various articles over the years). But in the second place, the Habsburg social background to the thought of Wittgenstein and Malinowski that he describes here was also his own background, or, strictly, that of his father. The choice that faced Wittgenstein and Malinowski was also the choice that faced every member of his family. On both sides my father was descended from secularised, German-speaking Jews, as was common in Bohemia, though less so further east in Poland. His grandfather was a loyal subject of Franz Josef who had nine children. The men became lawyers, doctors, even, in one case, a theatre director. One of his aunts was an active Zionist. His father, Rudolf, went to Berlin to study history and sociology the year after Max Weber died. Later he studied in Paris and made some money by writing for German newspapers. The birth of my father meant that his parents had to have a more regular income, so his father gave up being a student and returned to Bohemia. They endured real poverty, with Rudolf selling his books so they could eat. Eventually he began a small business and also started a Czech-language law review. Rudolf had had to learn Czech as an adult, after the creation of the Czechoslovak state, but his sympathies were with it rather than with Zionism.

As the 1930s progressed, the threat from the Nazis became clear and Rudolf prepared the family's flight to England, where one of his sisters was married to an Englishman. No one knew when or if the final catastrophe would occur, so it was only in 1939, after the Germans had invaded Czechoslovakia, that they escaped. Since adult males were not allowed to travel through Germany, my father, then thirteen, together with his younger sister and his mother, set off by train across Germany. Rudolf and a close friend, who was later to become his business partner, attempted to cross illegally into Poland. Twice they were turned back, but the third time they were successful. In Warsaw, by good fortune, they met some old contacts of Rudolf from Siberia where he had spent some years as a prisoner of war during and after the First World War, contacts now in the Communist Party. They succeeded in getting the all-important visas for Rudolf and his friend to proceed to Sweden and then on to London. In England my father's family lived first in Highgate and then moved out to St Albans. It was from St Albans County Grammar School for Boys that he won a scholarship to Balliol. He studied for one year before leaving to join the Czech Brigade and spent much of the war besieging Dunkirk. The Brigade went first to Plzen and then to Prague for victory parades. Apparently he was captured on film driving his half-track through Plzen, though he never saw the film himself. In Prague my father demobilized and attended lectures at Charles University. He was cured of his nostalgia for the city of his youth (in England he used frequently to dream about it) by the realization that the Communists were going to take over. This must have seemed likely to his family in England also, since they were worried he would be trapped there a second time. He returned to Balliol to finish his degree after a few months.

The atmosphere in the Oxford of the time is described below in sections 32 and 33. He found the local orthodoxy, which was inspired by Wittgenstein's later philosophy, complacent and trivialising. But so many people took Oxford linguistic philosophy completely seriously that, though he was always convinced that it was wrong, it was a long time before he felt able to tackle it head on. After two years teaching philosophy at Edinburgh University he moved to a lectureship teaching philosophy in the sociology department at the LSE. He published four conventional philosophy articles in 1951 in order to get tenure, but then published nothing for four years. He spent his vacations climbing or skiing in the Alps. The LSE at the time was a dynamic and stimulating place, with Popper dominating the philosophy department, Oakeshott politics, and the disciples of Malinowski in anthropology. On his own account, it was after he began to study anthropology seriously, and had decided to take a PhD in anthropology, that he found himself able to articulate his critique of Oxford linguistic philosophy. Victor Gollancz approached him after hearing him speak on linguistic philosophy on Radio 3 and the result was *Words and Things*. When it came out in 1959 it became a *cause célèbre* because Gilbert Ryle refused to review it in *Mind*, the leading philosophy journal which had published my father's first article. Bertrand Russell, who had contributed the foreward to *Words and Things*, wrote to *The Times* and, over the next eighteen days, there followed a whole series of letters about the propriety of Ryle's action, culminating in a leader article. The description of these events by Ved Mehta, *The Fly in the Fly Bottle* (1962), infuriated my father with its facile attribution to him of things he never said.

Clearly, then, the ideas of both Wittgensteins, the 'early' Wittgenstein of the *Tractatus Logico-Philosophicus* and the 'late' Wittgenstein of *Philosophical Investigations* and other posthumously published works, as well as the ideas of Malinowski, were central concerns of my father for most of his adult life. When he was invited to an Italian conference on 'levels of reality' in the early 1980s he produced a paper entitled 'Tractatus Sociologico-Philosophicus' which attempted to outline his fundamental position in terms of a commentary on seven gnomic propositions on the model of the *Tractatus* (Gellner 1987*g*, ch. 11; for references to my father's works see the special bibliographies below). Psychologically, it was the discovery of the 'school' of social anthropology created by Malinowski at the LSE that enabled him to produce his first critique of Wittgenstein in *Words and Things*. As with Wittgenstein, he never met Malinowski himself; but in both cases, he had prolonged exposure to their closest disciples.

Like both Wittgenstein and Malinowski, my father left Central Europe and had to make his way in England. Of course, he was younger when he came, and it was a generation later. Wittgenstein he always thought of as a brilliant curiosity, but in no way as great a philosopher as Karl Popper. Likewise, he makes it clear here that he believed Malinowski to have been far more original than Wittgenstein in the way he dealt with the Habsburg intellectual inheritance. He seems to have identified with Malinowski particularly in his attitude to nationalism, since he advocates, as the only humane way to deal with multi-ethnic situations of conflict, exactly Malinowski's combination of cultural freedom and decentralisation, on the one hand, with political centralisation, on the other (see section 28 below and *Nationalism*, section 16).

It is evident that in 1950s and 60s the theme of the present book – the roots of both Wittgenstein's and Malinowski's thought in the social and ideological conditions of the late Habsburg Empire – had not yet occurred to my father. He reviewed the Malinowski Festschrift edited by Raymond Firth very favourably without mentioning Wittgenstein

(Gellner 1958*h*), even though Firth, in his contribution on language, had already raised the possibility of a connection between the two (Firth 1957: 94). In the 1960s my father also briefly compared the two thinkers – very much to Malinowski's advantage – while reviewing A. R. Louch's *Explanation and Human Action* (Oxford, 1966), without considering their common Habsburg background. When *Words and Things* was reissued in 1979 the new introduction was sub-titled 'Wittgenstein-ianism Reconsidered in Historical Context'; its arguments prefigured much of the analysis given here, but there was as yet no mention of Malinowski or of the Habsburg Empire. It is my guess that it was at the centennial conference of Malinowski's birth, held in 1984 in Cracow, that the seeds of the present book were sown. By the time of his interview with John Davis (*Current Anthropology* 32 (1991): 69–70; Gellner 1991*a*) the argument was already clear to him (cf. Gellner 1991*d*, 1992*c*: 116–23). Furthermore, since his thought had consider-able unity, it is not surprising that certain parts of this book are prefigured elsewhere: for instance, the arguments on Hume and Kant in section 12 will be familiar to readers of *Legitimation of Belief* (1975*a*) and *Reason and Culture* (1992*e*), and much of the material on Frazer and Malinowski builds on or repeats arguments made in his essay 'Zeno of Cracow' (Gellner 1987*h*) and in *Politics and Anthropology: Revolutions in the Sacred Grove* (1995*x*). The arguments about nationalism are made at greater length in *Nations and Nationalism* (1983*e*), in an essay published in G. Balakrishnan (ed.), *Mapping the Nation* (Gellner 1996*i*), and in *Nationalism* (1997). They were also tried out in numerous other places, since nationalism was the topic about which he was most often asked to speak in the 1990s (see bibliography on nationalism below).

In short, *Language and Solitude* is a synthesis of several themes that concerned my father all his adult life: the thought of Wittgenstein, the history and theory of social anthropology, the causes of nationalism, the nature of modernity, and the social roots of rationality and irrationalism.

Since this book attempts to identify the social context of ideas, it is worth remarking that my father's approach was far from determinist. Although he clearly believed that Wittgenstein's development could not be understood without taking into account the 'Habsburg dilemma' which Wittgenstein himself was not consciously aware of, the substance of my father's critique of Janik and Toulmin is that they go too far in attempting to derive the *details* of Wittgenstein's philosophical ideas from the local context. In other words, my father allowed considerable scope for the power of ideas to work themselves out independently. One can contrast the procedure of Clifford Geertz who, being concerned only with Malinowski's text, draws attention to the constant juxtaposition of 'High Romance and High Science' in Malinowski's writing (Geertz 1988: 79) without any attempt to explain either the origins or the originality of his characteristic and unique combination of romanticism and positivism.

Another 'health warning' may be in order for those who are not familiar with my father's style of writing (he was both amused and pleased to have been included in an American collection supposed to illustrate fine essay writing). One should not be misled by his frequent metaphorical usages. I am reliably informed that Carpathian villages do not actually have 'village greens'; that should not detract from the point being made by his references to worshippers of it or them.

As noted, my father had been working on and revising this book for some years. The manuscript in its latest version was scattered with notes to himself, such as 'END OF PASSAGE PROBABLY DUE FOR EXCISION', 'WHAT FOLLOWS REDUPLICATES EARLIER PASSAGES BUT SOME BITS MAY NEED TO BE RETAINED' or 'QUOTATION FROM MACH TO FOLLOW.' In other words, he had yet to work through the entire book and revise it in the light of repetitions. I have adopted a fairly conservative policy, cutting out and rearranging as little as possible, but readers should be aware that it is not in the form that he would have given it and is certainly more repetitious than it would have been had he lived. I am responsible for adding the sub-title and the division into five parts. I have made numerous small stylistic changes that I certainly would have suggested to him anyway if given the chance (he always insisted, no doubt in deference to some distant lesson at the Prague English Grammar School, that 'a number of' should be followed by a singular verb; alas I have had the last word on this). I have tried to check all quotations and I have systematized the references, adding some relevant works to the bibliography that were in his library but are not quoted or mentioned. In the case of the quotation from Mach I had to select it as well. Most importantly, I have moved and amalgamated material as follows:

1 Section 12, 'Ego and language', was composed separately and has been slotted in by me;
2 What is now section 3, 'Genesis of the individualist vision', was originally section 5, coming after 'Romanticism and the basis of nationalism';
3 The last two paragraphs of section 9 originally appeared at the end of section 5;
4 What is now section 32, 'The impact and diffusion of Wittgenstein's ideas', originally appeared immediately after section 17;
5 There was a section called 'Populism to philistinism' appearing immediately after 'The impact and diffusion . . . ' which has been

absorbed into section 33, 'The first wave of Wittgenstein's influence';

6 Sections 15 and 20 have absorbed what were originally separate following sections;

7 The final section, 'Our present condition', seems to have originally had the title 'The truth of the matter II'.

Should anyone wish to make a scholarly study of the draft as it was, they should write to me at the Department of Human Sciences, Brunel University, Uxbridge, Middlesex UB8 3PH.

The painting that appears on the cover is by an unknown Russian artist, called Ella, who gave it to my parents in 1989. When he began writing this book my father always intended that it should be on the cover. Unfortunately all attempts to trace the artist or to discover her surname have failed.

Special thanks are due to Gay Woolven who spent many years trying valiantly to bring some order into my father's affairs and who typed and retyped versions of the manuscript over several years, digging out the final version after my father's death. John Hall, Ian Jarvie, and Chris Hann read through an earlier draft and made detailed suggestions for improvement, as did my mother, Susan Gellner, and my wife, Lola Martinez. Ian Jarvie provided the bibliographies and Steven Lukes kindly agreed to write a foreword. For all this help and moral support, I am deeply grateful.

DAVID N. GELLNER

Foreword

David Gellner is right to describe this exhilarating book as a synthesis of several themes that concerned Ernest Gellner all his adult life: 'the thought of Wittgenstein, the history and theory of social anthropology, the causes of nationalism, the nature of modernity, and the social roots of rationality and irrationalism'. Exhilarating and unclassifiable: at once a synoptic interpretation of the thought of Wittgenstein and Malinowski; a comparative assessment of their world-views – of their accounts of knowledge, language and culture; a brilliant sociological sketch of the common socio-political and intellectual background which they shared; a view of their influence upon their respective disciplines; and a passionate and polemical argument with them and some of their successors, in which Gellner once more and for the last time eloquently and succinctly expresses his own world-view. He expresses it here, with all his characteristic verve, by engaging directly with what he takes to be the egregious and wholly pernicious errors of Wittgenstein, early and late, in the light of what he sees as Malinowski's liberating but only partially developed (and partially retracted) insights into the interrelated themes that have together been central to his own life's work.

It is, moreover, a genuine effort at synthesis: a bringing together of purely philosophical theories, about the nature of reality, knowledge and language; contending accounts of what he calls 'socio-metaphysic, or philosophical anthropology'; and alternative political standpoints seen as expressing alternative responses to a common historically-given predicament. The essence of his argument can be briefly stated. These various elements are 'aligned' with one another, forming 'two poles of looking, not merely at knowledge, but at human life' and 'the tension between them is one of the deepest and most pervasive themes in modern thought'. The 'two poles' are given a variety of labels. One is the 'atomic-universalist-individualist vision', beginning with Descartes and Robinson Crusoe, typified by Hume and Kant, and reformulated by Ernst Mach and Bertrand Russell. It is variously identified with empiricism, rationalism and positivism, and with *Gesellschaft*, with economic markets and political liberalism, and bloodless cosmopolitanism. The other is the 'communal-cultural vision', the organic counter-picture, first lived and practised unreflectively, then articulated by Herder and by countless 'romantic organicists', 'nationalist populists' and 'romantic rightists', stressing totality, system, connectedness, particularism, cultural specificity, favouring *Gemeinschaft*, roots, 'closed, cosy' communities, *Blut und Boden*. The 'alignment' of the elements within these poles and the tension between them was especially strong in the Habsburg lands, not least Poland and Austria, as the Empire reached its end, where 'the confrontation of atomists and organicists . . . meshes in with the alliances and hatreds of daily and political life'.

Wittgenstein, trapped within this polar opposition, veered from one philosophical system to another, expressing in extreme form first the one and then the other of these polar alternatives. Malinowski, by contrast, recombined elements from both – romantic and positivist, organic and liberal – thereby prefiguring and expressing a version of Gellner's own position. This is that a 'third option' is available which combines the recognition that 'shared culture can alone endow life with order and meaning' with understanding that 'the notion of a culture-transcending truth' is inseparable from cognitive (notably scientific) and economic growth, that it is central to our culture and indeed that 'the possibility of transcendence of cultural limits' constitutes 'the most important single fact about human life'.

Clearly, Gellner's argument, as presented here, relies upon his construction of the two poles. The text begins with the dramatic claim that there are 'two fundamental theories of knowledge,' standing in 'stark contrast to each other,' which are 'aligned' with 'related, and similarly contrasted, theories, of society, of man, of everything.' This 'chasm', he writes, 'cuts right across our total social landscape'. The confrontation is 'deep and general'. Yet we are very soon presented with a variety of telling examples of British thinkers whom it does not fit. In Britain, Gellner suggests, the confrontation between atomists and organicists 'cannot be tied in with, and reinforce, any political cleavages in the country.' On the other hand, it 'really came into its own within the Danubian Empire', with individualist liberals, often Jews, defending the idea of a pluralistic, tolerant, patchwork empire and nationalist intellectuals offering the alternative of 'a closed, localised culture, idiosyncratic and glorying in its idiosyncrasy, and promising emotional and aesthetic fulfilment and satisfaction to its members.' Generalising the point, he suggests that 'the opposition between individualism and communalism, between the appeal of *Gesellschaft* ("Society") and *Gemeinschaft* ("Community")' is a 'tension which pervades and torments most societies disrupted by modernisation'. In any case, it was, he claims, deeply embedded in the Central European world, from which he himself came, where it was 'closely linked to the hurly burly of daily political life and pervaded the sensibility of everyone'.

This claim suggests that there is a distinctly personal, even autobiographical aspect to the present work. Its argument proceeds, one might say, from exposition to exposure. Gellner first expounds by reporting on the apparent naturalness and self-evidence of the linkages between the components of these two great complexes of ideas and attitudes and of the tension or confrontation between them. He then exposes that naturalness and self-evidence as an illusion. The overarching dichotomy in question is a massive but historically contingent construction urgently in need of deconstruction. And he makes this argument through a multiply paradoxical interpretation of the thought of his two principal *dramatis personae*, which in turn provides a commentary upon his own intellectual choices.

Thus Wittgenstein, explicitly assuming these to be the only alternatives, first expressed 'the solitude of the transcendental ego,' by giving an account of 'what the world looks like to a solitary individual reflecting on the problem of how his mind, or language can possibly "mean", i.e. reflect the world'; and then offered a second philosophy, transplanting 'the populist idea of the authority of each distinctive culture to the problem of knowledge', concluding that 'mankind lives in cultural communities or, in his words, "forms of life," which are self-sustaining, self-legitimating, logically and normatively final'. Wittgenstein did this, Gellner argues, even though he was totally ahistorical and lacked 'any sense of the diversity of cultures, and indeed of the very existence of culture' and, moreover, was uninterested in social and political questions. In short, Gellner's Wittgenstein is a sort of unwitting transmitter of prevailing cultural assumptions, with a 'ferocious narrowness of interest', whose expression of 'the deep dilemma facing the Habsburg world' was all the more effective because 'it was never consciously thought out and never at the forefront of his attention', expressing those assumptions in successive, one-sided philosophies, the later of which retains enormous cultural influence.

Malinowski, on the other hand, was able to escape the tyranny of those assumptions, partly because they were less dominant in Cracow than in Vienna and because his life situation and temperament made him more inclined to 'doubts' and 'rational thought', but principally because he applied a biologically-based philosophy of science to cultural objects. Malinowski combined the radical empiricism he had learnt from Ernst Mach with a penchant for ethnographic fieldwork, which in Eastern Europe had a 'culture-loving and culture-preserving' significance inspired by populism and nationalism. In consequence he was able to develop a powerful new, scientific methodology within modern social anthropology, whose founder he became, combining an 'empiricist abstention from the invocation of unobservables' with 'a both functionalist and romantic sense of the unity and interdependence of culture'. At the same time, according to Gellner, while allowing that language could be 'use-bound and context-linked', he also allowed (though subsequently mistakenly denied) that in scientific and philosophical contexts, it properly strives to be context-free. He further reflected in a fruitful and original way upon the relation between cultural and political nationalism, exhibiting a 'remarkable freedom' from the latter. He argued, in a way that foreshadows Gellner's own position, that the only hope is to 'limit the political power of nations, but permit, indeed enhance and encourage, the perpetuation of all those local cultures within which men have found their fulfilment and their freedom', thus 'depriving boundaries of some of their importance and symbolic potency'. Thus in these several but allegedly related ways the social anthropologist Malinowski reflected critically upon assumptions that the philosopher Wittgenstein merely reproduced. Gellner's own intellectual career, which began with a sociological as well as philosophical critique of Wittgensteinian philosophy, went on, among other things, to explore the philosophical contribution of Malinowskian social anthropology.

This structure of argument, moving from the construction of an overarching dichotomy to its deconstruction, has several significant virtues. It gives a satisfying unity and direction, even drama, to the present work. It provides a challenging basis from which to interpret and compare the thought of Wittgenstein and Malinowski. And it raises the highly interesting issue of just what the relations are between the extremely various theories, doctrines and political positions gathered around the two supposedly opposite polar views of knowledge.

Yet here Gellner's readers will doubtless be provoked to ask a number of pertinent questions. First, just what are they to make of his arresting claim that 'the universalist-populist confrontation pervades Habsburg culture and consequently, for those who are immersed in it, it has the power of a compulsive logical truism'? How is this to be squared with his argument (against Peter Winch's cultural holism) that our world consists of 'unstable and, above all, overlapping cultural zones' with 'conflicts or options within them' and 'multiple competing oracles'? And why would the inhabitants of the Habsburg lands be so 'immersed' in their culture that the indicated polarity should be so inescapable and 'compulsive'? Why should that cultural zone – and, more generally, those of 'most societies disrupted by modernisation' where, on Gellner's theory, nationalism tends to flourish – be particularly inhospitable to the doubts and rational thought that would put it in question? David Gellner is right: Ernest Gellner was no social determinist in relation to ideas. Yet his argument seems here to require (at least in 'less blessed parts of the world' than Britain) a pervasive 'compulsion' that only a fortunate few can escape.

Moreover, the polar opposition in question is of course a massive reduction of complexity – a caricature of the history of ideas which, however, as a caricature, would succeed to the extent that its simplifications capture the essentials of what it simplifies. But here too several related questions arise. Max Weber once remarked that 'Individualism' embraces the utmost heterogeneity of meanings. It has been assigned innumerable origins and meanings and characterised from many different points of view, often hostile, ever since it was first identified by de Maistre in 1819 as a corrosive threat to social order and by Tocqueville in his *Democracy in America* as a new term to which a new idea has given birth, a turning away from public involvement that threatens what we now call civil society. Since then virtually every writer on the subject offers a different constellation, with a different purpose in view.

Gellner's version here is one such. The 'individualist', he writes, 'sees the polity as a contractual, functional convenience, a device of the participants in pursuit of mutual advantage' as opposed to the 'holist' who 'sees life as participation in a collectivity, which alone gives life its meaning'. Individualism is a tradition:

The Crusoe tradition, which begins with Descartes, finds its supreme expression in Hume and Kant, and is reformulated again in the second positivism and the neo-liberalism of recent times, offers the story of how a brave and independent individual builds up his world, cognitively, economically, and so forth.

But is this really a 'tradition' or does it only look that way through a seriously distorting lens (in this case, perhaps, that used by an archetypal Central European nationalist)? Does Defoe's fable really illustrate Cartesian doubt? Are Humean empiricism and Kantian rationalism really bedfellows, and is the anti-contractualist, custom-favouring historian Hume really an arch-individualist? Are there not innumerable elementary errors involved in this agglomeration, confusing, for instance, abstraction, reductionism and the search for universal laws? Epistemology, economics and political theory have complex links, but not of this simple kind. Liberals (whether neo- or not) have differed extraordinarily widely about economics and politics and can be rationalists or empiricists or positivists and much else besides. And from within this so-called tradition, there is unending disagreement and contestation about all these issues, and not least about what individualism is. And the same, of course, goes for the many versions and varieties of collectivism-communalism-communitarianism.

Of course, the first person to acknowledge this is Ernest Gellner, who writes, immediately following the passage just quoted, 'All this simply will not do either as an actual descriptive or as an explanatory account.' We 'have come to undestand our world a little better than when its nature was disputed by two parties'. But was there really such a time and place, rather than the construction or illusion of it? It is not clear why the illusion should only now be unmasked and why we needed to wait for Malinowski to see through it. If it simply will not do, then, of course, it never did. Which raises the interesting and important question of what account Gellner himself offers of how these ideas, doctrines and political positions properly fit together.

His position, well-known and often expressed, is a distinctive contribution to current debates embracing postmodernism and relativism, the so-called culture wars, post-positivist philosophy of science, and method in social and cultural anthropology. His case, as formulated here, is a defence of 'individualism' (or 'the Crusoe model') as an '*ethic of cognition*': a 'normative charter of how one particular tradition, namely our own, reconstructs and purges its own cognitive and productive worlds'. It maintains that 'all cognitive claims are subjected to scrutiny in the course of which they are broken up into their constituent parts and individuals are free to judge as individuals: there are no cognitive hierarchies or authorities'. It is thus atomistic, egalitarian and universalistic in that it is committed to the practice of criticism by reference to a 'notion of culture-transcending truth'. As he has put it elsewhere, one cognitive style, namely 'science and its application', is governed by 'certain loosely defined procedural prescriptions about how the world may be investigated': 'all ideas, data, inquirers are equal, cognitive claims have to compete and confront data on terms of equality and they are not allowed to construct circular self-confirming visions' (Gellner 1995x: 3, 6–7). This (broadly Popperian) account of the validation (though not the origination) of cognitive scientific claims marks out the ground that Gellner has, over the years, sought to defend against relativists, idealists, subjectivists, interpretivists, social constructionists and other exponents of 'local knowledge' – inheritors all, he believed, of the (late) Wittgensteinian error that this work, once more, aims to expose and uproot.

In what way can it be seen as carrying the debate further? In large part, it is, as I have suggested, a defence and restatement of Gellner's anti-relativist stance in respect of what he calls the new style of cognition constituted by science and technology that is central to our culture and has transformed our world. Here he argues that what he variously calls 'universalism-atomism' and 'individualism' 'probably gives us a correct answer to the question of how valid and powerful knowledge really works, and, in that sphere, deserves a kind of normative authority'. But what is the scope of that sphere? Is the understanding of our natural environment inherently unlike that of our social environment? And how and where is the distinction between natural and social to be drawn? In the last paragraphs of the book, he expresses a genuine and honest uncertainty concerning the reasons for science's limited success in the realm of social and human phenomena, and further uncertainty as to whether these limits are in principle surmountable or not. Furthermore, he writes of values as 'instilled by contingent and variable cultures'. And yet his intellectual heroes, notably Hume and Kant, and other thinkers of the Enlightenment, were universalists in respect of morality as well as knowledge. Is not the notion of culture-transcending moral principles also central to our culture, and do they not also deserve a kind of normative authority, and, if not, why not?

These are, of course, old, classical questions but they will not go away. Yet a further virtue of Ernest Gellner's last work is that it raises them once more in a new and unfailingly provocative way.

STEVEN LUKES

Part I

The Habsburg dilemma

1   Swing alone or swing together

There are two fundamental theories of knowledge. These two theories stand in stark contrast to each other. They are profoundly opposed. They represent two poles of looking, not merely at knowledge, but at human life. Aligned with these two polar views of knowledge, there are also related, and similarly contrasted, theories of society, of man, of everything. This chasm cuts right across our total social landscape.

In order to seize the gist of this deep and general confrontation, it is perhaps best to begin with knowledge. In this field the contrast is particularly stark and has a sharp profile.

There is, first of all, what one might call the individualistic/atomistic conception of knowledge. Knowledge, on this view, is something practised or achieved above all by *individuals alone:* if more than one person is involved, and collaboration takes place, this does not really modify the essence of the activity or of the achievement. In principle, the acquisition of knowledge is something open to Robinson Crusoe, and perhaps to him especially. It is our suggestibility and gullibility, especially in youth, perhaps our desire to please and conform, which above all leads us into error. We discover truth alone, we err in groups.

Crusoe's isolation saves him from following a multitude to commit folly. He is spared the worst temptation to err – conformism. Mutual aid may advance an inquiry, but it does not affect its character. Knowledge is a relationship between an individual and nature. Society, its hierarchy and its customs may sometimes be of help; but rather more often they constitute a hindrance. They stand in the way of objective, lucid perception. Above all, society never constitutes an authority or a vindication. If society itself, or some institution within it, makes such a claim, then that is a usurpation and one to be strenuously resisted. Society has no right to impose its authority either on inquiry or on its outcome. Neither its views nor its idiom is authoritative. Truth stands outside and above, it cannot be under social or political control. Legitimation of ideas by authority, by consensus, or the social creation of truth, is an abomination.

This vision is atomistic as well as individualistic. It not only makes the solitary individual a foreigner in his own world, separating him from it, requiring him to assert his independence; it also makes the part sovereign over the whole. The whole is made up of its parts and owes its existence and its characteristics to its parts. The bricks of knowledge – and on this view, knowledge must use bricks of a sort – are individual, isolable sensations or perceptions or ideas: granular entities of some sort, which accumulate so as to form large, and perhaps massive structures. These, however, for all their possible grandeur, are ultimately composed of cognitive atoms, and owe everything to them. Whatever truth may be affirmed about the larger totalities depends on the truth concerning the constituent elements.

The stuff of knowledge begins, as it were, in a disaggregated condition: aggregation or totality is achieved or constructed, but is not there at the start. It adds nothing, and the ultimate reality of which it is composed is, in the end, atomic. And even if this were not a true account of the sequence of events in time, of the actual progression to discovery, and if, in the beginning, there were some initially unsegregated totality – even then, the validity or otherwise of claims concerning it could only be established by disaggregating it, and considering the merits of affirmations about its constituents. Men are atoms, but the material they use is also atomic. In the beginning there were the constituent atoms. Their aggregation is indeed but a summation, which adds nothing to that which is being assembled.

Separation, segregation, analysis, and independence are at the heart of this approach. Everything that is separable ought to be separated, at least in thought, if not in reality. Indissoluble, inherent linkages are to be avoided. Alliances and alignments, like those occurring in a free society (of which this vision is both a model and a support and an echo), are contingent and freely chosen: they are not prescribed, obligatory, or rigid. Ideas behave like individualist men: not born into estates or castes, they combine freely and as freely dissolve their associations. Likewise, ideas make free contracts and form free associations among each other, rather than being suborned by status imposed on them from above, by some theory more authoritative than they are themselves.

The main device for achieving innovation and discovery is the recombination of elements: in order to have a keen eye for the possibility of new combinations, one must first of all not be overly wedded to and overawed by their habitual associations. Neither man nor facts nor ideas are allowed to act in restraint of trade, by combining into guilds and improving their own terms through monopoly. The freedom of association applies to ideas as it does to men: no castes or estates are allowed or imposed, for us or for our ideas.

The movement in psychology and in the philosophy of mind known as Associationism might just as well have been called *Dis*sociationism: it did indeed make a big fuss of the way in which the *a*ssociation of ideas lay at the base of our construction of our world. But it could do this precisely because it began with an acute sense of the *dis*sociability of all elements. It was just because the world had been atomised into the smallest elements that could be found or imagined, that our environment could thereafter be interpreted as the result of the association or aggregation of those elements. The associations actually found were all treated as contingent. They might have been other than in fact they were. The associated clusters had not arrived as clusters but had been assembled by us; they had neither stability nor authority. So they might just as well be rearranged. The patterns we find have no permanent legitimacy, and they are not rooted in the nature of things.

In fact – on this view – there is no such thing as the nature of things. The constellations of things and features we find in our world do not constitute a God-given, hence sacred and normative order; they are an accidental by-product of the interplay of natural forces. We explore the world by seeing actual patterns as contingent variants of deeper factors, and these we explore by rearranging actual patterns, in real or imaginary experiments. Freedom of experiment is analogous to freedom of trade, and each leads to growth in its own sphere, and the forms of freedom and consequent growth aid each other. Each is opposed to the imposition of hallowed rules or rigidities, whether based on tradition or revelation.

It is just this which distinguishes the atomic vision from the more customary way of seeing the world, which accepts habitual linkages as inherent in the nature of things, and has little if any sense of the fragility or contingency of these associations, and does not presume to experiment with them. Cultures freeze associations, and endow them with a feel of necessity. They turn mere worlds into *homes*, where men can feel comfortable, where they belong rather than explore, where things have their allocated places and form a system. That is what a culture is. By contrast, atomistic philosophy loosens and corrodes these linkages. Atomistic individualism is custom-corrosive and culture-corrosive. It facilitates the growth of knowledge, and of productive effectiveness, but it weakens the authority of cultures and makes the world less habitable, more cold and alien.

Deeply contrasted with the atomic theory of knowledge, there is what one might call the organic vision. First of all, this vision repudiates the individualism of its rival. No man, least of all when he endeavours to know and understand the world, is an island unto himself. Knowledge is essentially a team game. Anyone who observes, investigates or interprets the world, inevitably deploys concepts which are carried by an entire cultural/linguistic community. He cannot on his own understand the rules of its operation, if indeed he can understand them at all. They work through him, rather than simply being his self-created tools. Their wisdom is greater than his own.

No single individual is capable of excogitating the system of ideas required to make a world: only the unconscious cunning of a culture and a language is capable of such an achievement. Man cannot act on his own, but only when sustained by and interacting with other participants in this collective game. The ideas of a culture, of a historic tradition, of an ongoing community, work through him. He is their agent, and cannot be their author, or even, perhaps, their critic.

Likewise, the objects deployed in the construction of a world are not some homogeneous assembly of similar grains, differing only in – What? Colour, shape, hardness? – as the individualist/atomic tradition would have it. On the contrary, the constituent elements form a system, whose parts are in intimate and intricate relation with each other. Separation of all separables is not the heart of wisdom, but of folly. Any strong striving in this direction is a symptom of poverty of spirit, of lack of true understanding, of narrowness of vision, of a failure of comprehension. The sensitive mind and heart see and feel the totality; they appreciate the connectedness of all its parts and do not seek to break up that unity.

2 The rivals

The standing of the two philosophic visions is not altogether similar. Their histories, their places in the world, are not fully parallel. The atomistic one was the first to receive deliberate formulation, but not the first to come into existence. Partisans of the organic vision would say that just because it is the primordial and normal form, it needed no articulation. It was at its best when it was free of self-consciousness, when it had no need to reflect on its own existence. Its innocence was its glory, the sign of its primordial and legitimate place in human life. Formulating it and presenting it as a theory may well soil it. Its validity lies beyond argument, arguing its merits only demeans and contradicts it. A real traditionalist does not know that he is one, his tradition simply is his life and his being: once he knows it as *a* tradition, one among others, or even as opposed to reason, he has been corrupted by his knowledge of something else.

The fact that the atomistic view was formulated before ever it was lived may likewise be a sign of its artificial, indeed pathological character. Live first, think after: those who need to think out their identity before living it betray their unfitness to live. Nobility is conveyed by the priority of being over thought, which is but a kind of embellishment, not a refuge or fortification. Aristocrats simply *are*, parvenus *do*, the rootless try to *argue* their identity. Such, at any rate, would be the 'organic' view of the matter.

Descartes was perhaps the chief, certainly the most famous and elegant, progenitor of intellectual individualism, the Samuel Smiles of individualist cognitive entrepreneurialism. He insisted that true knowledge could best be obtained by a single individual, who had bravely and ruthlessly freed himself from the incubus of the conventional wisdom of his own culture and had built up a new capital exclusively from neat, distinct, clear elements, separate from each other. Acting alone, step by separate step, *that* is the basic rule of procedure. Such an inquirer kept good accounts and incurred no cognitive debt. He trades only with his

how (without argument)?

7

own self-made capital and need fear no taint which might devalue his future achievements.

The programme of individually erected and checked, socially disembodied and detached, carefully erected cognitive accumulations, was carried further by the school of so-called British empiricists. It was they who in the end provided a picture of knowledge constructed from homogeneous, granular elements – perceptions, sensations or ideas – standardised bricks in a neat edifice of knowledge. The culmination of this tradition is to be found in the work of David Hume. What really distinguished the school was its acute sense of the independence of the atomic elements which went into the erection of a world-picture. Nothing was inherently linked to anything else, the base-line of knowledge was an assembly of disconnected atoms.

The organic counter-picture was formulated explicitly only in reaction to the atomistic/individual vision. Previously it had needed no formulation, but now it needed vindication against the new solitary men. So, in this sense, but in this sense only, it was *later*. Its adherents, of course, would deny that it was in any real sense 'later'. Its overt articulation might indeed have come later; but what it describes had long existed, indeed it had been the normal and healthy condition of mankind. It had been *lived* and practised, long before it had been turned into a theory. It feels distaste at its opponents, who have soiled it and deprived it of its innocence and, in some measure, reduced it to their own level, by forcing it to argue, to articulate, to render life subject to abstraction. If forced to do so by the need to reply to its opponents, it does so only with distaste.

Men had been members of organic communities as they had spoken prose, without knowing they were doing so, taking it for granted: without being in possession of a concept or a word for expressing what they lived, and without feeling the lack of it. It was only when an unnatural, scientist vision of knowledge, which detached cognition from all that was social and human, had appeared on the scene, that the organic perception was provoked into consciousness and self-definition. Goaded into defending itself, it remained uneasy about its own articulation: it senses a betrayal, an excessive concession to its opponents. Its protagonists certainly prefer a position of strength, from which a smile of contempt is more appropriate, and indeed more effective, than an argument.

The confrontation of the two visions is not something which occurs only in the intellectual, literary, or academic spheres. It is far more deeply rooted in life and pervades social and political conflicts and options. In some places it does so neatly and conspicuously. It may tie in with the principal fissures in the society in question. Sometimes, on the other hand, it may cut across them. For instance, romantic organicists are not unknown in Britain: Burke, Wordsworth, Coleridge, Scott, and, later, D. H. Lawrence, Hoggart, Raymond Williams, Oakeshott, Scruton. As for the atomist individualists, there is of course a great lineage leading from Hobbes to Russell.

But this deep philosophical opposition does not, in Britain, define the confrontations of political life: it cuts right across it. In fact, it is represented, in extreme form, in *each* of the major parties. The Tories contain both romantics and formalistic market enthusiasts. The partisans of rustic hierarchy somehow align themselves with irreverent opportunist yuppies: they are at one in their dislike of do-gooding egalitarian paternalism. The Burke–Oakeshott poets of deferential rural idylls cooperate amiably in the Conservative party with the 'smart-aleck' operators and insider traders, sometimes of less than prestigious social origins. Labour has both its sentimental William Morris romantics and its technocratic welfare engineers, its Tawneys and its Webbs. The Fabian dream of government by benign statistically informed bureaucrat blends with the vision of the unspecialised craftsman, fulfilled in his work, earthy and authentic, unconnected to modern sanitation, untouched by modern vulgarity. The nostalgia for an unspecialised, profit-spurning, natural economy is aligned with the humourless bureaucracy of welfare.

In other words, although the English are perfectly familiar with the basic contrast and are endowed with a wealth of fine literary expressions of it, it would be quite impossible to give an account of their political life in terms of it. If you can identify a man as a romantic or a rationalist, you cannot infer from this which way he will vote. The main cleavages of actual, effective political life simply cannot be plotted onto the deep intellectual distinction which concerns us. They defy it. In Alan Macfarlane's version of English romantic populism, the archaic-traditional element he identifies is at the same time presented as highly individualistic, and as having made an important contribution to the emergence of modernity (Macfarlane 1978). If he is right, the English were at their most individualist when they were also most traditional. Other nations had to do violence to their traditional nature so as to become modern: the English only needed to remain true to themselves.

Continental romanticism tends to be populist. The unconscious, earthy wisdom which it often idealises, and contrasts with abstract barren reason, is generally credited to the peasantry. In England such an attitude may perhaps be found in, say, Wordsworth but, all in all, it is badly hampered by the sheer absence of peasants. It is hard, though perhaps not impossible, to hold up something that barely exists as a model. There was not much yeomanry left after the Enclosures and the move to the cities. In some cases, notably in Burke and Oakeshott, there is a kind of inverse populism, which it is rather odd to call by such a name at all: unconscious political wisdom is credited to the ruling class. It is an elitism really, an elitism invoking, not the formal training of the rulers, but its alleged redundancy. Their wisdom is located in what they *are*, not what they learnt, and it cannot possibly be taught. The attribution of a superior wisdom beyond the reach of formal instruction, indeed antithetical to it, cannot be credited to the unlettered, as you might expect on the analogy of other forms of anti-intellectualism. It is in the hands of those who, although they have received formal education, know full, in virtue of their superior breeding, that they need not and must not take it seriously. There is also, in men such as Hoggart or Raymond Williams, the attempt to romanticise the culture of an old working class: this is the nostalgia provoked by the disappearance, no longer of the old yeomanry, but of Bethnal Green, its age-mellowed culture swept away by high-rise council flats. (Something similar happened in Czech society under Communism, when populist ethnography turned from the farmers to the urban working class – but this happened under political pressure!) There is also the unusual romanticism of a D. H. Lawrence in the form of the interesting view, never seriously tested, that gamekeepers make better lovers than landowners. So all in all one must say that the attribution of deep, trans-rational, organic wisdom in Britain is so untidily and multifariously related to social strata that it simply cannot be tied in with, and reinforce, any political cleavages in the country. The Wisdom of the Deep is variously credited to a whole range of diverse social strata and interests, and so its political impact is liable to cancel out. Organic intuition against cold ratiocination – this is not often the dominant issue in general elections.

There are less blessed parts of the world where this is not so, where the confrontation of atomists and organicists does capture much of the central emotional charge, the underlying inspiration, of real, concrete political life, where this profound philosophical opposition meshes in with the alliances and hatreds of daily and political life. This was nowhere more so perhaps than in a dynastic empire which ended in 1918, was located in the Danube valley, and controlled extensive areas outside it: the Alpine lands, Bohemia, Galicia, wide stretches of the Balkans, and even (though much of this was lost in the course of the nineteenth century) northern Italy.

Once upon a time, notably in 1848, liberals and nationalists could be allies within this Habsburg Empire, united in their shared opposition to the authoritarian, hierarchical, traditional, though not specifically ethnic centre. But later, all that tended to change. In the end virtually all the 'ethnics', including even or especially the German speakers, turned against the centre, which, however dynastic and traditional, was finally only able to rely on the support of the new men: the commercial, industrial, academic, professional meritocrats, interested in maintaining an open market in goods, men, ideas, and a universalistic open society. This was the great paradox of its terminal condition. Its loyalists were the *nouveaux riches* and the newly emancipated, often not altogether integrated and accepted, and often made to feel uncomfortable, notably if they were Jewish: all this being so, both economic and political liberalism was to their taste. They were liberal but they needed protection by the state against ethnic illiberalism. The fact that in the past, this dynasty had persecuted them – Jews were expelled from Vienna in 1670 because they were blamed for a royal miscarriage – and that it was snobbish, sclerotic, hierarchical, formally absolutist, and intimately associated with an intolerant, absolutist religion – all this now mattered little. Unless the regime survived and maintained and fortified its perhaps reluctant but significant *de facto* liberalism, the Jews' position would be precarious, perhaps untenable. Were the regime to be replaced by ethno-romantic, nationally specific states, the liberalism would surely lapse and the position of the newly freed and newly enriched would be grave. The newly freed had good cause to sing *Gott behalte, Gott beschütze, unsern Kaiser unser Reich* [God preserve, God protect our Emperor and our Empire]. In the end, the fears which had led them to be loyal Habsburg subjects proved to be only too justified.

To some extent, even before the coming of nationalist sentiment in the early nineteenth century, the Empire had known the conflict between centripetal and centrifugal forces. Enlightened despotism, eager for efficiency, tried to strengthen the centre by means of bureaucratic control and standardisation, whilst *Landespatriotismus* strove to preserve the ancient liberties and powers of local institutions. Such local patriotism was territorial and respectful of hierarchy. Some, like the Czech philosopher Jan Patočka, later looked back with nostalgia to this staid hierarchical order, relatively free of ethnic self-definition. In the nineteenth century, a Prague philosopher such as Bolzano, had been eager to combine non-ethnic, non-linguistic patriotism with greater social equality, and even with ecumenism. But that was not yet nationalism. Genuine nationalism, centred on culture and language rather than antiquity of institution and territorial association, only came to be powerful later, and then struggled against the European system set up at the Congress of Vienna.

It was with the rise of nationalism that the deep confrontation with which we began really came into its own within the Danubian Empire. The opposition between individualism and communalism, between the appeal of *Gesellschaft* ('Society') and of *Gemeinschaft* ('Community'), a tension which pervades and torments most societies disrupted by modernisation, became closely linked to the hurly burly of daily political life and pervaded the sensibility of everyone.

Hence the deep irony of the situation: an authoritarian Empire, based on a medieval dynasty and tied to the heavily dogmatic ideology of the Counter-Reformation, in the end, under the stimulus of ethnic, chauvinistic centrifugal agitation, found its most eager defenders amongst individualist liberals, recruited in considerable part from an erstwhile pariah group and standing *outside* the faith with which the state was once so deeply identified. The dynasty had accumulated a patchwork Empire not because it was theoretically committed to pluralism, but largely because it was lucky and had married well – *tu felix Austria nube* – and also for the simple reason that in those days cultural homogeneity was of no consequence. You might ask about the quality of land, but never about the dialect of its peasants. The dynasty had indeed once been committed to a political and religious absolutism. But now the logic of the situation led it to be the patron of a pluralistic and tolerant society. It was the Hayeks and the Poppers who produced the classics of twentieth-century liberalism under the impact of this situation.

There were also, of course, the opponents of the liberals. The ethnic groups on the margins of the Empire were not quite so interested in their own absorption into the cosmopolitan culture of the centre or in winning places in its pervasive bureaucracy, as were the *nouveaux riche* and newly emancipated. They could do better when in control of their own closed unit than when competing in the cosmopolitan centre. Initially, at the very beginnings of centralisation in the age of Enlightened Despotism, individuals were indeed eager to avail themselves of the opportunity of becoming incorporated into the dominant idiom and language, and thereby becoming eligible for maximum career opportunities. Originally, the language that needed to be mastered was Latin; it was only replaced by German relatively late. Separatism was fostered by the competition between individuals *and* between languages.

Some no doubt persisted in the old attitude – upwards by assimilation – even during the later periods. But many – and this was the essence of the new age of nationalism – preferred to agitate for the full recognition of their own idiom of origin, for its elevation into a fully *gleichberechtigte* language, fit for bureaucratic use and a pathway of entry to a bureaucracy. The culture they fought for may once upon a time, in the Middle

Ages, or even up to the end of the Wars of Religion, have had its court use and its courtly literature; or it may, since ever the beginning of time, never have been anything other than a peasant dialect. This difference mattered relatively little, though some historians make much of the difference between 'historic' and 'un-historic' nations.

What did matter was that now this lowly idiom had to be elevated from a primarily or exclusively peasant use, whether or not it had once long ago known better days, to a language properly recorded and codified, and suitable as a medium of instruction in schools and for bureaucratic and commercial deployment. The first step towards such an elevation in status was its scholarly exploration in the context in which it was still alive, namely, in the world of peasants. In this part of the world, the first stage of national 're-birth' (in fact, quite often, simply *birth*, for the 'nation' in question may never have previously had a self-conscious political and cultural existence) was scholarly ethno-graphy of peasant life, not always carried out by members of the same culture as the one under investigation (Hroch 1985). Such scholars were what you might call vicarious 'Awakeners'.

The peasant culture did not merely need to be explored, it had to be advertised and glorified; its charms and that of the milieu in which it flourished had to be extolled. And this was indeed the characteristic stance of the romantics-populists, the opponents of the universalists-individualists. They rhapsodised about the charms of the village green and of the idiosyncrasy and earthiness of its folk culture. They explored it, but they also loved it and sang its praises. They defended it against bloodless cosmopolitanism. What mattered was its specificity, its dis-tinctiveness, its *roots*. These theorists could not be universalists.

Such, then, was the great confrontation of rationalistic individualism and romantic communalism in a society where it *did* permeate and dominate political life and provide it with its basic outline, the contours of its fundamental opposition.

3   Genesis of the individualist vision

The emergence of the individualist spirit in Europe is a complex and much discussed phenomenon. How did men come to switch from accepting social authority to choosing their own vision, values, aims, style, identity?

This book cannot contribute to the discussion concerning whether the roots of this individualism are to be found in ideological or social and economic factors. Wherever the prime mover may be found, what is indisputable is that when a more individualist society does eventually emerge, it manifests itself at all these levels.

In the ideological sphere individualism manifests itself in the emergence of a whole set of new theories. These explain and validate social arrangements in terms of ultimately individual concerns. Such theories emerge in a whole variety of diverse fields. In politics the emergence of the polity, and its justification, comes to be found in a contract made by pre-social individuals in their own interest: they will be safer and more prosperous if they establish a civil society, and see to its protection and the enforcement of its rules. In ethics a theory emerges which in the end equates the good social order with one which maximises the contentment of the individuals composing it, the individual pains and pleasures being added and subtracted in accordance with some agreed or self-evident algorithm. In economics production is seen as the interaction of individuals, ideally untrammelled, or minimally restrained, in the choice of contracts they make with each other, and in the means and methods they deploy. The famous transition from status to contract, in Maine's phrase, is but an aspect, or rather an alternative expression, of this individualism: statuses emanate from society, contracts are made by individuals. A status society subordinates individuals to the community, a contractual society subordinates the community to the individuals. We have focused primarily on the expression of this transition in the field of knowledge, which is indeed an extremely important but by no means the only area in which the great transformation can be observed. But knowledge is crucial; what

14

is acceptable in other fields in the end depends on what the individual can or cannot know.

In each sphere, the theory can be read as a description, as an explanation, and as a legitimation. It can of course also be read as all three and, quite often, both the theorist and the reader fail to distinguish between these aspects. The just-so story about the origins, about how it all started, is at the same time treated as a specification of the elements in human nature which require the emergence of the institutions in question, be it the contractual state or the free market or what have you.

But in each case, the legitimation starts from the individual, conceived of, at least in principle if not in fact, as a pre-social, pre-cultural being. If it is held – as is most plausible – that no such pre-cultural man either exists or possibly could exist, this does no doubt highlight a genuine defect of the individualist theory as a descriptive or explanatory account of how this or that institution actually came into being. If men were never pre-social or pre-cultural, then a story concerning how pre-social or pre-cultural men invented language, the state, religion, or anything else, cannot have a great deal of merit, at any rate as history.

This defect, as a descriptive or explanatory account, is however at the same time an actual merit when the theory is used as a way of highlighting, normatively, just what feature (not necessarily what origin) accounts for the distinctiveness and power of individualist practices. What is it that makes modern science so uniquely powerful? The great theoreticians of science were often naively individualistic and no doubt this was a weakness if we want to know what actually happened in the emergence of science, or how it really works. For this end, we may be well advised to look to the markedly anti-individualist trend in recent philosophy of science, and heed those who insist on 'shared paradigms', the social nature of science, and so forth. Yet is not the society-blindness of the great theories of knowledge, which accompany and try to explain the rise of science, itself illuminating? Is it not precisely the asocial nature of modern science and the ultimate sovereignty of individual judgement which constitute the clue to its distinctiveness and its power? Is not the ultimate equality of theoreticians, the absence of sanctified and permanently authoritative and politically underwritten hierarchies, part of the clue, perhaps even the central clue, to the unique cognitive power of science?

The theory of knowledge has probably been (and in my view, rightly) the main and most important tradition in modern philosophy ever since the seventeenth century. Initiated by Descartes, continued above all by the great British empiricists, it finds its culmination in Hume and Kant. The individualism remains prominent and basic: the basic model is that of an individual facing his data and constructing a world from them in the light of and under the guidance of principles which he finds within himself. The nineteenth century sees a bit of a retreat from individualism, notably in the Hegelian tradition, though the theory of knowledge found in Schopenhauer continues to be individualistic. However, by the end of the century, individualism and its epistemological articulation find a kind of second wind, and the vision of Hume and Kant is reformulated in thinkers such as Ernst Mach in Austria and Bertrand Russell in England. It is the very distinctive formulation of this vision by a man deeply influenced by both Mach and Russell which provides us with a crucial specimen.

4 The metaphysics of romanticism

The model of man engendered by the empiricist/individualist tradition is very distinctive. The solitary Crusoe-like individual faces the world or, rather, assembles the world out of the accumulated bits of experience. He carefully sifts out impurities introduced into his experience by the pre-judgments, the prejudices of his social milieu. Within this world, his egoism has a curiously cold quality. In Kant this is made very explicit: to be moral is to abide by *rules*. Sin for Kant *is* the making of exceptions. This was the morality of the Prussian bureaucrat: *Ordnung muss sein*. But even in Hume, in whose thought morality is based on our sensibility rather than on our rationality, it is *impartial* feeling which is at the root of morals. So impartiality and symmetry, *Ordnung*, hence human universality rather than cultural specificity, is the basic message.

So the individualist/rationalist acts on principle. He deals with all like cases in a like manner – that is his honour. Clearly, this is a trustworthy reliable man, but not exactly exciting and stimulating. You might be pleased to have him as your bank manager, but be less thrilled to find him your dinner companion. A moral man, on this description, would display exactly the same sentiments in similar circumstances: to behave in any other manner would be to display partiality, asymmetry, arbitrariness, caprice, in fact all he abhors. Consider what this involves: it means that a decent man must love all similar objects – all landscapes, all countries, all poets, all women – in precisely the same manner and to the same extent, in as far as they possess the same relevant characteristics. He may not have a passion for this particular hillside, or that line of poetry, or that woman, unless he can show just how the object singled out for special affection differs from others, in a relevant way, and one which, moreover, would induce him to feel the same partiality for any other object similarly endowed. But who would want to be loved by such a precision-machine? Friedrich Schiller ironised this aspect of Kant's moral philosophy.

This is the charge of the romantics against the men of the Enlightenment. There are aspects of life in which symmetrical rationality, the like treatment of like cases, has no place. It may be all very well in law, in public examinations, in trade, and it may indeed single out the practitioners of those professions and be their pride. But what about love, faith, the appreciations of beauty, heroism and sacrifice? Is symmetry of consideration and cold evaluation to be invoked there as well? Would it not go against the very spirit of the thing, would it not destroy its beauty? Have spontaneity and passion no place in life? Must a romantic lover commit himself to feeling the same sentiments for any woman who resembles his beloved in the relevant respects? Must a true believer extend his commitment to any revelation formally similar to the one he had accepted? To do so looks like a contradiction . . . these men loved or believed in *this* rather than anything else, not in virtue of general principles, but in defiance of them.

Romantics may be moderate and be willing to live and let live, saying to the cold calculators: You keep the economy and we shall have love and poetry. But they have not always remained so modest. They may go on the counter-offensive and wish to take over larger parts of life, or devalue those aspects of life where their preference for passion is inapplicable. They may hold warfare dearer than trade not because it is a quicker way of amassing wealth – to hell with that – but because it is inherently nobler. They may say not merely that the irrational part of life is essential, but that it is at the very heart of humanity, and that its rival, barren reason, is an accretion or worse, a cause or sign of ill health. Man fulfils himself not in the rational appreciation of the universal, but in his passionate commitment to the specific. There comes a time when they are not content with the dominance of feeling and specificity in art or personal relations, their home territory so to speak; they come to insist that they are even – or especially – at home in politics. If liberalism is the politics of the universal, then nationalism is the politics of the specific. It may be specific culturally or genetically or both. Its object is selected by passion not by reason and just that constitutes its legitimacy.

Thus at the core of romanticism there is a metaphysic of man. It is in headlong confrontation with the rationalism of the Enlightenment. And it fits in very well with the claustrophilia of the partisans of *Gemeinschaft* against *Gesellschaft*. They are, after all, the advocates of specificity, of the distinctiveness rather than the universality of culture. They are not saying that Ruritanian culture should be universalised and adopted by everyone. On the contrary, they are irritated when foreigners ape it and try to penetrate it. They dislike such intruders intensely, just as they deplore deserters from the ranks of Ruritanian culture, seduced by the garish attractions of metropolitan civilisation. They do not claim that their own culture is meritorious because it embodies universal values:

they love it because it does *not*, because it incarnates its own values, and displays its own distinctive style, which is not the same as that of others.

And what they hate above all else are just those damned cosmopolitans, who lack roots of their own and wish to impose their rootlessness on others, and try to make it a universal norm in virtue of some grey general humanity. These rootless people are, not surprisingly, engaged in activities such as trade or thought, which lead them to these bloodless values. But that is not for us, say the romantic nationalists: we are rooted to the soil, peasants or warriors or both, we *feel*, we do not calculate . . . and we spurn those who do . . . and it is we who represent true humanity, and the others are but a parody of man.

So the cult of community and specificity receives reinforcement from the entire romantic tradition and its claim that the best, or even the only, truly human elements are to be found in the non-reasoning aspects of life. Reason is defied twice over: by the love of the *specific* rather than the *universal*, and of the *passionate* rather than the *calculating*. Love, or passion, as it were, is enlisted in the political arena: political confrontations are presented as the conflict of life with sterility, of vitality with disease, a disease which masquerades as reason and compassion. (It was a romantic English novelist, after all, campaigning happily for sexual rather than nationalist liberation, who actually introduced the expression 'anti-life' to characterise cerebral attitudes he did not like.) For the latter-day romantics, the specific and the passionate are to be pursued not only in courtship or on the nature walk or in one's the choice of music, but also (perhaps especially) in the council chamber or the chamber of commerce. The new spirit is to pervade the whole of social life and not merely special reserved areas (sex, wilder forms of life); it is to be at the service of the polity, and the polity is to serve it. Politics are to cease being instrumental and become theatrical, ritualised, and expressive.

In due course, the cult of community and specificity receives another powerful ally: the authority of literature is reinforced by biology. Not only poetry but Darwinism too teaches that strong and violent feeling is closer to the centre of our being than cold cogitation. Aggression not reflection helped man the hunter to survive . . . Aggression, courage, cohesion, discipline, loyalty, are the virtues which helped communities to overcome their enemies and so the argument from natural selection reinforces the arguments from literary appeal, psychic health and fulfilment, and authenticity of ideal. The mainsprings of our life are not cool impartial sentiments or a rational preference for symmetry and rules but, on the contrary, powerful instinctual drives. The contrary rationalistic and universalistic doctrine, far from being the voice of something 'higher', is but the devious, distorted, pathogenic servant of those very instincts it pretends to oppose. (This was the message of Nietzsche and Freud.) So, the argument between the universalistic liberals and the romantic rightists is an argument about the very nature of man. When the general issue plays itself out in on-the-ground politics, we find ourselves in a remarkable situation in which the political stakes of philosophic visions are very great.

5 Romanticism and the basis of nationalism

The universalistic-atomic and the romantic-organic vision are indeed the two great rivals, the poles of a fundamental binary opposition. Much of the intellectual life of recent times can be spelt out in these terms. However, the two visions do not exhaust the world. (As we shall see, the contrary supposition, that there is no further option, can be a terrible mistake.) Other options are in fact available. Other forces are in operation. The polarity which concerns us might never have become quite so conspicuous, had not one further vision entered the scene: nationalism.

The traditional organic way of life is probably imperceptible to itself. It is lived, it is danced, it is performed in ritual and celebrated in legend, but it is hardly articulated in theory. It is only when the snake of abstract theory appears in the garden, that the garden is suddenly perceived and named Community. Only then does one begin to sing its praises. The real traditionalist, al-Ghazzali observed, does not know himself to be such. Community is sung and praised by those who have lost it.

Even when an Enlightenment castigates tradition for its arbritrariness, cruelty, and injustice, tradition does not initially defend itself *as* tradition. The first reactionaries tend to be absolutists. They defend their tradition because they consider it to be revealed and valid. They use a language similar to that of their critics. Or one might put this the other way round: just *because* the 'higher' religions already used theories with universalist pretensions, they prepared the ground for their eventual opponents. By giving reasons at all, they implicitly invited their critics to challenge them with better reasons. They may of course invoke tradition as an auxiliary argument: de Maistre observed that superstitions were the outer bulwarks of faith. He did not, however, say that they constituted the inner citadel. That is the position reached by later, sophisticated traditional*ism*: the defence of a position not as true but as traditional. So the crucial change comes when this role is inverted: when it is no longer tradition that is maintained because it embodies the absolute, but the absolute is used as an idiom for perpetuating a specific tradition. This curious development took place on the way to modernity.

It was widely believed by many of the early commentators of the social transformation, both Liberals and Marxists, that there would be a kind of direct transition from the traditional closed worlds to a kind of universal human society. In other words – and this, notoriously, was their greatest and deepest mistake – they failed to foresee nationalism. What did in fact take place was a transition from the old world of endless cultural diversity and nuance, not directly linked to the political order, to a new world of mass, anonymous, but *not* universal, societies. And it is these internally mobile, but externally closed, societies which discovered and made a cult of *Gemeinschaft*, of the closed society, and claimed (quite falsely) to be implementing and exemplifying it. In forging new state-linked 'high' (educationally transmitted, codified) cultures, they used folk themes and invoked the *Gemeinschaft* of the village green: but they were neither establishing a village green, nor did they greatly appeal to those who were still in the village. They were creating a new kind of society based on a shared educationally instilled culture, and their clientele were the new entrants into that society. Nationalism is born of the needs of *Gesellschaft*, but it speaks *Gemeinschaft*.

Liberals and Marxists both believed that the closed and differentiated communities would eventually be replaced by an open universal one. Boundaries and closures depended on those arbitrary cultural specificities and distinctions; industrialism would inevitably erode them. So, in the end, nationalism would wither away, for it would have no cultural boundaries to work on. It would perish for lack of suitable nourishment. Liberals and Marxists differed a bit concerning the detailed mechanics of this process: the former thought it would be achieved mainly by free trade and an international division of labour, and the Marxists, in a more sombre variant of the theory, expected universal human nature to reveal and assert itself in the dreadful melting pot of a global, nation-less proletariat. But notwithstanding these differences on points of detail, there was a shared and, one must add, most plausible expectation of the universal replacement of *Gemeinschaft* by *Gesellschaft*.

Plausible and reasonable though this expectation was, it did not come to be fulfilled. What happened instead was the coming of the age of nationalism. This is a system which in a curious way blends both the closed culturally delimited community and a certain openness, anonymity, mobility and structurelessness. The world of national states has the following characteristics: inside each nation-state, there is a high degree of anonymity and mobility. Accredited fully qualified members of the culture move legitimately from any one position in the society to any other. No caste, guild, estate, territorial or kin-group or other restriction inhibits employability, commensality, or eligibility for marriage. The partial survival of such barriers is viewed with shame and disapprobation, at best with ambivalence and amusement. *But*: the boundary between this mobile, *gesellschaftlich* pool and its neighbours acquires an enormous potency and is deeply underwritten by symbolism. The membership of one of these pools is, both practically and affectively, the most important possession a man has. It is the precondition of the attainment or enjoyment of all others.

It is not entirely clear why this has happened, why the old man-tied-to-his-niche should have been replaced, not, as the Enlightenment taught and hoped, by Universal Man committed to a corresponding universal brotherhood, but by an ethnically specific man, detached from rigid links to the old niches, but mobile only within the limits of a now formally codified and state-protected culture, i.e. within the bounds of a nation-state. *That* it has happened is one of the most significant facts of the last two centuries. The explanation is no doubt related to the uneven diffusion of the new mobility-stimulating and homogeneity-engendering industrial order: the uneven facility and timing of entry creates great cleavages between different cohorts of entrants into industrialism. Early ones have no wish to share their benefits, and have them diluted or destroyed, by a flood of migrant late-comers. Late arrivals, and especially their leaders, have a great deal to gain from setting up new cultural-political units, 'building nations', within which they will not need to compete with better qualified early adepts of the new dispensation. Whatever the full explanation – and this is an important topic deserving further exploration – it has happened, and we must needs live with the consequences, and indeed we have done so to the cost of many of us.

This new system needs ideological support. It replaces the old complex, hierarchical, highly diversified (vertically and horizontally) system by a set of large, internally homogeneous and externally delimited, sharply bounded 'national' pools. The new boundaries are seldom given by either nature or history: sometimes, genetically transmitted traits or well-established territorial boundaries, correlating with cultural ones, help to set up the new borders. More often, an appallingly complex ethnic map and a culturally marked division of labour make the new borders highly problematic. The new emerging units compete for both territory and recruits; they fight each other for ethnic catchment areas.

Under the old order the majority of the population were peasants. In some cases the new national culture may be based on a court or hieratic language and a high tradition, but more often it is based on the standardised and formalised version of a peasant dialect. One reason for this is that the old court regimes are frequently too compromised by the real or attributed weaknesses of the old system to have much appeal, and the new nationalists prefer to invoke a populist legitimacy.

The new nationalisms enter into violent competition with each other, and the new standard and rallying cry is, above all, folk culture. This is the deep paradox of nationalism: it is a phenomenon of *Gesellschaft*, but it is obliged to use and invoke the imagery of *Gemeinschaft*. The moral sovereignty of ethnic culture is nationalism's central principle. It was the nationalists who really rammed home, persistently and to great effect, the vision of the closed community, final and sovereign.

When the community really existed, it did not preach itself. It danced itself and took itself for granted. In the more complex and larger agrarian societies doctrinal and absolutist religion reinforced the authority of tradition: revelation claimed authority but deigned to spell out its own teaching, thus setting a precedent (which was to cost it dear) for *reasoning*. If the scholastics can use reason as an auxiliary to faith, their opponents will use it in subverting it. The Enlightenment deployed reasoning in the opposite direction, on behalf of a symmetrical, human, and humane revelation allegedly inherent in human reason or nature as such, rather than in some privileged Information Point with its direct line to the transcendent. But the idea of communal tradition as morally and politically authoritative came into its own when deployed on behalf of specific, non-universal, but no longer genuinely communal units, namely, 'nations'. In fact, these were neither immemorial nor 'organic': they were based on a rational economy with a mobile meritocratic labour force, but one which needed easy impersonal communication, hence a shared high culture, and so came to delimit itself culturally. The idiom used for this was that of community of culture. Henceforth, the social pool was to be culturally homogeneous: the modern 'nation' was born.

The new order had to tell people that their identity, vitality, and integrity were dependent on their (ethnically specific, though not over-specific) *roots*. Roots are everything. Rootlessness is not just wicked but deeply pathological and pathogenic. The relatively gentle Herderian insistence on the life-enhancing quality of a local communal culture was in due course strengthened by a less benign element: Darwin mediated by Nietzsche. The vitality-conferring roots were to be not merely territorial-cultural, but also genetic. The legitimating community was not merely language-transmitting but also a gene-transmitting one. The

Darwinian stress on competition as a precondition of excellence could be combined with Nietszchean ideas (well diffused by Freud) about the pathogenic origins or consequences of universalism and aggression-denying conscience. The line of development towards extreme and racist nationalism was clear and plausible.

6   Individualism and holism in society

The industrial-scientific society which was emerging and rapidly becoming dominant in Europe, and was soon to spread throughout the world, has two possibly contradictory aspects: it has both an individualistic and a holistic bias. Their interaction calls for some comment.

The tendency towards individualism is more immediately obvious. How it all began remains contentious. That it must be such in order to function (though not absolutely beyond all questioning) at any rate seems fairly obvious, and perhaps is unquestionable at any rate for the early stages of the first and endogenous industrialisation. The new man had to choose his productive activity and his methods independently, in the light of his own aims and assessments of the circumstances, rather than have them dictated by his status, his location in the social hierarchy, his guild membership, and so forth. Status constrained him less than it had his ancestors, and he chose his contracts in the light of his own interests and views. Naturally he recognised himself in the new individualist philosophies which portrayed such an individualist procedure in the various spheres of life which concerned him.

So far, so good. His life situation made our new man into an individualist. Perhaps, as Weberian sociology would have it, he was an individualist first, in virtue of his Protestant religion, and he later, unwittingly, created a new individualist society in his own image. Be that as it may, an individualist world and ethos, and its accompanying individualist rationale, were emerging. It made, or was made of, so to speak 'modular' men, unlike the traditional men who came as part of communal package deals.

Modular man can arrange and rearrange himself with his fellows in social groupings and patterns which are not pre-fixed and imposed by society. Modern social relations can be, and frequently are, reordered and yet are not fragile. In the past, the only institutions which could survive were those which were multi-stranded, linking many activities and relationships, and which were heavily fortified by ritual and symbolic reinforcement. Not so now: our modular man respects single contracts which are not superimposed on entire networks of other relationships and are not sanctified by awe-inspiring rituals. In all these ways the new society of modular men is individualistic.

But there is another way in which it is not. To put it most simply: the society which emerged in the course of the nineteenth century was not only individualist and egalitarian, it was also, notoriously, *nationalist*. These two aspects are contrasted with each other and perhaps in conflict: they also have, in my view, the same roots. Both individualism-liberalism *and* that stress on cultural identification which is known as nationalism, are based on that transformation of human society which, for lack of a better term, can best be called industrialisation.

Why is this newly emerging modular man also a nationalist?

The society of which he is a member is committed to affluence and to economic growth. Its legitimacy depends on providing these: if it fails in supplying them, it loses the respect and loyalty of its citizens. They expect to live well, and they expect their standard of living to rise continuously. It is this expectation, and its satisfaction, which smooths over conflicts within society. Greed and expectation of material better-ment, not fear and pride of status, bind men to the social order and constrain them to respect its requirements.

But there is a price to pay: continuous improvement in economic performance requires continuous innovation, which in turn brings with it an unstable occupational structure. The mobility goes with that 'modularity of men' which we have already noticed. Men must be standardised, so that they can rapidly be slotted into new locations in the economic and social structure.

They need to be standardised for another reason and in another way, on top of all this. This requirement is inherent in what they do whilst they are in any one temporary social location, whilst they carry out any one job assigned to them. The nature of work itself has changed radically in this kind of society. Work has ceased to be physical and has become semantic. It consists not of the modification of things, but in the manipulation of meanings and people. In advanced societies actual manual work is something done only as part of recreation. In working hours people exchange messages or find themselves at the sophisticated controls of a machine. Literally manual work, calling for the deployment of brawn, is a rare and rapidly disappearing phenomenon. When required at all, it is often performed by cheap immigrant labour.

The standard or normative citizen of this kind of society, performing a socially acceptable and respected task and fit for full social membership, is doing something for which he needs to have been educated. Education means being trained to comprehend and emit messages, in speech or writing, or to use the sophisticated technologies which are a kind of extension of writing, in a *standardised* idiom. In other words, the modern citizen must be a member of a high, and not merely a low, culture. The sociological difference between the two is that a low culture is transmitted by the immediate environment, is locally specific and context-dependent; a high culture is transmitted by an educational system which trains its products to understand and articulate messages independently of context, and in accordance with rules which are equally internalised by all the other fellow-products of the same educational machine. Thus, for the first time in human history, a high culture, linked to literacy and formal education, its rules formally codified in writing, ceases to be the privilege of a minority and becomes, not so much a privilege, but a precondition of effective social and economic participation for the generality of the society. It comes to define any one given society. The need to protect such a society-defining culture, and the enormous cost of establishing and maintaining it, means that it needs its own state as its protector.

In agrarian society cultural differences between men were in the main used to indicate their location in a social structure which was both complex and fairly stable. On the other hand, cultural differences do not mark the very boundaries of major political units. Quite often there simply are no clear boundaries of that kind. In industrial society all this is inverted. Within each society, though of course status differences do exist, they are transitory and gradual and are widely held to be a social imperfection: ideally, members of the same society share the same culture. On the other hand, the boundaries of a culture and its polity are meant to be congruent. Cultural differences underscore those boundaries. Culture should *not* mark status differences within society, and it *should* mark the limits of a society.

So far so good. All this is dictated by the inherent requirements of industrial society, by the need for a shared and literate culture and for internal mobility and, hence, for the elimination of any deep, internalised, transmitted social differences. But the world initially invaded and conquered by industrialism does not at the beginning satisfy these requirements. Quite the reverse: its organisation goes counter to it. The world of complex, intertwined cultural differentiations, marking status rather than indicating major boundaries, has to be transformed into one devoid of culturally externalised status, but well equipped with culturally underscored boundaries.

This process is painful and frequently violent. Its driving force is known as nationalist irredentism, and the form it takes is one of ethnic struggle and wars of national liberation. This is, of course, somewhat of a misnomer and a retrojection because, in the sense required, nations did not yet exist and so could hardly be liberated. They had to be created, but this was presented as the awakening of ever-present, but submerged nations. The idea that they had been 'asleep', and had been woken and then struggled to cast off their chains, is part of nationalist mythology. What really happened was that nations were created out of the mass of cultural nuance and ambiguity, which filled out the available social space prior to the age of nationalism.

In some places all this is much less painful than it is in others. For instance, along the western Atlantic seaboard of Europe it just so happened that there was a series of strong dynastic states, very roughly correlated in their territorial extent with cultural zones, so that nationalism, requiring that polity and culture be co-extensive, had its political shells and cultural filling pre-fabricated, ready and waiting. Nationalism did not need to create either a state, or a standardised high culture: both were there and waiting and available. The most that needed to be done was to extend the zone of the normative high culture, previously restricted only to the court, the bureaucracy and the clerisy, and perhaps some urban centres, to the population at large, above all to the backwoods peasantry.

But it was all much more traumatic, difficult, anxiety-haunted elsewhere, for instance, in Kakania, to take Robert Musil's derisive name for the Habsburg Empire.

7   Crisis in Kakania

Kakania was an empire based on a dynasty with its roots deep in the Middle Ages, with a claim to a supreme authority in Central Europe even outside its own family domains, and with very important and intimate links to religion: it was the defender of Europe against the Turkish infidel and, at the same time, the champion of the Counter-Reformation against the heretic. It called itself 'Apostolic'. Though one language happened to be dominant in Central Europe and was naturally the language of the imperial court, the Empire was not an ethnic empire and did not have very special links to any one ethnic group or language. Rather, there was a certain ethnic division of labour within the Empire, or perhaps one should put this the other way round, and say that the division of labour was accompanied by cultural-linguistic differentiation.

The nineteenth century in effect pulled much of the ideological ground from under the feet of this polity. The Turks were no longer a danger: on the contrary, the danger to peace came only from the squabbling over their territorial inheritance. The weakness, not the strength, of the Turks constituted a danger to European peace. The Counter-Reformation was no longer a rousing cause. The Habsburgs had noticed the superior economic performance of Protestants and were eager to emulate their educational levels (the Weberian thesis about the economic role of Protestantism appeared among bureaucrats before it appeared among professors); in the same way, the Prussians noted the military superiority of free peasants over serfs. So modern ideas, then as now, spread thanks to the apparent success of the societies implementing them. So the Counter-Reformation only constituted a feeble barrier, stubborn but uninspired, to liberal ideas, which did seem to appeal to the enthusiasm of youth. The Counter-Reformation did not even always prevail in the Church itself: Metternich, upholding the old order, had to accommodate himself to the surprise, as he himself put it, of a liberal Pope. Nationalist striving became important. The cultural groups which had previously been content with their station in life within the imperial structure – some cultures to be used by the clergy, others by peasants, others by bureaucrats, others by traders, and so on – ceased to be so humble, and began to claim their rights. They wanted, for some reason, to be the cultures of complete nations, i.e. cultures endowed with all classes rather than being restricted to one social niche. And they wanted more than that: they wanted their own political roof, their own political institutions, perhaps their own defence forces and complete independence. The second requirement was in a way the crucial corollary of the first: a real nation has its own state, its own army, its own bourgeoisie, its own peasantry. Specialised cultures became offensive, a parody of the human condition, where they had once been the norm.

It had all begun with the Empire trying to increase its own efficiency and effectiveness by centralising and streamlining its bureaucracy. At first this provoked a hostile reaction from the old, initially often quite non-ethnic regionalisms, from the local institutions and the local nobility which manned them. But it also helped engender the new, non-regional but ethnic nationalism: by making bureaucracy more important and pervasive, it underscored the importance of culture and language. Full effective citizenship now belonged to those who could deal with the bureaucracy in an idiom it respected, and who were masters of that idiom. The formal rights of a free citizen were a necessary, but not sufficient, condition of real social incorporation. When government is distant and contacts with it are intermittent, its language does not matter much: who cares what the courtiers speak, when you never see them? But when government is all-pervasive and contacts with it are constant, the idiom it uses matters a very great deal. Latin was neutral: German was not. It favoured those whose mother tongue it also happened to be. Czechs and Germans are equal in face of Latin (Czechs may even have a marginal advantage, given the closer grammatical similarity between the two languages); but they are not equal in face of German. When German takes over, suddenly it begins to matter whether the ancient Kingdom of Bohemia is a fiction or a reality and what language is employed by its servants.

At first, in their conflict with the centre, the old *Landespatriotismus* of the local aristocracy, the new ethnic nationalism of the newly risen classes, and the liberalism of those opposed to the dogmatism and authoritarianism of the centre – all of them could make common cause. This seemed to be so in 1848. But it was not to last. In the end, a curious, acute, and perhaps rather dangerous polarisation took place in the politics, the hearts, the minds, and the literature of Kakania.

The new nationalism of the ethnic-cultural-linguistic groups

assumed, in the main, a strongly populist tinge. It was *Völkisch* or
narodny. Such nationalist ideology was about as clear a case of false
consciousness as you might wish to find anywhere: it had no relation to
reality. The nationalists themselves were quite unaware of this. What
they were in effect forging was a new high culture, to be enshrined in
texts, with its written literature. The new high culture was to be
perpetuated and transmitted by a formal educational system manned by
full-time and devoted personnel, who were to be the clerisy of a national
culture-faith. The schoolmaster was the nation-builder, the professor
was the prophet. They did not usually invoke the high culture of an
existing court or clerical organisation. Some of the ethnic groups in
question had never had such a court, others had possessed one only in
the dim distant historic past, but had lost it, and others still had doubts
about their identification with an existing dynasty which was not
exclusively committed to the ethnic group in question. They all preferred to define the new culture, whether 're-born', or first-born, or
allegedly 'historic' (endowed with its own and continuous political
cover), in terms of that peasant culture from which the new entrants
into the mobile new society were being recruited.

Nationalist propaganda had begun with a fairly timid and modest
defence of peasant culture and idiosyncrasy against the normative
cultural imperialism of the French court or the French Enlightenment
or Manchester commercialism or rationalism-scientism. But in due
course it passed from gentle defence of cultural diversity to an aggressive
affirmation of the virtue of peasant roots. Roots were everything, and
roots were to be found in the soil. Peasants were virtuous and they also
made good soldiers. Cosmopolitanism was treacherous, alien, feeble
and enervating.

So the ethnics turned against the centre in the name of peasant roots,
of community and togetherness, as against abstract rootless cosmopolitanism. And who remained with the centre? At first, no doubt, those
representatives of the old order who would have too much to lose from
its disintegration: the nobility, the bureaucracy. Initially, they were tied
to it by interest. But in the end, even their loyalty became doubtful. And
now the centre acquired a new and surprising ally: the beneficiaries of
liberalism. The rickety structure which was a survival from feudalism
and baroque absolutism, somehow endeared itself to, and only to, the
free-thinking liberal individualists! A strange metamorphosis indeed.

The Empire was big and contained many cultural, linguistic, and
religious groups. When the Empire began to modernise and industria-
lise, naturally some individuals and some groups did well out of it,
better than others. There were fortunes to be made, social positions to

be ascended. The new wealth was not necessarily or exclusively or even predominantly acquired by the previously privileged strata: perhaps they were too comfortable to be eager and active enough to avail themselves of the new opportunities. Their values may not have impelled them to go into trade. But some of those who had previously been stigmatised, and hemmed in by social restrictions, had the motivation, the energy and the ability to make excellent use of the new openings.

The very fact that such a high proportion of the new professional bourgeoisie and the new wealth belonged to a previously stigmatised category, namely the Jews, meant that the stigma continued to attach to such origin, even if it no longer had any formal legal sanction, or was losing it. If only a few of the new men of success had been of this origin, it would have been obscured and ignored. But when there were so many, it could only be highlighted and be a cause of envy.

The newly successful, previously stigmatised category had every reason to be attracted to liberalism, to the cult of equal opportunity for all, and a free market in goods, ideas, and men – and they had every cause to combine this liberalism with a loyalty to the centre, whatever the past history and formal affiliations of that centre. An old and rigid dynasty, long linked with hierarchy, authoritarianism, and obscurantist dogmatism, did not exactly look like promising material for being the symbol of the Open Society. But, comic though it might be, the logic of the situation made it so.

The pariah-liberals had little to hope from the irredentist nationalists and their return to the village green, and the fetishism of the peasant culture from which they themselves were inevitably excluded. A few determined pariahs might be accepted into the pseudo-*Gemeinschaft* of the Ruritanians, but when the newly independent kingdom of Ruritania (a bit later, the Socialist People's Republic of Ruritania, and a bit later still, the Federal Republic of Ruritania) proclaimed and above all practised the principle of Ruritania for the Ruritanians, the prospect for the average pariah was none too bright.

If only the Empire could be maintained, things would be different. The Empire had lost its erstwhile religious zeal, in fact it hardly took its religion very seriously any longer, and, instead, was addicted to a national style of *Gemütlichkeit, Schlamperei und Schweinerei* [literally 'geniality, slovenliness and like a pigsty']. No danger there. And the Empire had at most only rather loose links to any one ethnic group, even though the monarch might prefer one language over the others; he was not fanatical about it.

The Empire failed to satisfy the ethnics. It wasn't so much that it was rigid and unwilling to accommodate itself to their requirements: on the contrary, many of them did exceedingly well. It was rather that, given the complexity of the ethnic map, and the distribution of the ethnic groups both on the map and in the social structure, there was simply no way of satisfying them all. As they saw it, it was a zero-sum game, or probably even a minus-sum game. There was no way of simultaneously satisfying the demands of the Magyars to retain their historic kingdom, and the demands of the Slavs and Rumanians, who jointly amounted to an enormous proportion of the population of the said kingdom, for their political expression. There was no way of satisfying the perfectly reasonable request of the Czechs, that in the historic Czech kingdom of Bohemia local officials should be able and willing to function in the Czech language, with the equally reasonable preference of the German-speaking Bohemians to operate in German in purely German regions and towns of Bohemia. The Empire could only satisfy the demands of some by infuriating others. It could easily infuriate *all* of them and only with luck accommodate *any*.

This, above all, was the basic, pervasive cleavage of the Empire during its terminal decades (which were not known to be terminal, for few anticipated or even desired its demise). But the ethnics went crazy about roots even though some of their leaders were quite moderate and wished to combine their nationalism with a general humanism; and, irony of ironies, the old centre, the dynasty of obscurantism, was in the end deserted by all except the pariah-liberals . . . The village green stood against the Café Central of Vienna, or so it seemed.

Such was the basis of the ideological life of the Empire. The consequence for the history of ideas, culture and literature was curious. The pariah liberals were gifted and clever, they were exceedingly good at thinking and writing, and as on balance they were debarred from easy access to political positions, they had time to write, and they produced the great masterpieces of twentieth-century liberalism. The ethnics, as far as I know, did not produce many *general* masterpieces of organic communalism. They borrowed their ideas from Herder, who had preceded them, and was not a local figure anyway. Perhaps they were too busy forging the national literatures of the re-born nations, recording those peasant songs and customs, or establishing political networks, to work out profound thoughts. Perhaps they could not surmount the contradiction of formulating a general justification for cultural and political specificity.

8   Pariah liberalism

As described above, the new men who had risen by their own efforts were naturally drawn to liberalism, especially as their own social acceptance and recognition was partial, vacillating and ambivalent. They had good cause to fear both the exclusiveness and the communalistic leanings of the new nationalisms. They had every reason to wish the Empire, precluded by its ethnic pluralism from becoming ethno-chauvinistic, to remain in existence and to move in the direction of an open, non-ethnic state and society of individuals. So the philosophy to which they were naturally drawn was an individualistic-liberal one, which saw the acquisition of knowledge, the production of wealth, the creation of beauty, as primarily individual achievements. They valued their own assimilation into the dominant linguistic culture, their detachment from their erstwhile roots, especially when these had constituted a stigma. Their penchant for individualism may have been strengthened by the constant inflow into Vienna of new migrants from the provinces, provocative by their non-assimilation (as yet), and reminding their predecessors in the move to the centre of the fact that they hadn't been there all that long and that their acceptance was not wholehearted or beyond challenge. The new migrants not only were not yet assimilated, they had a stronger sense of the kin collectivity and did not exemplify real individualism, thereby aggravating the offence of their existence. The Open Society was to be seen in the successful professional bourgeoisie, the Closed Society in the new migrants, with their ethnic politics and a personal style which put the achievements of the earlier comers in jeopardy. This, or something like it, was the line-up. What wonder that the most passionate, brilliant and profound paeans to liberalism in the twentieth century came from the pens of Viennese authors?

The political fate of the liberals is well described in a passage by Carl Schorske:

Austrian liberalism . . . had its heroic age in the struggle against aristocracy and baroque absolutism. This ended in the stunning defeat of 1848. The chastened liberals came to power and established a constitutional régime in the 1860's almost by default . . . Even during their two decades of rule, the liberals' social base remained weak, confined to the middle-class Germans and German Jews of the urban centers. Increasingly identified with capitalism, they maintained parliamentary power by the undemocratic device of the restricted franchise. (Schorske 1981: 5)

According to Steven Beller's remarkable book, *Vienna and the Jews, 1867–1938,* the situation was even worse than this. The German intellectuals did not support liberalism, or at any rate, deserted it by 1885 (Beller 1989: 45). The only real social base of liberalism was the attempt of the erstwhile pariah group to escape their stigma or, rather, to resist its re-establishment. Those not subject to such a threat found the appeal of liberty and liberal values less than irresistible. They preferred a return to the old or invented totem poles. The non-Jewish liberal bourgeoisie, which Schorske's account presupposes, to all intents and purposes did not in fact exist (Beller 1989: 243).

And Beller also observes:

The assimilated Jews were indeed the 'Kerntruppe' of Austrian liberalism; not only did they depend for their life's meaning on the principles for which liberalism stood, they also brought to the movement a fervour for the creation of a new type of man which only they, who had most radically accomplished the sloughing off of the traditions of the past, could bring. (Beller 1989: 141)

If all this is so, one must look at the logic and the ambivalences of pariah liberalism.

9 Recapitulation

The great *ideological* confrontation was between the closed, cosy Community and the open, icy, individualist Society. In certain parts of the world, notably the region which concerns us, it pervaded both politics and general sensibility.

This confrontation was in a sense unreal, a case of false consciousness. It wasn't Community and Society which really confronted each other. In reality, it was stable supra-ethnic hierarchy versus mobile culturally homogeneous units, 'nation-states', about to become the new political order. So the apparent confrontation mirrored, in a highly distorted and misleading manner, another and real one. The real contestants were a hierarchical, stable, absolutist but morally debilitated *ancien régime* and the new nationalist order, internally mobile and anonymous, but with accentuated and well-defined cultural boundaries. This new nationalist order was not universalistic but culturally specific and bounded. Thus, partly because each nationalism was defined by a shared culture and legitimated as its protector (in fact: progenitor), partly because such nationalisms were engaged in the struggle for the conversion of culturally ambiguous peasants with neighbouring rival nationalisms, the self-image and self-presentation of the new nation-states was in terms of the model of a closed, localised culture: idiosyncratic and glorying in its idiosyncrasy, and promising emotional and aesthetic fulfilment and satisfaction to its members.

In this struggle nationalism employed the distinctive socio-metaphysic, or philosophical anthropology, provided by romanticism. *Roots* are everything. Those endowed with roots are healthy and vigorous, those devoid of them are pathological and indeed pathogenic. Man was true to himself when his specific, soil-bound or blood-bound culture spoke to him through spontaneous and powerful *feeling*; he was false to his true nature when he linked himself to some anaemic universalist humanitarian ideal or heeded the claims of a *déraciné* dynasty claiming apostolic endorsement.

The struggle in which each nationalism was engaged had two

enemies: rival nationalisms and rootless cosmopolitanism, whether it be the cosmopolitanism of a non-ethnic Empire claiming apostolic but not ethnic vindication or the cosmopolitanism of an internationalist socialism or liberalism, which invoked either the Brotherhood of Man or free individual choice of aim and culture. This was, it must be remembered, prior to the days of socialists and their communist successors themselves choosing to play the nationalist card when they considered it convenient.

In this struggle, the new nationalism used to the full, and very effectively, the romantic vision of man, invoking roots and repudiating cosmopolitanism. No doubt it could not have been so effective in this if the social and intellectual climate had not been so favourable – but it was. It ensured that this vision was deeply and powerfully internalised in the hearts and minds of men – those it favoured, but equally, or perhaps even more, those it rejected. It condemned them to self-hatred and self-hatred was their lot: as many of them had very considerable literary talents, they expressed and recorded it with eloquence. Most of the audience were of course not placed quite so unfavourably: they had been displaced from closed rural communities in which ethnicity was hardly an issue. In their rural settlements of origin status was what counted, even if often (though not always) it had an 'ethnic' (better: cultural, linguistic, and/or religious) marker. They had entered a mobile urban environment, in which culture, now 'ethnically' self-conscious, was the crucial factor determining the limits of a man's aspirations and mobility, and his relationship to political power. The new role of cultural differentiation was presented as the 'awakening' of something old, not the invention of something new. The boundaries of the newly emerging cultural/ethnic groups were not really fixed and, very often, they were easily crossed: in many cases, those who controlled the borders were only too eager to welcome new entrants, so as to enlarge their own nation's demographic strength or to extend the range of its territorial claims. Not always, however: the boundaries were less easy to cross for categories of people too profoundly tainted by the stigma of rootlessness, especially if their talents (due, for instance, to a long tradition of urban commercialism and a scripturalist tradition, which constitutes good training for the literacy-oriented style of modern life) made them dangerous rivals for the best positions in the emerging 'national' community.

Such was the new human condition. There is a nationalist commandment which reads: Thou shalt not covet another man's *Gemeinschaft*! But, like other commandments, it is frequently broken. And the transgressions, as in the case of other commandments, are liable to be punished, both by inner anguish and by external sanctions. Moreover, as in the case of other commandments, the imposition of punishment is liable to be selective rather than fair. The punishment, when self-imposed, is also liable to be tortuous and sometimes bears remarkable literary and philosophical fruits.

This was in the end the ideological confrontation: closed roots against universalism, *Blut und Boden* against 'bloodless' cosmopolitanism. Nowhere was this confrontation as pervasively and deeply felt as in the Habsburg Empire, for the reasons indicated. The pervasiveness of this antithesis must have made many men simply assume, without consciously thinking about it, that these two alternatives were the only ones open to mankind. What else could there be?

Suppose such an assumption is made by a man who, without enthusiasm but with a certain masochistic satisfaction, works out the nature of the human condition, thought, and language. He explores the implications of that imposed solitude, solitary confinement in effect, which is the ultimate corollary of the atomic-universalist-individualist vision. Suppose then that he finds this vision unacceptable, for whatever reason – whilst still tacitly embracing the underlying metaphysic that there are two and only two choices. He has grown up in the world in which the partisans of Community and Society, of national particularism and universalist cosmopolitanism, are fighting it out, in philosophy, literature, parliament, and sometimes literally in violent conflict. What they are all agreed on is that this is *the* fundamental and exclusive dilemma of human life and of social organisation. That, at any rate, is shared and uncontested ground. Where can such a man turn?

Part II

Wittgenstein

10 The loneliness of the long-distance empiricist

There are diverse paths to loneliness. One man may tread more than one of them. Solitude may well be overdetermined.

One path is that taken by the mainstream of Western philosophy. It began with the Promethean defiance of René Descartes, who decided to go it alone, to step outside the custom and prejudice of his own age and culture and to seek truth on his own. He thought it would be possible to judge the culture in which he had been reared from the vantage point of a solitary individual purified by doubt, who accepts nothing other than that which his own reason compels him to accept. Cosmic exile, as Quine aptly named it, was, above all, cultural exile. It expresses extreme distrust of culture, one's own and all others. Moreover, Descartes felt an acute contempt for culture, which he called 'custom and example' and considered to be the source of all error. The human mind was so made as to ensure that, on its own, it would find the truth: this was Descartes' solution to the problem of evil, for it enabled him to exonerate God from the charge of leading us into error. It was not man as made by God who erred, but man as perverted by culture.

The punishment in due course meted out to this Promethean presumption fitted the crime perfectly: the sentence eventually imposed was – *solitary confinement*. If you accept the cognitive authenticity of nothing other than your own directly accessible data, in the end you are confined to a prison whose limits are indeed those data. If they are constituted by *your* immediate consciousness, by *yourself* in effect, then your self eventually becomes your prison. The self is your world, the world is your self. Nothing else is allowed you. The terms of reference you yourself chose preclude all else. For Descartes, the ego was a starting point. What he did not realise, when he started off on this quest, was that his point of departure was destined also to become his terminus.

The argument is simple, even if it took a little over a century to work out fully. Assume that one realm only is accessible to you (it is in effect defined as that which is indisputably accessible to you, and, *as* itself, not open to doubt). Furthermore assume that another realm, of external reality, in principle is *not* directly accessible. Can you infer, from the entities drawn from within the first category, which are indeed accessible to you, either to the mere existence, or the character and distribution, of entities of the second kind? Remember that whatever theories you postulate about the connection between entities of the first kind and those of the second, you can never, ever, check on the correctness of your surmise about such a connection. You only have access to the first lot, but never to the second. How could you check connections between what you can see and what you can never see?

Call the first lot 'experiences of the individual' and the second lot 'external reality'. Inescapable conclusion: neither the pattern, nor even the mere existence, of external reality, can ever be substantiated. All you have is your own data, *yourself*. The conclusion, given the premises, is inescapable. This is the Loneliness of the Long-Distance Empiricist.

In this way an abstract argument in the theory of knowledge led to the total isolation of the individual: from plausible premises – our own data are all we can reach – it concludes that we are locked into those data and can never attain an external world of independently existing things or other minds . . . The philosopher who excogitates this position may or may not, in his private and as it were philosophically off-duty life, also feel lonely. David Hume, for instance, did argue himself into a kind of philosophical anxiety state by such argument, but his normal, personal sociability acted as an effective antidote. A game of backgammon would dissipate the mood and turn it into something artificial and unconvincing. Philosophically induced solitude could be dispelled by temperamental gregariousness. Perhaps, as we shall see, it can also be dissipated by a philosophical demonstration of compulsory gregariousness.

However, a philosopher who has excogitated and worked through the epistemological, empiricist calvary to solitude may also be liable to other forms of solitude. The empiricist argument became fashionable and persuasive in a definite historical context, although it was available earlier. It became fashionable at a time when a rigid system of ranks and social and economic practices was being replaced by a commercial order, in which men were free to choose their own paths and practices and to seek their own achieved position in the world. The privatisation of statuses accompanied, perhaps preceded, the privatisation of knowledge. Loneliness could now have more than one source.

In modern society some men will indeed feel lonely and socially alienated, without necessarily being pushed in this direction by the epistemological argument proving that they must be locked into the island of their own consciousness. The system of ranks was dissolving, the supportive sub-communities conferring positions on individuals were being eroded, and some individuals may have risen economically whilst not gaining corresponding acceptance in the world to which otherwise their wealth would entitle them. They may have lost the support of their erstwhile community, either because they had left it or because it no longer existed, or both, and at the same time they may be stigmatised as unwelcome upstarts in their new milieu. They may be caught between a liberal doctrine, on the one hand, which tells them they are full members of society and, on the other, an illiberal romantic mood which denies them full membership, and tells them into the bargain that they are the perfect example of anti-man, of dehumanised rootlessness, of all that is wrong with the modern world. The eloquence of the romantic poetry and metaphysic which carries this message may be so persuasive that it convinces its victim even more than its bene-ficiary. Alienation, Anomie, Disenchantment, Déracinement are some of the terms associated with such a condition. This is the loneliness of the Man Without Qualities, or of the Viennese Jew, and, particularly perhaps, the formally converted Jew. Whether the condition is further aggravated if the individual in question is also homosexual, which appears to be so in the case which concerns us, probably doesn't matter. He had troubles enough anyway. As the New York black reading a Yiddish newspaper said when asked whether he was a Jew, *Das fehlt mir noch*.

So the Cartesian twist in philosophy inevitably led to the solitude of what Kant called the Transcendental Ego. The social mobility of a market society and the partial, incomplete dissolution of a system of ranks, which emancipates those who had previously been pariahs but does not allow them to feel at home in their new world, leads to the solitude of the Viennese Jew. What happens when the Transcendental Ego is a Viennese Jew, or a Viennese Jew is the Transcendental Ego?

11   The poem to solitude, or: confessions of a transcendental ego who is also a Viennese Jew

Ludwig Wittgenstein's *Tractatus Logico-Philosophicus* (1922) is a poem to solitude. It is also an expression of the individualistic-universalistic, atomic vision of knowledge, thought, language and the world. That vision logically engenders solitude – though the sense of solitude may well also have had other roots. The multiple origins of this sense of solitude is what gives the story its interest.

The poem is all the more effective for its dogmatic, oracular style: the ideas are presented not as an option, which is to be argued against some possible alternative vision, or against mere doubt, as one case among others; but rather as an unquestionable, self-evident set of verities, which do not permit legitimate questioning and whose status is somehow far beyond that of mere earthly affirmation. The dogmatism is brazen. This was ever Wittgenstein's style. Contingent truths did not interest him much: he was eager to reach the very limits of conceptual choice.

There is, in effect, no sense whatever within the *Tractatus* of the possibility of any alternative vision: it is presented as the one and only possible vision. The key premises are abstract but seemingly cogent: the world is the summation of the facts which constitute it. This in effect is the re-statement of the basic atomic intuition: totalities are nothing but the summation of their constituent parts. This is somehow quite particularly true of the world as a whole. The intuition receives a kind of strengthening from the basic rule of the propositional calculus, itself a crucial foundation of modern logic: complex propositions (propositional wholes, if you like) depend for their truth and meaning on nothing other than the truth and meaning of their constituent part-propositions, and the manner in which they have been combined. Nothing extra, so to speak, is accumulated in the course of summation.

The fundamental elements of the world can be reported by being as it were echoed or mirrored. Naught else can be said, not even *that* naught else can be said, so the author notoriously had to withdraw it after saying it. The whole human predicament is contained in this situation.

Wittgenstein's *Tractatus* is of course not the only work in which this particular vision can be found. In the end, the greatest classics articulating this vision will remain David Hume's *Treatise on Human Nature*, and, in somewhat different form, Kant's three *Critiques*. Their terms of reference are the same as those of Wittgenstein's *Tractatus*: an individual, assumed to be the standard exemplar of an invariant humanity, faces the world or his world. How can he think it, conceptualise it, comprehend it? How does Wittgenstein's version differ from them? What is new in it?

It is, for one thing, much, much shorter. It is more dramatic, so to speak revelational, and incomparably more dogmatic. Hume for instance *argues* his case, sometimes vacillates and displays diffidence and anxiety, pursues details, makes concessions. All these weaknesses of the flesh are wholly absent in Wittgenstein's oracular style and they seem to have been altogether alien to his spirit.

Within Hume's soul, there was a contradiction, which has enabled his commentators to present at least two radically distinct Humes: there is the uncompromising formulator of the radical empiricist vision, the solitary Crusoe thrown upon the shores of our island/world and working out a checklist of what he knows and can discover about his habitat. The Crusoe/Hume checklist drastically revises our previous vision of our world, so as to allow within in it only such entities as can be constructed from atomic observables, for faith in anything else would be unwarranted. But there is also a kind of benign, tolerant Tory who sees custom, self-sustaining and beyond the reach of proof, as the only base we can have for our world, whether social or cognitive. The two Humes are both in opposition and in collusion: when Hume/Crusoe cannot stand his isolation any longer, the Tory steps in and assures Crusoe that where reason fails, custom will do perfectly well. This tension is wholly absent from Wittgenstein's *Tractatus*, though not, as we shall see, from his subsequent life and development. The duality which was synchronic in Hume, in the end appeared as two successive stages in Wittgenstein's life.

There is another difference between Hume and Wittgenstein – their respective styles and spirits – and it is extremely important. If you wish to have the atomic vision presented in slow Augustan prose, at leisure, with the dignity of tolerance and doubt and occasional confessions of anxiety and ambivalence, then, unquestionably, Hume is your man. You cannot do any better than that. His is, as you might say, the Lord Chesterfield version of the empiricist loneliness. In defence of Hume it should be said that he was a Scot: the complacency which pervades his reasoning on morals, for instance, can be seen, in the context of

Edinburgh, as defiance of the Calvinists rather than as lack of any sense of the seriousness of the problem. If, on the other hand, you wish to read a dramatic poem, full of fireworks and aphorism, in Viennese *fin-de-siècle* style, with all the defiance of an intellectually autistic young man – well then, turn to Wittgenstein's youthful work.

But there is also a difference of content and intellectual background. Hume's atomism was psychologistic. It is rooted in a certain image of our psychic life which assumes that we build up whatever is in our mind by accumulation and association, from elements which are, as it were, sensory atoms. As a matter of descriptive psychology all this is quite wrong, ignoring as it does the important role of pre-programming and of 'Gestalt'; though it is a good account of how, in a scientific age, our world is *re*-organised. What is misguided *psychology* is at the same time a very good allegory for a plausible, or at any rate widely accepted and very effective, *ethic of cognitive comportment*.

By contrast, Wittgenstein's atomism pretends to be innocent of this kind of psychological background picture: in any case, important parts of the argument can be formulated without crediting him with any specifically psychological premises. The overt, highlighted roots of his atomism lie not in psychology (atomistic associationist psychology was old hat in his time), but in logic, and in the state of logical theory at the time he was thinking and writing. This was not old hat, but a new, vital and rapidly developing subject, with which he was preoccupied and to which he contributed in the very work under discussion.

The underlying argument seems to be: logic captures the way we think, if we think at all. We can no other. The laws of logic being what they are, the world we think, the world we know, must be of a certain kind. The so-to-speak agglutinative world, the world as summation of elements, reached by Hume on the basis of – or so he claimed – attentive introspection, was reached by Wittgenstein without any avowed introspection.

Can the picture of the world offered in the *Tractatus* be maintained? The answer must be an emphatic *No*, for a whole variety of reasons. The reasons are interesting and relevant. Here we shall list six of them. They are not fully independent of each other.

(1)   Framework

In the calculus of propositions, individual propositions do not, so to speak, have a place. They accumulate, but they form no queue: they are not placed in relation to each other; there is no order. (Connectives, such as 'and' or 'or', do of course relate them to each other and, sometimes, as in the case of the use of 'if-then', they do relate them in a definite order, which makes its contribution to the actual sense of the complex proposition. But this does not affect the basic principle that propositions live a place-less life.) *A and B* means exactly the same as *B and A*: the conjunction is true if and only if each constituent is true. It *sums* them up. But the *order* in which they appear is wholly irrelevant. They know no order.

Is our world like that? Obviously, it is not. Any remotely plausible atomistic account of our world must inevitably make it resemble a *mosaic*. The stones which enter into the composition of the mosaic do ideally resemble each other in shape, so that any one of them can replace any other: they do all of them *fit* the slots. It is this which makes them atomic and independent of each other. To that extent, but to that extent only, they resemble the atomic proposition in the calculus of propositions. But the world, the picture, which emerges, is not merely a function of the available stones-elements, but also of the availability of a framework into which they are placed, and above all of the order in which they are placed in it. Hume and Kant, who also offered a version of this atomic-mosaic account of world-construction, did each of them have a theory of the framework, of the manner in which it related the pieces of the mosaic to each other. For Kant, the structure preceded the elements, which makes him a proto-*structuraliste*; for Hume, the structure is a product of the tendency of the elements to combine and clot and associate with each other, which is what makes him an Associationist.

Hume made the elements cluster together as they came; they constituted groups or 'bundles' as he called them. These bundles aggregated partly in terms of the order in which the elements-atoms had arrived on the screen and partly in terms of their inherent properties. They 'associated' and Hume's work contains an account of the various principles of association, of bundle-formation. Kant, on the other hand, was much more preoccupied with the pre-existing screen onto which the elements were to be placed and his *Critique of Pure Reason* is largely an account of the properties of this screen and its structure, which he believed to be universal and invariant amongst men.

Neither of these two principles, nor indeed any other, is to be found in Wittgenstein's *Tractatus*. The elements exist, as they do in logic, without any ordering or queuing, like some undisciplined rabble which has never been taught to behave in an orderly manner. The world *is* their accumulation, but not their pattern – the pattern is irrelevant and absent. Can a *world* really emerge in this way? It cannot. The world presented in the *Tractatus* is a bizarre summation, an accumulation of elements devoid of order. It would remain exactly the same world, *whatever* the order in which its elements appeared. The calculus of propositions in logic does indeed display such indifference to the order in which propositions appear in conjunction or disjunction, and of course it is quite blind to their order of appearance: it can have its Dramatis Personae, but no order of arrival on the stage. For that very reason, it is not a very good model for a world. A *world* is not indifferent in this manner to the *placement* of those seated at the world-table. *La place à table ne ment jamais* (F. Mauriac). The *Welt-Tisch* also has its protocol.

Why was Wittgenstein so indifferent to this obvious problem? I can only suggest a possible explanation: he was more concerned with his literary effect than with the question of how our world is possible. To produce his desired *Entfremdung-effekt*, he needed a dreary world of blindly accumulated atoms, and the model borrowed from the propositional calculus served well enough for that purpose.

Order is of the essence of our world: it does not simply consist of its elements, but of those elements related to each other in such a way that each of them is located in a definite place, in relation to all the other places. The world is not merely a totality of things, or even of facts (which is what Wittgenstein claimed), but also of *locations*. And even if locations were merely derivative from facts and things, a kind of sum total of relations which they brought with themselves (as Hume thought), rather than having them imposed on relations (Kant's version), there would still have to be some mechanism, some procedure, for engendering them.

The world we actually inhabit is made up of certain characteristic clusters, *things*, and the manner in which the accumulation or organisation of these things is achieved is an important question, which preoccupied Hume and Kant. Wittgenstein does not face it: his world is a random summation of elements. This no doubt helped satisfy his *Weltschmerz*, but it does not make a good account of our real situation.

(2)   Overlap or chain-links

In our normal life we build up our world not merely by slotting individual atoms, whatever they be, into places on a pre-existing space, with positions waiting for them: we also are able to erect the picture because the individual items overlap, are linked to each other, in a manner which indicates how they are to be related in the picture that eventually emerges. (Hume actually thought these kinds of principles were sufficient for the construction of a world.) For instance, we see an object first from one angle, and then all at once from a slightly different angle, but the two successive pictures have an important overlap or affinity, encouraging us to link the two to each other, as belonging alongside each other, and revealing slightly different aspects of the same 'thing'. Wittgenstein, though he does speak of 'things' being related to each other like links in a chain within 'facts', says nothing of such overlap between what he considers independent facts. He uses the term 'things' for elements within atomic facts, and it is not clear whether such 'things' (in our normal sense, i.e. bridges between facts) can be incarnated in diverse facts, in other words whether they have any real similarity to what we call 'things' in ordinary life.

Extreme empiricism is liable to deal with this kind of overlap, and the, as it were, fact-transcending 'things' which are so engendered, by treating it as a kind of theory-construction. Adjoining perceptions contain similar elements which are linked together and are called 'one thing'. For instance: aspects of a kitten seen successively from slightly different angles engender the 'theory' of a continuous, solid kitten. The *Tractatus* tells us nothing of 'things' in this ordinary but important sense: the argument seems to proceed on the assumption that things occur only within isolated facts, presumably partaking of their solitude. The existence of 'things' in a more normal sense would then simply be an entirely contingent fact about the patterning of the actual cognitive elements of the world. If it so happened that neighbouring facts possessed no similar elements – and as all facts are totally independent of each other, there quite literally can be no reason in the world which might cause this to be so – there would be no 'things' in the ordinary sense.

This particular objection may or may not be fatal to the vision. But in any case, it reveals it as an exceedingly odd vision. It fails to account for the most obvious feature of our world, namely, that it is indeed a habitable *world*, consisting of usable and perceptible *things*. It doesn't merely fail to explain it, it does not even bother to mention the problem. Wittgenstein seemed only to be interested in sketching a dead, inert world, so that he could bewail his alienation within it: other important features of the world we actually inhabit were beneath his attention.

(3)   Absence of a Turn-over Ontology

A curious and very conspicuous feature of the world-picture presented in the *Tractatus* is that it has a fixed, permanent ontology, i.e. a kind of definitive inventory of the 'things' (in *his* sense, whatever they be) which make up the world. This *seems* logical enough: before we play a game, we need to know the elements which go into it, the objects which it is legitimate to use in making moves. The first thing which needs to be done when explaining a game is to specify the nature of the pieces which can be used in it. Knowing or exploring or characterising a world is a kind of game and the same point might well be expected to apply. We must know just what the things are we are dealing with before proceeding to characterise them further. The basic elements should be *given* and stable. This argument seems plausible, but is actually false. The game of cognitive exploration of the world consists, above all, of changing the elements . . .

In the seventeenth century, much philosophising was in fact carried on in this style: the philosopher would begin with identifying the 'substances', which were to be the ultimate world-bricks, substance being defined as that capable of existing on its own rather than being a feature or aspect of another substance. It was important to find such 'substances' and separate them from ontologically second-class entities, which only inhere *in* substances but cannot exist on their own. Descartes, Spinoza, and Leibniz proceeded in this manner, differing only in the number of substances they came up with, rather than in the overall strategy – Descartes working with two (possibly three), Spinoza with one only, and Leibniz with some very large or unlimited number of them. They differed in doctrine, but not in the underlying assumption which led them to the formulation of the question.

Now it seems logical enough that we should have a definite inventory of elements before proceeding to do something with them. The inventory should come first, before other activities, should it not? If you don't know what the things or elements are, if you only have some undifferentiated messy continuum, how on earth can you do something with it? How indeed. Inventories first! *Then* you can start saying things about the items in it.

Notwithstanding the *prima facie* plausibility of this argument, this is in fact *not* how our world works. Ontologies, world-inventories, come not at the beginning but at the end of inquiry; or rather they come in the middle, because they do not seem to be definitive, but are frequently and indefinitely revised. We start with one set of 'things' and then find that the theories articulated in terms of them do not work too well. The way out turns out to be not to ascribe different attributes to the same things, but to re-think the inventory, the units into which the continuum of the 'world' has been divided, i.e. to find *new* 'things'. The world is like a play in which the Dramatis Personae are forever changing, sometimes radically. We do not have stable inventories and variable theories: both theories and ontology change, and the important changes often occur in the latter. What distinguishes cumulative and genuine science from pre-scientific thought is precisely this: science has become habituated to, as it were, expendable, replaceable ontologies, whereas pre-scientific thought tends to make them rigid.

There is no room whatsoever for any turn-over quality of ontology in the scheme proposed in the *Tractatus*. It proceeds as if a fixed and firm ontology-inventory were there from the beginning, a very precondition of thinking, of mirroring the world at all. It is in this respect a curious revival of a seventeenth- and early eighteenth-century style of thought. It is, in fact, precisely in this manner that the issue is presented. He could defend this approach by saying that unless there was a firm base, we could not think the world at all. Thinking in terms of fixed given basic substances had in fact been out of vogue for some time, and had been displaced in physics, where it had been very much at home for some time. Why on earth did Wittgenstein return to it? Why billiard balls in logic or ontology at the very time when physics had definitively abandoned them?

Once again it is modern logic, and the part of mathematics on which it is primarily based – set theory –, which seems to provide the explanation. That area of inquiry seems generally to operate in terms of quite unidentified but none the less definite 'objects', which then do or do not fall into classes, sets, and do or do not possess attributes that assign them to classes defined by them, etc. Set theory seemed initially to be designed to apply to a world of definite and clearly defined objects, falling or not falling into definite sets. Apparently it has also of late adjusted itself so as to operate with so-called sloppy rather than well-defined sets; I do not know whether it can also adjust itself to apply to sloppy objects, whether it can deal with jelly-like or cloud-like entities, with mushy viscous messes that do not break up into manifest units. I suspect that nothing is beyond the technical ingenuity of men and that, if it does not already exist, a set theoretical technique will be developed applicable to jellies and clouds. But it does not appear to have existed at the time when Wittgenstein was composing his *Tractatus*. The ontology it projected onto the world was neat, clean, firm – or so the language of the *Tractatus* emphatically suggests.

(4)   Homogeneity of Things

Once again – and this point is closely related to the preceding one – the *Tractatus* talks as if the elements which enter its ontology, its things/substances, were all of one and the same kind. But the most striking feature about our normal talk about the world is that what we call 'things' differ tremendously in logical type, so much so that it makes little sense to add them up or put them alongside each other. A shoe is a thing, and so is a pair of shoes, but a pair of shoes is not three things. (But for a set theoretician, they *can* be three things.) On a map we can see countries and we can see boundaries, and we can refer to both as 'things', but they are not things in the same sense. Sometimes people get logically conscience-stricken about this and like to have some criteria of 'real' things, e.g. entities occupying space, and will then say things like 'boundaries are imaginary lines'. They seem to think that countries occupying territory are real but the lines separating them are somehow imaginary.

The *Tractatus* seems to presuppose that the 'things' which enter into facts and thus provide the furniture of the world are all neatly of one kind, and do not reduplicate each other in the way that individual shoes duplicate the pair and boundaries duplicate the territories which they delimit.

I rather doubt whether a language endowed with such a neat and hence philosophically aseptic basement, a list of real and logically homogeneous objects to which it refers, could actually function and perform the services which our language in fact does perform. We do not merely need turn-over, unstable ontologies; we also need messy reduplicative ones. We need to handle, to think, 'objects' of radically distinct kinds. If this is indeed a valid principle, the *Tractatus* violated it.

(5)   Ambiguity

The *Tractatus* fails to explain how the individual items making up the world/self mosaic are fitted into their specific locations; how they overlap and share content and coagulate into on-going and persisting entities; and why it is that their basic constituents are not forever fixed, as the book claims, but on the contrary change with the advancement of knowledge. Over and above this, the book fails to account for the pervasiveness of ambiguity, of alternatives, and of interpretation in human life.

One of the most important aspects of our life is that what we 'experience' is open to reinterpretation. This is of enormous importance in our life and our world would be quite different from what it is, were this not so. The world presented by the *Tractatus* is indeed utterly different in this respect: just as the basic inventory of the world is alleged to be given and unchangeable (which is quite false), so 'facts' appear to be hard, firm, unambiguous.

In fact, Wittgenstein notices this problem in the *Tractatus* (Wittgenstein 1974 (1921): 54, proposition 5.5423). He observes that the drawing of a cube can be seen in two ways, with certain edges forming either the front or the rear part of the cube. When we look at the schematic drawing of the cube, does it constitute one or two facts? Wittgenstein opts for the second alternative: we really have *two* facts here. Wittgenstein notes that there are other similar phenomena.

What he fails to notice is how disastrous this concession is to the vision presented in the book. First of all, it is wrong to say that there are 'similar phenomena', in as far as this suggests that there also exist phenomena which are *not* like this, which are hard and totally unambiguous facts. Are there *any* such reinterpretation-resistant facts? Alternatively, if one treats the open multiplicity of such interpretation as a plurality of facts, a number of problematic consequences follow. Diverse 'facts', for one thing, now lose that total independence of each other which is one of the cornerstones of this vision. What the class of diverse interpretations of the same drawing or whatever have in common – that which makes them members of the same class – is that they share a certain invariant base. This base, i.e. the drawing minus the variable interpretations, is rather difficult to name, now that the status of 'fact' has been assigned to each interpretation and not the drawing. If 'facts' are the ground, the bottom storey of the world-picture, there now seems to be an under-base even more fundamental, standing in a curious one-many relationship to the 'facts'. It also becomes rather difficult to speak of that summation of facts which for early Wittgenstein constitutes the world. If one thing is obvious about interpretation, it is that it is open-ended, that new ones can always be added. This undermines the finite summation-of-facts world presented in the work.

Wittgenstein's remarks about the cube play a role in his system similar to that of the patch of blue in David Hume's *A Treatise of Human Nature* (Hume 1888 (1789): 5–6). In that passage Hume notes that the principle, central and vital to his system, that ideas can exist only as after-tastes of sensations, is contradicted by the fact (which he admits) that if we are familiar with a series of shades of a colour, and one particular shade happens to be missing, we can visualise it even if we have never actually experienced it. With commendable honesty Hume remarks on this and then happily goes on – without also remarking on the fact that, once such an exception is allowed, the whole central argument of the *Treatise* goes by the board. We are then free to say that what comes first is our capacity to recognise a certain series, into which we place actual experiences, rather than that we construct all series *ex post*, from the experiences. Similarly, once Wittgenstein recognises the multiplicity of 'facts' in the same data (or whatever you want now to call the new basic raw material of experience), two crucial features essential for his system – total independence of facts from each other and the finitude of their number – go by the board.

This is far more than merely a technical criticism. The multiplicity of possible interpretations of any experience is a really essential feature of our world, and an account of our world which denies it is grossly inadequate. The central feature of our intellectual life is that we can oscillate between radically distinct styles of interpretation, in addition to rival interpretations in the same style; we live in a realm in which diverse conceptualisations are possible and practised, and their relationships to each other are complex. There are quite diverse ways of seeing situations. This is what makes life interesting.

Wittgenstein does of course use just this feature, the denial of a conceptually plural world, to secure his desired literary effect: the solitude, dreariness, and grey deadness of the cell he paints hinges on this mute, unambiguous, and, as it were, terminal quality of the 'facts' which constitute it. Pascal induces despair in the inhabitant of the human cell through the awareness of being *condemned*: Wittgenstein's prisoner is spared the anticipation of an ending of his predicament (he cannot, says Wittgenstein, conceive or visualise it), and the hopelessness of his condition lies in its greyness, in the present not in the future. In a curious way Wittgenstein's account of the human condition anticipates the methods used to break down prisoners through 'brainwashing': the environment of the prisoner is made dreary and lifeless. There is no pattern in the world to endow it with interest or, if there is, it is so contingent as to merit little attention, and it is known to have this accidental quality. There is no hope, for the dreariness itself is a necessary consequence of the very nature of things, of knowledge, of the language which alone is capable of recording it all.

(6)   Structure

In our life, we are much more like a child crawling through a complicated climbing frame and exploring it in all its variety than like an unutterably bored fly crawling over a mosaic and noting its repetitiveness. The *Tractatus* suggests the opposite: that is why its author feels such *ennui* with the world, and that is also why he is wrong.

The world has structure or, rather, complex multiple structures of all kinds: the bits we bump up against are connected in all kinds of ways with other bits, and it is the exploration of these connections which makes up life and endows it with excitement. The structure is much more than the summation of propositions about inert and unutterably isolated atoms. It is the structures, the way things are parts of systems, which interest us. The world is full of systems, it is not a summation of dreary 'facts'. The complex interrelatedness of objects, the changes in constellation, the possibility this offers for combination, intrigue, adventure – that is our world. It is so much more than the mechanical summation of inert, pointless elements. The structure *is* the thing. This complexity of structure, which is somehow connected with the multiplicity of alternative visions and angles, is what we find in life, but not at all in the *Tractatus* . . . which simply constructs a world deduced from the assumption that there is nothing but echo-and-summation, the brass-rubbing of atoms, and the aggregation of the rubbings. It then lovingly luxuriates in the anguish induced by the unutterable dreariness of such a world.

One might exclaim in reaction to this: but the world simply is not a summation of dreary mini-brass-rubbings! If you find the world dreary anyway, you may endow your depression with philosophical depth by a putative demonstration that the world *must* be like that, because that is all that language will allow you to say. The proof is spurious: the world is indeed depressing, but for quite different reasons, and not because it is obliged to fit into the conventions of the logical notation of a given period.

What has really happened in this work, what state of mind does it express? It conveys the despair of a solitary and alienated individual, well in the tradition of pessimistic romanticism: so far, nothing new, other than, perhaps, the originality and effectiveness of the literary methods deployed for this end. But there *is* something new: the desolation of the soul is presented as a corollary, a consequence, of general, simple, and indisputable contentions concerning the nature of thought and language. The situation in which this despairing individual finds himself is not a contingent misfortune, but a *necessary* fact, a philosophically demonstrated affirmation. In other words, if all this were true, it would not merely depict our prison, but prove that there is no way out. This is of course part of the predicament. There cannot be any escape: the demonstration constitutes the locks and bars of this dreadful prison. Is there a way out? Can Bond/Wittgenstein get out of this one? Wait for the later part of the story . . .

One might of course also put it the other way round: here we have a restatement of the old ego-centred empiricist epistemology, new in part in virtue of the injection of the logical and linguistic theme (language as well as the self is made solitary), but above all by the form of its literary presentation, by placing the initially aseptic solitude established by the theory of knowledge at the service of romantic despair. Poetry, and literary effects, are used to enhance the experience of isolation. Here, of course, Wittgenstein was anticipated by Schopenhauer, who invoked idealism to confirm desperation: the world was unreal as well as horrible, and this somehow, to Schopenhauer's satisfaction, made it worse.

12 Ego and language

The *Tractatus* was the simultaneous expression of two kinds of anguish: that of the solitary explorer of the world propelled into 'cosmic exile' and finding himself in total solitude, and that of the Man Without Qualities, without any attributes imposed on him by his roots: lacking roots, and so lacking any genuine identity, he is doomed to opportunist volatility, superficial emulation of others, and self-hatred. The distinctive trait of Viennese individualist empiricism of the terminal decades of the Habsburg Empire was the intensity with which it combined these two elements. But there is another duality which can also be discerned in the *Tractatus*: alienation through the solitude of the self, and alienation through the inert superficiality of language. Let us turn to the latter, because the former has already been discussed above.

The *Tractatus* is a squeal of pessimistic woe, an expression of despair. What, strangely enough, the so very numerous commentators have failed to spot is that it contains two totally independent paths to despair. Either would be quite sufficient on its own, neither needs the other, though possibly they reinforce each other. This dualism, as we are stressing, is crucial when we examine the manner in which the 'later' Wittgenstein escaped the gloom of his earlier position.

One of the two paths leads through the nature of *language*. Speech, being bounded by the range of logical forms available to it (and revealed to us through modern logical notation), is only capable of echoing, mirroring, the structure of inert, pointless, meaningless and isolated 'facts'. The insulation of facts from each other is guaranteed by the first principle of the 'calculus of propositions', which requires all elementary propositions to be totally independent of each other. Nothing interesting can be said and what is interesting cannot be said. What a dreary world to be in!

William James, writing a decade or so earlier, noted, in *Pragmatism*, how the complex tangled reality of the world contrasted with the simple elegance of the constructions of the philosophers (James 1990 (1907): 8). What he had in mind was the elegant simplicities of the Hegelians and their then New England disciples. In that context the simplicities, also justified by logic though in quite a different tradition, were invoked to provide a vision which was not only incomparably simpler and tidier than the reality we live in, but also more edifying, comforting and reassuring. The Anglo-Hegelians taught that the world, properly understood, was a simple elegant unity in which man and sound values were, in the end, properly looked after and assured of a dignified and secure place.

The curious thing about the empiricist tradition and one of its terminal culminations, the early Wittgenstein, is that it too bizarrely simplifies the world (the *Tractatus* tells us *everything* about it in seven short propositions!), but it does it not so as to cheer us up, but so as to depress us. The summation of isolated cognitive atoms, which was ever the empiricist world-model, was never particularly exhilarating, and it was never less so than in Wittgenstein's youthful work. Here it was made quite specially dreary by the logical internal structuring of the basic propositions and basic facts, which somehow obviates the possibility of any joyful flow or continuity. These facts or the objects which compose them all hang together like a piece of machinery, all the screws and bolts discrete. Each might just as well have been placed in some other piece of machinery, none of the elements have any elective affinity with each other. Nothing *belongs* anywhere, it is a world made up of distinct, dead, indifferent, isolable and isolated bits. Our intellectual life can only consist either of not reflecting this machine-like desolation, and hence talking nonsense, or of reflecting it, thereby expressing sense – but of the utmost drearyness. An unpalatable set of alternatives. In such circumstances, it is only too understandable if the thinker decides that the rest is silence.

What however is noteworthy about this particular pathway to despair is that it invokes *only* the nature of language (summation of basic propositions, and naught else) and/or the meaning relation (echo, mirroring). This says absolutely nothing about what sort of consciousness may exist in the world, if any, whether it is a world-soul or, on the contrary, it is multiply incarnated in a whole set of individual beings. All this is ignored and, indeed, not required: it is simply the nature of language on its own, irrespective of who uses it or whether there is anyone to use it, which guarantees universal dreariness and pointlessness. Despair is, as it were, self-sustaining, or language-sustained, and requires no selves or consciousness to suffer it.

The other and more conventional path to despair is by solitary confinement, imposed on the investigative self as it examines its data to see how far they will allow one to proceed, only to find that the data themselves are the limit of the world, and that self and world are coextensive and identical. This theme is also conspicuously present in the *Tractatus*. It too guarantees total solitude, emptiness and despair. It is also self-sufficient and does not really need any theory of language, and can be stated without it (though in Wittgenstein's case one suspects that the atomisation required was engendered by the atomism of the logical calculus).

Thus in the *Tractatus* the two despairs, though endowed with logically independent foundations, are presented as *one* desperation. If, however, one is inspired by a theory of language, which is then shown to be false, then *both* despairs, having been made into one, are conjured away! This, in a way, is a summary of Wittgenstein's development and the place he accorded to himself in the history of thought: the empiricist theory of the solitary thinking/sensing being is conflated with the logicist-inert model of language; and the latter being shown to be wrong as an account of language, the entire problem is dissipated.

The self/language dualism is not the same as the duality of sufferers (the epistemic investigator versus the rootless wandering Jew). But both these polarities are there, hidden in the argument, and help explain both the driving force and the mechanics of the escape from the Viennese predicament.

13   The world as solitary vice

Arthur Schopenhauer had spoken of the world as either Will or as Idea. He was, it would seem, one of the few philosophers actually to have directly influenced Wittgenstein. Wittgenstein worked out an image of the world not merely 'as Idea', but as an idea inherently held by a lone individual consigned to conceptual solitary confinement. This is, in effect, the plot of the *Tractatus*, or rather one of them: as we have stressed, that work has two superimposed themes, not distinguished and clearly separated. Apart from the solitude of the individual, bounded by the limits of his perceptual field which he cannot even see, let alone transcend, there is also the alienation of an unutterably dreary language, restricted to soulless photocopying of isolated 'facts' and their mechanical summation. The nature of language, as well as the condition of the self, is enough to drive one to despair . . . The loneliness of the transcendental ego is old hat in philosophy: alienation and solitude in virtue of the very form of language is rather more original. The basic plot of Wittgenstein's philosophical life was to be that the two predicaments are conflated, and then the alienating theory of language is decreed false, the realisation of which is held to liberate the prisoner from *both* sets of chains.

One of the most striking statements in the *Tractatus*, which is not short of striking statements, reads as follows: 'Death is not an event in life' (Wittgenstein 1974: 72, proposition 6.4311). He also observed that life has no limits, rather in the way the visual field has none (if we look at it, the limit is no longer there). The two points are meant to illustrate each other. A man cannot experience his death, for if he experienced it, it would no longer be his death. Nor can a man focus on the edge of his experience, his death, for if he experienced it, it would no longer be his death. These passages are of interest, among other reasons, because they illustrate that Wittgenstein was *also* concerned by the isolation of the *self*, and not only by the alienation of and by *language*. In other words, he was not so far removed from the phenomenalist vision of the world as constituted by the sensing of an individual.

One is tempted to expostulate in reaction to his remarks about death – what exactly is it that people experience when they sit at deathbeds, when they minister to the dying, or indeed are present at executions or take part in battles? What exactly is it that happens at funerals and cremations? If death is not an event in life, just how would you describe the events in the final act of *Hamlet* or *Romeo and Juliet*? The limits on what can be said proposed by the *Tractatus* would proscribe much of the world's literature, if not all of it. (This is not a trivial point.) Wittgenstein seems to be talking not about the world, but about a single stream of consciousness, as if it were the world. For a markedly autistic individual, perhaps it was.

If death is not an event in life, then at any rate it would seem that the death of others would be a part of life. But the *Tractatus* appears to be an autistic work in which there simply are no others . . . If there are no *others*, then indeed, death cannot be a part of life. For the author of the *Tractatus*, evidently this was so. There is a certain irony in all this: much later, Wittgenstein was to acquire fame as the man who had shown, or so he and his converts claimed, that there could be no 'private language', that community was imposed on us by the very fact of speech.

The curious thing is that in his youth he assumed (rather than argued) that there could be nothing other than a private language, referring exclusively to a private world, and moreover one without death, for the world itself was extinguished with the snuffing out of its solitary observer and so could not conceivably incorporate its own termination. It appears that this world had no other significant inhabitants. A single consciousness mirrored a single world and was co-extensive with it. That is all. It had long been evident that if you formulate the problem of knowledge and existence in the terms commended by radical empiricism – what can consciousness apprehend, without allowing itself question-begging, unwarranted inferences? – then one does indeed end in this solitary black hole. What was original about Wittgenstein was that in his early thought the romantic despair-monger of *fin-de-siècle* Vienna (or indeed the First World War soldier who noted that his existence had been reduced to nothing but the performance of basic physical functions, including masturbation (Monk 1990: 126, 146)) received philosophical underwriting from the classical epistemological tradition – the sorrows of Werther confirmed by the reasoning of Hume and the logical notation of Russell and Whitehead.

This leads us to a correct formulation of what it is that the *Tractatus* is trying to do. It is an attempt at giving an account of what the world looks like to a solitary individual, who is reflecting on the problem of how his mind, or language, can possibly 'mean', i.e. reflect that world.

The exercise is carried out on the assumption that the notions and/or the notation of modern logic capture the nature of our thought, our language, so that what is meant or reflected must reproduce the general formal features of logic, on the assumption that actual language, though it knows it not, speaks logic as M. Jourdain spoke prose. When Jacques is asked to bring slippers, much though it might surprise M. Jourdain, this injunction, it would appear, has the form of the notation of *Principia Mathematica*. (Alternatively, it is devoid of sense.) If there are other people (this is not explicitly denied, though the *Tractatus* comes very close to implying it), they are irrelevant. Presumably they occupy their own private black holes, each endowed with its own structure just like all the others. Given that in all important features they simply reduplicate each other, they are really quite irrelevant and philosophically redundant. The world would be exactly the same if they did not exist: their existence does not really either amplify or complicate the world. They constitute a kind of contingent and uninteresting replication, more of the same. If there is more than one centre of consciousness, then each centre is doomed to solitude. As in Leibniz, the monads neither need nor are able to communicate. But Leibniz postulated a pre-established harmony to make up for the lack of communication: if they could not communicate, they were at least so finely synchronised that they could go through the motions, and it came out much the same as if they really were communicating. In Wittgenstein's version, they are so totally irrelevant to each other that no pre-established harmony is required. The whole point of the story is their loneliness, and so the question of how they can overcome it is not raised.

14 The mystical

The above formula, though it does capture some of the truth about the *Tractatus*, does not capture all of it. The idea that we apprehend the world through the logical equipment enshrined in set theory, which had such a remarkable hold over the thinking of the young Wittgenstein, did not dominate it without qualification. For one thing, as we have seen, the dreariness of language was grafted on to the solitude of the mind confronting the world. But there was also a further theme.

Wittgenstein also had a strong religious or mystical sense, which is very prominent in the later passages of the *Tractatus*. The notation of set theory may dominate and circumscribe what can be said but, for all that, what can be *said* does not exhaust our mental life. On the contrary, the dreariness of what can be said is highlighted by the luminous quality of that which cannot be said.

Not how the world is, but that it is at all, is part of the mystical. The mystical escapes the limits imposed by set theory and the calculus of propositions. In other words it escapes the atomism; a sense of totality is allowed provided it is not articulated, or provided it is not articulated legitimately (but, in true Wittgensteinian style, it is affirmed, decreed indubitable, and then withdrawn from the realm of the sayable). The ineffable, and this is very important, escapes neither Wittgenstein's autism nor his tacitly assumed universalism. The unsayable, like the sayable, observes the assumption that minds, though utterly isolated, resemble each other in all important features. The mystical, in Wittgenstein's *Tractatus*, is just as solitary as the referential; like the mind or language it merely photocopies atoms and then aggregates them. (These, interestingly, are the only activities allowed to rational thought in that work.) It never meets others in some collective ritual ecstasy, which is what most students of mysticism would expect. The autistic individual is still contemplating his own awareness of the world, and its ineffable aspects, in splendid isolation. The transcendence of the limits of articulate speech is possible, but it fails to overcome loneliness. The mystical does grant us a sense of totality (as opposed to those miserable, inert cognitive/linguistic atoms), but it does *not* grant us togetherness. Even the mystical is solitary. Totality yes, community no!

So Wittgenstein remained a universalist even in this sphere, where one would not expect universalist individualism to be at home: there is not the slightest hint that the mystical might assume quite different forms in different people, in different moods or social contexts, in different cultures, perhaps even in diverse, genetically differentiated species, or that it might be a bridge or a means of union. If such a thought ever crossed his mind, there is nothing in the book to suggest it – and a good deal to suggest that no such thought had troubled him. It was outside the terms of reference in which he wrote that work: individualism/ universalism was taken for granted; he was still firmly at that end of the crucial polarity. Human beings are not only doomed to isolation but also to fundamental similarity, indeed qualitative identity. The blindness to cultural diversity and its importance, the superimposed individualism and universalism so characteristic of the Enlightenment and so dear to the liberalism which perpetuated and developed its ideas, remains his unquestioned assumption. We are still dealing, even when he is in his mystical mood, with the Viennese *haut bourgeois* liberal and not with a worshipper of the Carpathian village green.

In reality, the really important features of the mystical in human society are, first of all, that it is tremendously variegated and, second, that it is often exceedingly gregarious. Men like to partake in the mystical together: if Durkheim is to be believed, it is of its essence that they partake in it collectively and it alone bestows true togetherness on us. For Durkheim, ritual is the social contract; it is also the only possible one. Durkheim's account of the social contract runs as follows: it is only in the mystical elation of collective ritual that men acquire shared concepts and shared obligations (for him, the roots of moral and conceptual compulsion are the same, as they are for Kant), and only in this manner do they become both human and social. Both the capacity for thought and a sense of obligation have the same origin, and it is to be found in *shared* mystical experience induced by collective ritual. But the manner in which diverse societies practise it varies enormously. How many tomes did it take Frazer to cover the diversity of magic and religion? – and, of course, he far from exhausted the possible range of material.

Thus, it is here that Wittengenstein committed himself to what is perhaps the strangest of all his strange beliefs. He bestowed upon the mystical that very atomism or isolation which was part of his own inheritance and his predicament. He himself evidently indulged his mysticism in an individualist style, as he did virtually everything else, but it is truly strange to project this on mankind at large. Rational cognition may indeed be part of an individualist culture; to assume the same for mysticism is odd indeed.

Other rationalists of his philosophical generation may have spurned the mystical: he neither despised nor repudiated it, but projected onto it the uniformity or conformity which, on his then views, logic had already imposed on the rational. You could, it seems, escape the bounds of reason but not those of solitude, which pursued you even into the realm of the mystical. Conventional rationalists were fully aware of the luxuriant diversity of superstition and spurned it, partly for this very reason: rich, undisciplined variety was one of the features which damned it. It had so many forms precisely because those who indulged in it had been unable to discipline their own thoughts. Genuine thought was more elegant and restrained; to romantics, such thought appeared impoverished for that very reason. That is the strange message of his poem, the *Tractatus*. He does not even preach: Mystics of the World Unite! It is assumed that they are already separate but equal, united in their total but solitary resemblance. This is the strange universal mysticism of a lonely rationalist.

15 The central proposition of the *Tractatus*: world without culture

The *Tractatus* is so arranged as to consist of a mere seven, fairly short, propositions. The actual book is, of course, somewhat longer as there are sub-propositions intended to illuminate the seven pillars of wisdom by filling in the detail. This, as it were, interstitial material is allocated decimal numbers, so that proximity of the number to a full numeral in theory indicates its closeness to the mainstream of the argument: the more decimal places, the further away a sentence is from the trunk, as it were. This, at any rate, was the intention of the author: in fact it seems to me that on occasion some decimally low, upstart propositions are more important or interesting than some hierarchically, numerically senior ones. Some of these low-decimal parvenus will be considered in detail.

But the point to be made here is another one: the book might well be summed up not in seven, but in one single proposition. What would it be?

There is no such thing as culture.

What the book in effect does is to explore, in a formal and *a priori* way, the relationship between a single mind and its world. It also says, as we have stressed, that this relationship is the same for all minds. Its central features are predetermined by the very conditions of the encounter between any mind and its data, or a world constructed, or rather just accumulated, from its data. Alternatively, and this is the crucial duality of theme, it is predetermined by the very possibilities of the encounter between any language and any world, and it makes no difference whether that language is used by one, two, many individuals, or none at all. Underneath the surface, it is and must be the same language. As for the diversity of what we normally call 'languages', this is entirely superficial: genuine referential content has the same form in all of them.

The possibility of decreeing in advance what that encounter will be like is indeed made possible in part by the linguistic turn which Wittgenstein gives to the empiricist formulation of the problem. The encounter is mediated by language and language is conceived in the idiom, indeed in the notation, of the recently developed symbolism of mathematical logic. As stressed, some of the oddities of Wittgenstein's position follow from this: for instance, the ideas that the world is simply assembled but lacks structure, and is made of permanent grains or atoms called 'things'; that these atoms are all of a kind, that their differences do not really matter, and that they do not change with the mood, personal or cultural, of the speaker.

That Wittgenstein should be blind to culture, when it comes to serious knowledge, is not surprising. This is something well established in the philosophical tradition to which he belongs. His predecessors also believed that truth was unique, whilst error and superstition were legion. As indicated, what was both unusual and odd about Wittgenstein was that he believed that the mystical too was unique, universal, and standardised. So culture was irrelevant, either way, to the serious business of life. Whether we relate to reality by reflecting it, or whether we were pervaded by the mystical, either way it is identical in all of us, and whatever cultural diversity there may be in the world is neither here nor there, and is barely worthy of the attention of either scientist or mystic. This is highlighted by one of the numerically low-status but important and revealing sentences, which refers to the 'enormously complicated' adjustments made by ordinary language (Wittgenstein 1974: 19, 4.0002). What Wittgenstein meant was that the enormous diversity of actual natural languages was but a surface phenomenon, covering complete identity underneath. The languages of men are basically alike. At heart, men are all alike, both in speech and in silence, in research or in prayer.

For the early Wittgenstein, the really serious business of 'meaning' the world, of referring and relating to it, but also that of relating to it ineffably as a totality, has a stark austere simplicity and universality. This simplicity follows from the very nature of meaning and the very possibility of significance. In each case, meaningful propositions are all at once solitary and universal. If meaning happens at all, it must always occur in the same way: there is no other. That it occurs more than once, is contingent and unessential and not really of any importance. So it is ever the same, and ever solitary. When engaged in serious business, all human minds are alike: they differ only in superficialities, in the contingent diversities of the tokens used and in arbitrary abbreviations and conventions rooted in historical and cultural accident. These hardly deserve much attention, and are dismissed curtly in a single observation.

In his focus on what is both individual and universal, in his conviction that what is of any importance in us is indeed universal rather than idiosyncratic, the young Wittgenstein was very close to Immanuel Kant.

What is wholly absent is the suspicion that an important part of what we understand by meaning might be intimately, inescapably, inextricably mixed up with the concrete and contingent activities of a given, specific and idiosyncratic culture; that meanings might be carried, not by individuals but, on the contrary, by on-going collectivities, by partnerships of the dead and the living and those yet unborn; that such collectivities have to cope with, amongst other things, the precariousness of the lives of their members, and are therefore concerned to ratify their births, realignments and decease. For such communities, death is – very much so – an event *in* life. Such on-going communities possess their own distinctive culture, and the functioning both of the referential and the mystical is intimately connected with the idiosyncrasies of that culture. The mystical does not in general remain unspoken: on the contrary, it is affirmed with ritual emphasis. Any such possibility is totally excluded by the *Tractatus*.

Likewise, the idea that the mystical might also be related to a sense of community, where the community is defined by what makes it *distinctive* rather than by what it shares with all mankind – all this is also wholly absent. The *Tractatus* does not so much deny this by explicit affirmation, let alone does it argue such a case; rather, and perhaps all the more eloquently, it conveys this by everything it takes for granted, by the assumptions which guide and limit its thoughts.

It is this hidden, though not very deeply hidden, doctrine which gives the *Tractatus* its flavour and interest. Its specific doctrines concerning the nature of language and the manner in which it relates to reality may have their points and, most certainly, they have their weaknesses and implausibilities, some of which we have briefly sketched; but what is really fascinating is this belated, passionate, uncompromising formulation of a vision of the world which assumes that all men are essentially alike, that their differences – above all, their cultural differences – are of no significance whatever, and relate only to superficialities, and that what is essential, is done alone. Collectivity, community, culture – all these are, on such a view, deeply irrelevant to our humanity.

16   Wittgenstein Mark 2

One of the commonest, oft-repeated remarks made about Wittgenstein is that he worked out and was famous for not one, but two philosophies. The first was contained in his *Tractatus*, and the latter in a long, seemingly unending stream of posthumous publications, but above all in his *Philosophical Investigations* (1953).

It is not clear precisely which of the many possible deficiencies of his first position persuaded him that it was untenable. Perhaps it does not even matter too much. Something or other persuaded him, and even that only in a certain limited sense, that his initial position was indeed misguided. The limited sense is important, because it is fairly obvious that he continued to believe that if philosophy in the old sense were possible at all, then indeed his early philosophy would be the correct and only possible version of it. The philosophical options of humanity were limited: it could choose the views of his youth or those of his middle age . . .

In order to move to his second position, the one which is held to represent his mature views, those destined to secure him enormous influence, two, and only two, premises were required. One was: *his early universalistic/individualist views, articulated on the basis of the idea that modern logic and its notation revealed the hidden structure of thought and meaning, were mistaken.* Precisely why he reached this conclusion remains something of a mystery. I feel I can guess his motives, but not his reasons. The motives are more important.

By contrast, the second premise required for the attaining of his final intellectual resting place, is supremely interesting and, moreover, it seems to me utterly obvious just how he reached it. He himself had no insight whatsoever concerning his manner of arriving at it and why it seemed so very cogent, so utterly indubitable, to him. Indeed, he lacked the equipment required for grasping this. He would have had to be able to think sociologically, and to say something like this: the universalist/populist confrontation pervades Habsburg culture and consequently, for those who are immersed in it, it has the power of a compulsive logical truism, even if, in reality, it does not exhaust human possibilities. Had he been able to see this, he might have understood himself – but for the same very reason, that development would have been closed to him.

Wittgenstein's second premise can be formulated as follows: *there are two, and two only, options available to human thought on these crucial issues.* Of these, Wittgenstein's early philosophy is *a* version; the other option is represented by Wittgenstein's later, 'mature' thought.

By a simple and entirely cogent logical operation, this, together with the exclusion of his early views, leads inescapably to his final position. 'Either p or q' and 'not p' jointly entail 'q'. If only two options are open in the very nature of things, and one of them is shown to be mistaken, then, if truth on these matters is available at all, the second option must be the correct one. QED.

The second option views human thought and language as embodied in systems of social custom, each tied to the community which employs it, and each logically ultimate, self-validating, and beyond any other possible validation. The custom of a community, expressed in speech, is the only law mankind can ever know or live by. Just this was of course the doctrine of the nationalists/populists of the Habsburg empire, *nur mit ein bisschen anderen Worten* [in almost the same words]; and they delighted in applying it to the political issue concerning the limits of the legitimate political unit. They did not apply it to the epistemological question of the validity of thought, logic, and inference. Wittgenstein, who gave virtually no thought to politics, applied their doctrine in this area. There he was indeed an innovator, in transplanting the populist doctrine of legitimacy to the theory of knowledge. The doctrine was not valid but, had it been sound, the Cartesian problem of the validity of knowledge would then have had a populist solution. The 'linguistic philosophers' who followed Wittgenstein and his later philosophy said and practised precisely this. This view would then refute the supposition that there could be a logical Natural Law, or Law of Nations, standing above idiosyncratic contingent customs. It would indeed demonstrate that this supposition is *the* delusion which is responsible for all false philosophy, i.e. all philosophy other than Wittgenstein's later position and its derivatives.

This is the real essence of Wittgenstein's development: the populist idea of the authority of each distinctive culture is applied to the problem of knowledge. In answer to (say) Hume's question, what justification is there for inductive inference, the answer would be: the peasants on our village green have always done it and we, as loyal sons of Ruritanian culture, will defend Ruritanian customs (including induction) to the death! Our cosmopolitan enemies, eager to dominate us and to assimilate us to the bloodless civilisation of their metropolis, are trying to deprive us of our customary dances, music, and induction. But they underestimate our resolve, the bravery and resolution of our young men. We shall fight in our mountains and forests, and we shall preserve our culture, our customs (induction included, specially in its distinct Ruritanian forms, which have many charming nuances, quite distinct from those tedious standardised inductive procedures of the metropolis).

17   *Tertium non datur*

The 'two options only' assumption was the really important, intriguing, fascinating and tacit premise: either universalism or epistemological populism. That Wittgenstein held it to be true, unquestionably so, seems clear. It alone makes sense of his development, but there is also direct evidence of conscious endorsement of it. Consider the following passage: 'he told me once that he really thought that in the *Tractatus* he had provided a perfected account of a view that is the *only* alternative to the viewpoint of his later work' (Malcolm 1958: 69; emphasis in the original). Assumptions built deeply into a cultural atmosphere and, more than that, assumptions which are corollaries of the objective social situation in which that culture is operating, can and do appear to men living within that world as overwhelming, indubitable truisms.

The 'two and only two' idea – the reduction of available alternatives to the choice between an individualistic, universalistic, liberal centre and a rival particularistic, communalistic, culture-revering vision – was deeply built into the whole life of the terminal period of the Habsburg Empire. There is no evidence that Wittgenstein was ever consciously interested in social and political questions, that he was preoccupied with issues such as whether a Danubian federation should be preserved, or whether, on the contrary, the rival ethnic cultures of the region should secure their wholly sovereign states, each dedicated to the protection and maintenance of its own national culture. The speculation of the Austrian Marxists about cultural pluralism and political unity appear to have left no mark at all on his mind. Should the National Theatre and Opera House, and National Museum – all of these, in effect, shrines to the national culture – be complemented by independent Ministries of Education, Finance and Defence? Must we go all out for full independence and sovereignty, or should we be content with cultural independence and maintain a federation so as to protect joint interests of economy and security? That was the question and its impact on Ludwig Wittgenstein appears to have been – nil.

Perhaps for this very reason, just because it was never consciously thought out and never at the forefront of his attention, the sense of the deep dilemma facing the Habsburg world may have pervaded his mind all the more effectively. Never properly brought to consciousness, it could hardly be the object of critical scrutiny or doubt. Nor was it. In his youth, he unconsciously excluded the romantic, culture-specific vision of thought, though, strangely enough, he combined romantic despair with a universalist/individualist model of thought and language, and indeed used it to vindicate that despair: in his later years, he affirmed it, with barely more self-awareness, and certainly without any self-critical spirit. Doubt concerning his own deep philosophical intuitions was not exactly one of his habits.

Wittgenstein's communal-cultural mysticism was wholly unoriginal in itself. Every little nationalist demagogue was capable of affirming the self-validating authority of local custom (though the idea of applying it to the problems of knowledge would not occur to him, largely because he would be unaware of those problems). If Wittgenstein did end as a communal-cultural romantic, he was only one among God knows how many. He did not invent the position, had no priority in formulating it, and his literary capacity for expressing it, though not negligible, did not surpass all the numerous other expositors of it. The fact that he expounded the position in a stratospherically abstract form, without any concrete specification or exemplification (no concrete culture was ever named), so that the local and idiosyncratic culture he deified was devoid of any local habitation or name, perhaps actually put him at a disadvantage amongst the preachers of romantic populism. Fundamentally, the overall position in itself, as he articulated it, was wholly devoid of any originality. Yet there were certain important new aspects in it.

One of these new aspects has already been mentioned. He reached the position by an altogether new path. The normative universalism he repudiated was not in his case a rejection of the domination of Europe by the French court and French cultural models, nor was it a repudiation of Manchester economics and British industrialism, or of a Jewish-Masonic-Bolshevik conspiracy, and it was not even, at any rate in any conscious way, a repudiation of Viennese haute bourgeois liberalism. The universalism he was officially repudiating (and which he had also so uncritically and dogmatically embraced in his youth) was that of the pretensions of the new logic and its notation to capture the essence of human thought and language. If arrogant, imperialist cosmopolitanism is to be rejected, *Principia Mathematica* and Logical Atomism certainly make quite a refreshing change from World Jewry or Capitalism or Communism or Free Masonry. The anti-semitic populist Mayor of Vienna, Lueger, would never have thought of this one. Here was a very strange new enemy of *Gemeinschaft* and human warmth, and there certainly was a kind of originality in this. The English populist, D. H. Lawrence, did in fact denounce the cleverness of Bertrand Russell's circle and their talk, but Wittgenstein went further and denounced the central idiom of Russell's philosophy. Many things, from universality via the Enlightenment to Marxism, have been relegated to the rootless alien spirit of cosmopolitans, enemies of any communal warmth and/or concrete historical identity. Set theory and formal logic make an interesting addition to this list of enemies of the people . . .

But an even more important innovation was to be found in the ends which his variant of romantic populism was to serve. The other, politically more specific and incarnated romantics wished to defend, glorify, and fortify the life of the village green against the anaemic universalism of the Stock Exchange, of a market society, of rationalist thought, of bloodless socialist brotherhood. They taught that the organic unity of a traditional, rural community was preferable to the extreme division of labour, the functional specificity, of a modern urban society. They set out to record and codify the old peasant cultures, and use them as the basis of a new ethnically defined sense of nationality, which was to become the new basis of politics, replacing dynastic loyalty, religious identification, and pride of status by pride of culture. The irony was that they preached the good life of the old village, and the eager consumers of their doctrine were mobile anonymous members of the new society, anxious to identify with one ethnic but codified and school-transmitted culture, and anxious to bring political units into line with this identification.

Wittgenstein turned to the communal vision of thought and its relation to life, but he was not interested in social and political problems. He continued to be interested in the philosophical issues which had led him to logic and the foundations of mathematics in the first place: the basic philosophical problems concerning the validation of our thought styles, the justification of the assumption or hope that, when we think, we are entitled to suppose that our thought does succeed in relating to reality. Why do the abstract and *a priori* laws of logic apply to reality? How do the abstract proofs of mathematics constrain reality to observe it? How can we infer from specific observations to general laws which can guide our conduct in the future? These are the traditional problems of knowledge, which are at the very centre of modern thought. Philosophers have been more successful in highlighting these problems than in answering them. If a Wittgensteinian conceptual populism is valid, and only it is valid, then we have all been looking in the wrong place for the answers, and a far more easily accessible answer awaits us in an area so close to home that we had never bothered to think of it: examine your own conceptual custom, for it is self-sufficient, self-validating, and sovereign. And why should the argument leading this way be cogent? We have already seen: there are only two options open to the human spirit, and one of them is closed. Which leaves this one alone . . .

The earlier romantics and Herderians had not adopted this path. When they defended folk culture against universalistic pretensions of one kind or another, what they meant was that somehow such cultures were closer to the springs of human vitality than the aetiolated cosmopolitanism which they opposed. The problem of vindicating the validity of mathematical or scientific reasoning, against Humeian scepticism or against Russell's paradoxes or whatever, was not uppermost in their minds. In fact it was not really present in their minds at all. They were not saving scientific inference or mathematical reasoning from a sceptic: they were saving the village dance and the folk song.

So an important feature of Wittgenstein's philosophy was that he deployed the communal-cultural vision of thought not for the solution of socio-political problems, not to rouse peasant cultures against alien or centralising policies but, instead, to solve or dissolve abstract problems of knowledge, to proclaim that they do not really arise, that our customary thought processes stand before no bar, face no indictment, have no case to answer. His 'dissolution' of the problem of the validation of our thought styles, our habits of reasoning and inference, was profoundly populist: our conceptual customs are valid precisely because they are parts of a cultural custom. It is not merely the case that no other validation is available: no other validation is either possible *or* necessary. The very pursuit of such extra-cultural validation is *the* error of thought. Custom is all we have, all we can have, and all we need. And this use of the populist idea was both paradoxical and original. Never before was the use of populism so ambitious. Tolstoy may have thought that muzhiks possessed moral wisdom and could teach it to the learned: he did not think they could tell Descartes, Hume and Kant that the problems they faced were muddles, to be cleared up by attention to ordinary speech.

It was left to Wittgenstein to go all the way and, there, rather than in his premises, he was original. If there cannot be truth outside culture, if there is neither individual knowledge nor external or universal validation, if knowledge simply must be communal and the speech community is ultimate and final, then this applies to the problem of the authority of science and mathematics as much as it does to anything else. Populist or culturalist epistemology had presumed to defend the moral or aesthetic sensibility of the Carpathian village against the imperialism of Versailles manners or of Manchester commercialism, or more specifically against the Viennese or Budapest bureaucrat, but it had not presumed to argue with Hume and Kant about the nature of inference or about logical antinomies. It had not occurred to it that they might be involved in the same game. Wittgenstein's strange originality lay in doing precisely this.

18   Joint escape

As stressed, the Wittgensteinian vision, as born in his bosom in the Viennese context, had deep populist roots. The underlying assumption, profoundly built into the Viennese world, was that man really had but two options in this world: either to become one of the individualist, universal, free-floating, cultivated *haute bourgeoisie*, with its distaste for the cousin-infested ethnic newcomers, who were both an enemy and a painful, humiliating reminder of its own *parvenu* origins – or to embrace one of the ethnic cultures, 'forms of life', and treat its voice as ultimate and authoritative. You could be liberal or nationalist. Strictly speaking, there were people seeking a third option, which would preserve the wider and liberal state and at the same time satisfy the nationalist craving. Perhaps one could turn nations into non-territorial cultural associations, which would leave the political and economic order to a non-ethnic central agency . . . Perhaps, let us hope so, mankind will yet turn to such an option, because the alternatives to it are horrible to contemplate. But, in Central Europe as it actually was during the earlier parts of this century, this – alas – persuaded few people. The third way was not followed. *Tertium non datur*, it seemed.

In his youth Wittgenstein fought rather bravely, and with a strange appropriateness which I am sure he never perceived, for the Habsburg Empire. He was a soldier of that non-ethnic empire, and in the intervals of fighting he worked out, with great conceptual frugality and economy, the structure of a world as it might appear to a culture-free individualist. The Empire was about to succumb to the onslaught and intrigues of the nationalists. One man who did fight for it loyally was (then) an ultra-individualist, for whom there might have been room in Vienna if the Empire had survived, but who was destined – had he not emigrated – for the camps when it did not. Psychically isolated as a front-line soldier on the Galician and Italian fronts, he sketched out what the world must be like for a solitary mind, devoid of cultural links. Whilst he was formulating it, he also proclaimed that it was the only possible world. How wrong he was, in a number of senses. Had he been right, *per impossibile*, the Empire might have survived as the only home fit for such individualists.

The world he constructed was a sad world devoid of hope or meaning. Nothing that could be said was worth saying, and everything that was worth saying was unsayable within it. The *Tractatus* was an essay in masochistic pessimism, well in the style of its period, and although there was unquestionably an element of literary affectation and posing in it, it was also sincere. There could be little joy in living in such a world.

As an exercise in the description of the solitude of the transcendental ego, of the solitary explorer who has shed all earthly links in the pursuit of cognitive purity (as Descartes had commended, though Wittgenstein was quite unaware of most of his intellectual ancestry), the *Tractatus* was already a bit unusual, in that it had two themes, not one: it dealt with the confrontation, the interface, between reality and the self, but also between reality and language. In fact, the world-language relationship initially predominates, and we only switch to the self, without anything in the way of explanation, later in the book. Initially, the propositions which confront the world seem disembodied: presumably they are entertained by *someone*, but we are not actually told so. These messages are articulated and received by no one in particular, not only *to*, but also *by* whom it may concern. It is only later, when we are told that death is not an event in life and that the world described has no limits, that we learn that this is not merely an account of how language refers to things, but how language is used by some isolated consciousness, curiously endowed with deathlessness thanks to its own incapacity to perceive anything outside its own borders. It is, strangely, spared death by its own absolute inability to transcend its own experience. (In a way it all follows, but it is a most bizarre and left-handed form of immortality.) The stress on language was itself an innovation, and was absent in the earlier great classical treatments of the Cartesian egocentric predicament. In previous forms of cosmic exile, the émigrés took their language with them, as indeed émigrés generally do, and spoke their home language in their places of exile, untroubled by the thought that its rules might be dependent on the world they thought they had left behind: the idea that this might be illegitimate, that language is world-linked, was something at least popularised by Wittgenstein. So here there was, already in the *Tractatus*, the germ of a solution. Language could be the saviour, by guaranteeing a world of which it was part, by inhibiting that exile and the alienation which went with it. At this stage, however, even if Wittgenstein had refrained from reintroducing the solitary ego, he would still have been left with a cheerless cold world in which an atomised, in a sense mute language faces an atomised world in a cold, loveless contact. Language itself, quite apart from the ego using it, was alienated from the world. It was totally indifferent to its content, mirroring it with a kind of disdain. It prescribed the *form*, but the content was of no interest to it or to a philosopher. The features of the world which made it such a grim place were all a corollary of its form: nothing that happened within it could make any real difference or provide any solace for us.

So the solitary Cartesian transcendental ego did have a kind of escape tool in his cell – language. If language turned out to be different from what the book asserted, that might be a way out . . . But it wasn't, *on its own*, any use to him. *There was nowhere to go.* The *Tractatus* had made it quite plain that this was the only possible world. It was an iron cage indeed. The bars were fatal because there was nothing outside them.

Still, the impersonality of language offers just a glimmer of hope of escape . . . but where to? No bolt hole was available. What use is a device for escaping from your cell if, on reaching the outside world, you simply have nowhere to turn?

This is where the story gets really interesting and unusual. The actual cell we are concerned with contains not one but two prisoners, each condemned to solitary confinement. Both of them had undergone what can only be described as a Kafka-style trial, though it was a different trial for each of them. One prisoner we already know: he is the philosopher in the epistemological tradition, eager to answer the question – what can the individual know? – and inescapably ending with the reply: he can only know himself, he can never ever transcend the limits of his own consciousness. He cannot even see those limits, for they are, like the limits of the visual field, forever out of reach. His self is his prison and he may never escape from it. The most cogent argument in the theory of knowledge ensures his perpetual solitary imprisonment: he can never check the correspondence between *his* data (which are his very self) and anything external, for he cannot reach that second class of entities, and so can never make that comparison, the only experiment which could ever tell him that his data refer to the world.

But there is another prisoner. He too, like the first one, reached his sad predicament through a painful process of persecution, certainly worthy of Kafka's pen and, in fact, his predicament really is the subject matter of much or all of Kafka's work. He too, like the first prisoner, is a *man without qualities*. The first one lost them in the process of becoming the pure observer, a transcendental ego and nothing else. His solitary confinement was the punishment for asking for the validation of knowledge. The other prisoner was scalped of all his personal qualities in an even more painful way. It was decreed, and accepted, in the new climate set up by the nationalist exultation and celebration of ethnic *Gemeinschaft*, that cultural roots alone, and nothing else, can make you human. The only qualities which are *echt* human are those imposed compulsively by an ethnic background, those which well up in your bosom in a surge of irresistible, *authentic* feeling, which leaves you no choice: your identity is imposed on you with all the unanswerable authority of blood and soil. By contrast, qualities easily acquired – and shed – in the commercial and intellectual market-place, in the hurly burly of culturally pluralist cosmopolitanism, where identities are for sale, where you can buy them in all kinds of finishing schools, simply do not count. Where you can choose or reason, authenticity ends. Identities born of thought, not feeling, lack all validity, they constitute a stigma, their possessors are not human beings, but mere parodies of human beings. And the more they wish to acquire the qualities, the ethnic clothing, of others, the more they give themselves away. A Jew in *lederhosen* does not become a Tyrolean. As a Viennese Jewish writer ironically put it: there are 500 million Chinese in the world and only 10 million Jews. How come that one never sees a single Chinese in Bad Ischgl?

So, for this cosmopolitan, *déraciné*, cerebral intellectual, there is no escape either. Just to depress him a bit further – as if he didn't have enough to cope with as it was – Nietzsche and Dr Freud assure him that the humanitarian, universalist ethic, which he invokes to confirm his standing as a human being, to protect him from ethnic particularism, is itself nothing but the fruit of *ressentiment* and the cause of further neuroses, and he would be foolish to expect it to help him. On the contrary, it will only make him feel worse.

But the situation of our *déraciné* cosmopolitan Viennese is not exactly the same as that of the solitary transcendental ego. Our Viennese Jew does know – only too well – that there *is* a place to go to. He knows everything about all those cosy communal *Gemeinschaften* with their village greens and folk dances and music, and their newly emerging political-cultural movements, each with its own National Theatre, National Museum, youth movement, forged historical documents, and so on. Oh, there most definitely is a place to go to, in fact, there are quite a lot of them: the Danube valley and the Balkans and adjoining areas are positively pullulating with them. You quite literally can't count them, not only because there are so many, but also because they simply won't agree where one of them starts and another one begins. In fact, they are at each other's throats on this account. What is an independent nation for one, is merely a dialectal variant for others. So there definitely

are places to go. No doubt about that. But you can't get in. As they used
to say on notices on Tyrolean hotels, until they switched to a Western
clientele during the economic miracle, *Juden unerwünscht* [Jews not
welcome].

The trouble is, though these populist communities most certainly
exist, they won't let you in. These new nationalists will stretch a point
about language and mastery of the culture and all that: as a matter of
fact, some of those National Awakeners don't even speak the very
dialect they are meant to be awakening, not properly anyway. They
speak it with a funny give-away accent, and they publish in the language
of the alleged imperial oppressor . . . but no matter, one can shut an eye
to this. Also, one stretches a point in eagerness to secure recruits. But
what, in general, the nationalists are less willing to welcome and accept
are recruits from cosmopolitan, urban milieux, who have no peasant
roots at all (rather than possibly having slightly 'wrong' ones). The
reasons for this fastidiousness are various: cultural/religious distance,
fear of competition from educated people who might usurp too many
good positions in the new ethnic unit . . . Who knows. Whatever the
explanation, there can be no doubt about the fact itself.

Note the asymmetry between the two predicaments. Prisoner 1 has
absolutely nowhere to go, nowhere to escape to, but he does seem to
have an escape rope, namely language, if only he knew where to go. The
other one, Prisoner 2, has no rope at all. He does know of places to go –
only too bitterly – but they won't let him in. What to do?

By a curious accident, the two prisoners are incarcerated in the same
cell. As long as each of them was alone, he was helpless, and no
amelioration of his condition could be expected. Either of them was
doomed to continue to suffer, without relief, without end, without hope.
But *together* . . . That is another story altogether. *Together*, their situation
becomes altogether different, and much less sombre. Once they
compare, discuss and understand each other's predicament, they suddenly realise, yes, if they cooperate, there *is* a perfectly good way out!
One of them has an escape kit, and the other knows of a hide-out . . .

The transcendental ego had been confined to his solitude, in the
Wittgensteinian version, by an account of *language*. It was the dreary
nature of language (which is and can be nothing but photocopying and
summation) that had landed him in his cell. Now suppose, however,
that this account of language were wrong, and were replaced by quite a
different account? Suppose language were not an infinitely tedious
collection of brass rubbings of atomic bits of reality, drearily stuck
together without even the slightest order, but that, instead, it was an
inherently gregarious, collective activity, one *only* possible in the context

of an on-going community, a 'form of life'. Suppose language, of its very essence, were a communal activity? What then? Ha!

The transcendental ego had the escape rope of language, but nowhere to go. The Viennese Jew or the Man Without Qualities on the other hand knew where one could go, but they wouldn't let him in. But what if the two of them are one and the same person, namely Ludwig Wittgenstein?

19 Janik and Toulmin: a critique

Allan Janik and Stephen Toulmin's *Wittgenstein's Vienna* (1973) contains an intricate, sustained, and elaborate attempt to account for Wittgenstein's thought and development in terms of his Viennese and Habsburg background. This idea is excellent; and it is an aspiration which the present work shares, though there are great disagreements concerning the execution of this aim. My argument is, above all, very much simpler.

The really crucial explanatory fact is the deep polarisation of Habsburg society and sensibility. It is the confrontation of an abstract, universalistic individualism on the one hand and a romantic communalism on the other. At a conscious level Wittgenstein was barely interested in socio-political issues and certainly gave them no sustained or sophisticated attention. None the less, or all the more, he simply could not but have been impregnated with an awareness of this opposition. He could not but have absorbed, assimilated and internalised the central intuitions of these two great competing visions. They impinged on his life and his feelings. Everything in his own background made him a natural adherent of the first of these two visions, and his first work was an almost perfect specimen of it – so perfect as to be in effect a parody of it. It was somewhat eccentric and unusual in its details, but it exemplified that outlook precisely in what it took for granted, what seemed so obvious that it wasn't even stressed, let alone argued. This assumption pervaded his early thought and is treated as utterly obvious: its implications are explored, but its premises are left unexamined. They are too obvious to warrant examination. And yet, the contrary position must at the same time have been the object of powerful longing. When he 'went to the people' and became a village schoolmaster, the experience was not a happy one. The yearning for simple community, whether conscious or not, was not to be satisfied, at any rate in any direct manner.

His later work is the sudden and, for him, the overpoweringly strong revelation that his basic premises could be challenged after all! Their inversion then becomes the stunning new illumination, which, once again, settles everything. Language is not what I had thought it was (tedious brass rubbings of world-atoms and their random summation – if ever there is a recipe for hell, that must be it): it is – oh bliss – an entry ticket to a closed community! Even better – it is not just a permission, it constitutes an *obligation* to join it! Community is not a *droit de seigneur*, it is a *devoir de seigneur*!

It is not fully clear whether, in Wittgenstein's own mind, it was technical defects in the elaboration of his earlier philosophy that condemned it or more general features inherent in the genre as such. Either way, when in the end he became convinced that his earlier vision did not work, a tacit premise was available which assured him that if his initial option did not work, then a certain other one *must* be valid. There were but two options in the world. The premise was not altogether tacit, for (as noted above) he actually articulated it in conversation with Norman Malcolm. So his later philosophy exemplifies, once again in a very exaggerated version verging on parody, a form of organic romanticism. Positivistic individualism and romantic communalism between them exhaust the options open to the human spirit: that much is obvious and beyond all question. In fact, this is not so: but it was close enough to the truth about Habsburg Vienna.

Why should the tacit premise seem so cogent? Far from being cogent, it is not remotely true. But it was deeply inscribed into the real life situation of the citizens, above all of the intellectuals, of the Habsburg Empire in its terminal period. Features which pervade the life situation of a person can and often do acquire the cogency of a genuinely irresistible logical compulsion . . .

The claim made here is that this is what did happen to Wittgenstein, and this alone explains his curious and passionate development. Other additional hypotheses, adduced by Janik and Toulmin and others, are really redundant, and possibly have other defects. All one really needs is the 'two options' assumption and the elimination, on the basis of whatever considerations, of one of them. The elimination in Wittgenstein's mind is well documented in his later work: it constitutes its dominant theme. The precise considerations which excluded the first option are less clear, but it does not really matter very much. We may speculate about his motives for wishing to escape the solitary cell to which his early position confined him: it is unlikely that we shall ever have direct evidence on this point, for it is improbable that he was conscious of it. He did not think in socio-historical terms, and was unlikely to say to himself – I wish to escape the alienation of rootless cosmopolitan intellectuals in a world where the dominant values are nationalist and populist, and my new theory of language both damns the universalist/individualist theory of language, and actually *proves* that anyone who speaks at all, is automatically a member of a community: 'Hurrah! At last we've made it to the world of the ethnics and the village green, even if we don't know which one.' He was unlikely ever to think and say this, and it is no use expecting a statement of this kind to turn up in those interminable posthumously published notes.

The Janik–Toulmin thesis is much more complex, and goes into details and nuances of Viennese intellectual life (though not always convincingly). Janik and Toulmin sum up their cental idea as follows. What Wittgenstein sought was 'some method . . . of reconciling the physics of Hertz and Boltzmann with the ethics of Kierkegaard and Tolstoy, within a single consistent exposition' (Janik and Toulmin 1973: 168). In a sense, the *Tractatus* can indeed be seen as something of the kind. Whether Tolstoy and Kierkegaard are as simple as the cryptic aphorisms of the latter part of the *Tractatus*, whether those two thinkers are consistent with each other and whether they (and in particular Kierkegaard) are really consistent with what Wittgenstein was trying to say at the time, are all problematic questions: Janik and Toulmin deal with the views of Tolstoy and Kierkegaard in a somewhat cavalier manner. But over and above such pedantic concerns with the history of ideas, serious difficulties arise for this interpretation.

What is certainly correct is that the *Tractatus* was meant to be the summary, a kind of delimitation of the very outlines, of the totality of human intellectual life, of what could be said, what could not be said, of what there was to be said, and what must obligatorily be left unsaid. It sums up the world, and human life and thought within it. The nature and limits of our psychic life were to be laid bare in stark, simple, brutal and, in its dark way, also poetic outline. The Janik–Toulmin case is that the situation in physics, the philosophy of physics and mathematics on the one hand, and the moral crisis of the Habsburg intelligentsia as commented by the unwitting Kierkegaardian Karl Kraus on the other, jointly presented Wittgenstein with his problem; the notation and ideas of Russell and Whitehead's work on logic and the foundation of mathe- matics provided the technical tools for the solution. The outcome: the *Tractatus*.

The implausibility of this interpretation hinges in part on the fact that this alleged 'solution' is so very unhappy, and could hardly have provided its author with much satisfaction. Janik and Toulmin would turn Wittgenstein into a refugee, not from the world as such, but specifically from Vienna:

If the culture and society into which Wittgenstein grew up offered no more prospect for the rational discussion of morality and values than it had offered, say, to Karl Kraus, the ultimate reasons for Wittgenstein's divorce of values and facts accordingly lay . . . in those features of the broader social context which had led . . . to the absolute alienation of so many serious-minded bourgeois intellectuals . . . Given life as it was lived in the Vienna of the early 1900s, no recognized public forum of opportunities existed for the sincere and serious-minded discussion of ethics or aesthetics. The man who truly understood the deeper character of value judgments could, thus, find room for them only in the private world of his own personal life. (Janik and Toulmin 1973: 237)

If this is what Wittgenstein was trying to escape from in Vienna, it is strange indeed that he did not make a better job of it. The flight into the recesses of his autistic consciousness, in which an inert language confronted a similarly lifeless world co-extensive with it, could hardly bring him much relief: the bolt hole was bleaker than the Waste Land from which he was escaping. It is even stranger that he should have been so satisfied with the result, and declared it, all at once, to be beyond both human articulation and all possible doubt.

There are many problems even in the technical part of the alleged solution, concerning the structure of what can be said and concerning the manner in which the world can be apprehended by language or language-using humanity. The notion of 'picturing' is a grossly inadequate or positively wrong account of how it is that sentences can ever refer to facts. But even if it were assumed that this part of the theory is acceptable, can it possibly be true that the whole of our cognitive interaction with the world consists of simple summations and combinations of allegedly atomic pictures?

However, the *Tractatus* did claim that these things were indeed so, that articulable knowledge (or significance) could be constrained within these astonishingly narrow and implausible limits; and Wittgenstein then proceeds to include the moral, the aesthetic, and the mystical within this very same seamless whole, by declaring them to be ineffable. Somehow or other, they are there, and more than that: Janik and Toulmin insist, quite persuasively, that they are supremely important for Wittgenstein, more so than anything else. They were not, as they were for conventional positivists, a kind of embarrassing residue, something which had to be admitted because it indisputably occurred in human discourse, but which one was a bit ashamed of, in as far as its standards did not match the rigour of the best kinds of human thought. But the fact that they were ineffable did not, it seems, prevent them from being unique and uniquely valid, traits which normally entail the most important additional attribute of articulability. Wittgenstein always had it both ways – the ineffable could not be shot at by his critics, yet remained under his own monopolistic control. It did not become, as the ineffable normally does, *freischwebend*, free-floating, unseizable, out of reach of control, accessible to other mystics. Wittgenstein knew precisely what its outlines were and would allow no rival views on this matter . . . though at the same time, being beyond speech, it could be spirited out of sight at any moment. In fact its temporary visibility or rather articulability was only a transient concession to the weaknesses of the flesh.

All this is a rather strange way of incorporating Tolstoy and Kierkegaard in modern physics. It is perfectly true that Kierkegaard was anti-rationalist, and that Tolstoy was anti-intellectualist. Kierkegaard believed it to be the essence of religious affirmations that they were logically offensive, that just because they were logically unacceptable, they set up a tension within the breast of he who would believe them, and it is this tension and it alone which endows us with our identity. Without it, we are nothing. Logically facile beliefs engender no self, but offensive ones do so. The logically unproblematic, articulable parts of the world of Wittgenstein's *Tractatus*, and the self-evident but unsayable extra allowed in the later parts of it, would hardly satisfy Kierkegaard: all too much plain sailing, the peace-of-guaranteed-despair rather than the tension of hope-and-faith-against-reason . . . Identity, for Kierkegaard, requires the tension of absurd faith, and he who lacks it also loses his very self in the process. It is the claim that there was this nexus between identity, unreason, and religion, which makes him the progenitor of existentialism, and provides the twist in Christian apologetics which links faith to identity rather than to conviction and a theory of the world. By insisting that faith must be *hard*, because it is the tension engendered by the difficulty which endows us with our identity, in the end Kierkegaard made it *easy*, which helps to account for his popularity: henceforth, believers no longer needed to worry about the disparity between evidence and conviction. (In the end, Wittgenstein's later position was to have a very similar role.)

It is also true of Tolstoy that he was anti-intellectual, at least in some of his views or moods, and much given to valuing the simple verities of the *muzhik* over the sophisticated ideas of intellectuals. Many *muzhiks* were no doubt inarticulate, and Tolstoy the writer knew well how to portray them, but as far as I know he did not actually equate this inarticulateness with validity.

But these thinkers were not all of them saying the same thing. The *Tractatus* might say, by implication, mystics of the world, unite! – or rather, it might claim that they were already united, whether or not they knew it, in the compulsory identity of their ineffable insight. Moreover, they might also be united in refraining from saying what on his view could not be said, with that special licence which he habitually accorded to himself to say that which it was forbidden to say. Other mystics might indeed have said that some things are beyond all speech, but there is nothing to suggest – and a great deal to contradict – the supposition that what all these diverse mystics were *not saying* was always, and in all of them, *one and the same*: ineffable, and identical with what Wittgenstein was illicitly, in defiance of his own rules, whispering. In any case, many of them also said quite a lot, and it certainly didn't all seem the same . . .

The whole intellectual, religious, spiritual history of mankind is, thank God, highly diversified. Neither that which is said, nor that which is not, is as unified as Wittgenstein, all at once autistic and confident, claimed. Wittgenstein was not merely utterly in error when he imposed, in the name of the calculus of propositions as developed in modern logic, total homogeneity on the fact-referring customs of all mankind, but he was even more preposterously, egregiously wrong in imposing a similar *Gleichschaltung* ['equalisation', rationalisation] on the ethical, aesthetic and mystical discourse of humanity. Men vary, and they vary a good deal, and long may it remain so: but Wittgenstein, never one to allow facts to stand in the way of his compulsive intuitions, would have none of this. That was of the essence of his youthful position. The curious thing is that he really did appear to hold that men, in all cultures and conditions, do exactly the same thing, not merely in their speech, but also in their silence. Even, or perhaps especially, the unsaid was not spared from the imposition of a single model.

Wittgenstein was always irritated by attempts of more conventional philosophers to argue and propositionalise about spheres such as ethics. Putting it beyond the reach of words sounds nice, even respectful. One does not want anything so deep and intimate to be sullied by words. But note that what it is that cannot be said apparently still – or all the more – remains uniquely determined and, apparently, he knew exactly what it was. He did it a multiple injustice. He pretended that a consensus existed, when in fact dissent and multiplicity of views is of the essence of the situation and may well be invaluable. He also implied that no good is achieved by articulation and that critical examination – which is hardly possible without verbal formulation – is of no value. By postulating a realm of insights, or whatever they are to be called, which are all at once unsayable, indubitable and accessible to himself, he conferred astonishing authority on himself. There are layers and layers of irrationalism and authoritarianism in his position.

As stated, the Janik and Toulmin position is that he was led to this despairing mutism-autism by the problems and crises of the Habsburg situation: nothing could be said under these dreadful circumstances. If only the surrounding society had been better, Wittgenstein would not have withdrawn into the ineffable. On the contrary, you would be able to find him at the Café Schwarzenberg, chattering away, eagerly discussing the latest football results with Arthur Schnitzler and Karl Kraus and Sigmund Freud. But as things were . . . the philosopher, it would seem, generalised his anguish, and argued that nothing could be said, full stop. The rest is silence. This view, which implies that under more favourable circumstances, something might after all be said about ethics and aesthetics, is somewhat in conflict with the authors' seemingly respectful endorsement of Wittgenstein's ineffability doctrine: they do talk of it as a deep insight, rather than a *faute de mieux* adjustment to difficult circumstances, a self-imposed transient abnegation, which might be lifted again when conditions turned more benign.

But, either way, the doctrine of the unique ineffable verity was a mistake. The religious, ethical, and aesthetic history of mankind is not simply one long pregnant silence, endowed with but a single, invariant, persistent significance. That is what the *Tractatus* would have us believe. This only highlights early Wittgenstein's total ahistoricity, his complete lack of a sense of the diversity of cultures, and indeed of the very existence of culture. It was and continues to be the *differences* in what men meant in these spheres, whether or not they articulated it, which matters. Very often the differences were articulated in words, and that too is a part of human history, and a supremely important one. A philosophy which denies that this happened, or indeed that it ever could happen, is a bizarre travesty of human experience.

The view that Wittgenstein's autism and the associated coldness of a value-free world is a reaction to the specific condition of the time is highly questionable. The sharp separation of the factual and the evaluative is not an idiosyncrasy of Wittgenstein's, but pervades the philosophical tradition of which he is part. It is at least as conspicuous in the philosophy of David Hume, and in its way even that of Immanuel Kant, as it is in Wittgenstein. Did Edinburgh and Königsberg in the eighteenth century suffer from the same malaise as *fin-de-siècle* Vienna? The resemblance of Calvinist Scotland and life on the Royal Mile in Edinburgh to life on the Ring in the days of Johann Strauss and Arthur Schnitzler is not immediately evident.

The fact/value separation, sometimes known in the trade as Hume's Law, is a fairly obvious and immediate corollary of certain basic premises shared by philosophers such as Hume and Wittgenstein, who start off by considering the differences between referring to facts and evaluating them. If an awareness of the fact/value chasm does in the end have deep social roots (and I believe it does), they are much more general. They are not specifically tied to the distinctive malaise of the terminal decades of the Habsburg Empire. They are tied to any society

endowed with science, i.e. sustained, cumulative, consensual exploration of nature by the experimental method, with the aid of mathematical
formulations and rendered independent of social dogma and requirement. Under such conditions, and perhaps under such conditions only,
the separation of fact and value becomes hard or impossible to avoid.
Scientific inquiry requires the separation of all separables, the replacement of rigid clusters of features by experimentation which sees whether
some new cluster might not work better. This then also involves the
separation of evaluative elements from others, the abstention from
including them as inherent in a cluster. (This is how Hume demonstrated the fact/value distinction: as a corollary of the separability of
anything from *anything*.) It is also a consequence of free inquiry: one
cannot change one's values with every change of ideas, so that, in the
sheer interest of stability, a society which encourages and practises free
inquiry cannot rigidly tie its values to theories about facts. Societies
without free and active inquiry can do so.

Whether the fact/value distinction is a universal truth which is merely
obscured under different kinds of social conditions, or whether it is
inherently linked to conditions of free inquiry, and owes its apparent
compulsiveness to them, is a very deep question which I shall not pursue
here. What matters at this point is that Janik and Toulmin do wish to
explain its presence in Wittgenstein's mind in excessively local terms,
whereas it seems to me that more abstract, philosophical considerations
led him to it. *If* the compulsiveness of the separation of fact and value is
a merely local phenomenon, it is connected with the entire Western
tradition since the seventeenth century; it certainly is not, like the
Sachertorte, a Viennese speciality.

There is a parallel here with Janik and Toulmin's view that it was local
circumstances which led Wittgenstein to the insulated, isolated, 'transcendental' self, the ego which is merely the limit of the visual field, and
possesses no more satisfying substance or identity. The disappearing self
is also deeply, logically inherent in a certain important philosophical
tradition, from whose premises it logically follows: hence the pursuit of
overly local, and unduly social, roots may well be misplaced. Hume and
Kant had been led to the same conclusion, without the anguish of late
Habsburg Vienna. Is one to say that Hume, like Boswell, did not want to
be a Scot, and therefore chose to be a bundle of perceptions instead? It
is a nice idea, but it is hard to accept. In this matter of an icy value-less
world of fact, as in the case of the disappearing self, I think the
philosophical reasons were more relevant than the *immediate* social ones.
However, the Janik and Toulmin sociologistic explanation deserves
investigation.

Solitary, universally identical, but inexpressible mysticism would seem to be a curious reaction to the ills of Habsburg society. An extreme individualism, the conception of life as the intercourse of a single observing ego with the world-to-be-observed, a vision which very clearly denies the relevance of other people or of any communally carried culture, is clearly present, and dominates in the *Tractatus*. The world of the *Tractatus* is nothing but a spectacle, and in no way a predicament. Moreover it is a spectacle of a rather curious kind. Only pure data, and pure data in atomised form, are what count: pure consciousness, which can never perceive itself other than through the limit of its own field, in the face of inert, ultimately homogeneous data-atoms, with no possible significance attaching to the contingent patterning which they may display – an icy and deeply unsatisfactory world, which is itself a predicament of a kind, precisely because it turns the world into nothing but a spectacle. It is indeed felt to be such, except that there is no alternative, no escape, and stoical silence is the only possible and commended reaction. It is hard to accept the Janik and Toulmin thesis that Wittgenstein entered this world as an *escape* from the ills of his time! This was the tragedy, not the solution. All you can say is that he revelled in it a bit, as romantics will: they take great pride in the depth of their despair.

The evidence suggesting that he was bothered by the specific ills of the time is less than convincing: and the bolt hole would seem to be a good deal worse than most ills one can think of – give me any world, but above all the joys of Vienna of the time, rather than such a world!

So it would seem that this philosophical world was Wittgenstein's problem, not his solution. He was driven into it *in part* because the logic of a certain important, and praiseworthy, philosophical tradition led to it, quite irrespectively of social or personal ills. Men of quite different temperaments, and with quite different backgrounds, are sometimes led to it. Ernst Mach was led to it, but was not a Jew and so not impelled, presumably, by social ambiguity; Bertrand Russell was led to the problem of the 'egocentric predicament', but he was not a depressive, nor the member of a socially ambiguous class. It is plausible to think that a kind of personal autism made Wittgenstein feel more acutely the icy solitude of this abstract situation. That may well be true, and it does have plausibility. But the escape-from-the-Habsburgs . . . no, that theory is redundant: it is unsupported by any facts and is possibly in conflict with some of them. The solitude of the long-distance empiricist was Wittgenstein's problem, not his solution. His emotional sensitivity to the problem may well have had (in my view, did have) another reason, namely that the solitude entailed by empiricism reminded him of a solitude which had quite other causes: but that is another matter.

But what really and conclusively militates against the Janik and Toulmin interpretation is Wittgenstein's subsequent development. It is generally recognised that the really crucial event in Wittgenstein's development was the transition from his early position, the universalistic, individualist atomism of the *Tractatus*, to the communalistic, 'organic', romantic reverence for collective conceptual custom. Commentators may disagree concerning whether this revolution was total or whether there was also some underlying continuity: but there can hardly be any doubt but that something dramatic did happen, that there was indeed a profound change. On the Janik/Toulmin interpretation, it becomes wholly puzzling why Wittgenstein should need to move any further, once the first position had been reached. He wished to escape from the horrors of Kakania, and found a bolt hole within the mystical. Why go any further?

Janik and Toulmin affirm: 'Clearly enough, too, Wittgenstein's change of philosophical method was for him only a continuation of his earlier intellectual policies by other means; it did not lead him *in fact* to abandon his long-standing ethical individualism' (Janik and Toulmin 1973: 235; original emphasis). A strange claim. What the passage declares to be clear enough is exceedingly implausible. Janik and Toulmin themselves proceed to wonder, rightly enough, whether Wittgenstein's later philosophy can tolerate (let alone provide support for) that fact/value separation to which, on their own account, he remained faithful.

The issues of fact/value separation and of the solitude of inquiry are closely connected – both of them are corollaries of the empiricist approach, and both haunt it. Janik and Toulmin observe: 'Wittgenstein's later philosophy of language could neither justify nor refute, *in principle*, any complete dissociation of the realm of values from the realm of facts' (*ibid.*; original emphasis). On the contrary, it seems to me quite obvious that his later philosophy is altogether incompatible with both philosophical individualism and the fact/value divide. The former he explicitly attacked in the form of the doctrine of the impossibility of a private language: we are all doomed to communality, conceptual commensality. Cosmic exile, private investigation of the universe, detached from the conceptual custom of a community, is not just difficult, but downright impossible. I do not know of any explicit attack on the fact/value divide in his work, but it seems to be clearly incompatible with his entire later vision. Its rejection follows, for instance, from Wittgenstein's use of the notion of language games. Language breaks up into sub-systems tied to concrete social purposes, and so these sub-systems simply cannot be value-free. The affirmation that language is inherently social, not individual, and is inescapably meshed into the purposes of social life, makes the imposition of the great divide between facts and values impossible.

If Wittgenstein had really been seeking, and was continuing to seek, a private haven as an escape from Kakania, he would never have ended with a position which banned all private havens, in principle, and declared them to be philosophically illicit. And if there is one thing which is obvious about natural languages practised by on-going communities, by 'forms of life', it is that their language is intimately, essentially involved in practical aims, and hence that it could not conceivably practise a logically puritan separation of fact and value. The only language which ever did anything like that was the artificial, purely referential language, invented as a model of culture-transcending, socially disconnected science by the empiricist tradition, and of which Wittgenstein himself had erected a rather extreme, and in some ways eccentric, version in the *Tractatus*.

In brief, the Janik/Toulmin interpretation, though entertaining, and endowed with the merit of trying to link Wittgenstein's thought with details of the contemporary intellectual scene, is untenable. Wittgenstein was fleeing *from*, and not *to*, solitude. Solitude was the destiny, the doom, the punishment of that logically puritan, scientistic tradition. It was also the doom of the cosmopolitans who lacked a soil-and-blood-linked culture glorified by the nationalists. As it happened, Wittgenstein suffered *both* these fates. He was both a philosopher and a paradigm of Viennese déracinement, having lost the old culture and not being admitted to the new.

His later philosophy guaranteed escape from solitude. It granted him, in abstract form, what the Austrian village had denied him in real life. The alleged impossibility of a private language, which shows that conceptual solitude is in principle not even possible, liberates him from the situation which the *Tractatus* had demonstrated as inescapable, and which had been his lot in the trenches in Galicia and Alto Adige. If it isn't even possible, then it could not have happened to him . . .

20   The case of the disappearing self

The individualistic, atomistic tradition began with the invocation of the
self. In Quine's excellent and already cited phrase, what Descartes
recommended was 'cosmic exile': the inquiring mind opted out of the
existing stock of ideas and information, and started afresh, relying on
the data which were indubitably in its possession. In reality, however,
the essence of this operation was *cultural* rather than *cosmic* exile. What
the Cartesian operation really required was sustained, systematic distrust of the assumptions of the local culture, and the erection of a body
of knowledge intended to stand outside it and be independent of it. The
self opted out of the culture; it was also initially rewarded with a kind of
hard, gem-like status of a 'substance', a thing capable of existing on its
own. Thought, at any rate, was credited with such a status by Descartes.
It was a substance, capable of existing on its own. It was independent
and, above all, it was independent of culture. When it liberated itself
from its culture, it nevertheless retained the tools for thinking about the
world, and retrieved them in a purer and hence more effective way.

But this metaphysical elevation of the self to substantial status was
not due to last very long. The very principles of sustained doubt, by
means of which the self had tried to liberate itself from culture, and
which it was meant to serve, also undermined its own status. Within
the tradition initiated by Descartes, a century or so later the existence
of that hard, substantial self was subjected to severe scrutiny. As David
Hume put it:

> For my part, when I enter most intimately into what I call *myself*, I always
> stumble on some particular perception or other . . . I never can catch *myself* at
> any time without a perception, and never can observe any thing but the
> perception . . . I may venture to affirm of the rest of mankind, that they are
> nothing but a bundle or collection of different perceptions, which succeed each
> other with an inconceivable rapidity, and are in a perpetual flux and movement.
> (Hume 1888: 252; original emphasis)

Immanuel Kant held much the same view: 'in what we entitle "soul"
everything is in continual flux and there is nothing abiding except (if we

must so express ourselves) the "I", which is simple solely because its representation has no content' (Kant 1968: 353).

The doctrine of the disappearing self, when it occurs in Wittgenstein, is attributed to the anguish of the Habsburg situation by Janik and Toulmin, and to the ambiguity attaching to personal identity in the circumstances it engendered. The conspicuous presence of the same doctrine in the work of Hume and Kant would seem to suggest that the idea has more general and philosophical roots. Kant had no grave doubts about his own personal identity and its location in the world, I think. Hume may have had them: his tranquil Augustan attitude may have been but a pose. It probably was. Perhaps he adopted such a posture in deliberate defiance of the Calvinism of his compatriots, so that the rather disagreeable complacency which pervades his moral philosophy should not be taken at face value but rather should be seen as a brave and independent defiance of the oppressive local orthodoxy. Had he been English, the complacency of his ethical theory might lead one to think of him as a mere philosophical Lord Chesterfield, but against a Scottish background he stands out as a dissident rather than a conformist. There is much anguish in his theory of knowledge, which emerges in spite of the air of tranquillity he affected. Be that as it may: whereas Jean-Jacques Rousseau could perhaps be recruited as a natural but premature companion of Weininger and Kraus, Hume could not. Yet the disappearing self is already present . . .

The disappearing self then turns up again in a philosopher who shortly preceded Wittgenstein and obviously did influence him: Ernst Mach.

The ego must be given up . . . If a knowledge of the connexion of the elements (sensations) does not suffice us, and we ask, *Who* possesses this connexion of sensations, *Who* experiences it? then we have succumbed to the old habit of subsuming every element (every sensation) under the same unanalysed complex, and we are falling back imperceptibly upon an older, lower, and more limited point of view. (Mach 1959: 24–6)

In Wittgenstein it all reappears:

The world and life are one.

I am my world. (The microcosm.)

There is no such thing as the subject that thinks or entertains ideas. (Wittgenstein 1974: 57, propositions 5.621, 5.63, 5.631)

And again:

The subject does not belong to the world but rather, it is a limit of the world. (*ibid.*: 5.632)

Here it can be seen that solipsism, when its implications are followed out strictly, coincides with pure realism. The self of solipsism shrinks to a point without extension, and there remains the reality co-ordinated with it. (*ibid.*: 58, 5.64)

Death is not an event in life: we do not live experience . . . Our life has no end in just the way in which our visual field has no limits. (*ibid.*: 72, 6.4311)

It is quite obvious what has happened. The empiricist insistence on refraining from trespass beyond the immediate data ends up by eliminating both an independent world and an independent, persisting self. Both dissolve and, moreover, flow into each other. The dualism goes: self and world meld into each other, and both disappear. The solitude is total. This surely was the problem, and not a solution, for Wittgenstein. He was not seeking a bolt hole from Kakania, he was looking for an escape *from* the bolt hole.

The new escape

The one and only alternative theory of meaning, by contrast, promised and provided liberation from this solitude, and a kind of guaranteed gregariousness. Language as a mirror of reality led to loneliness; language as a cultural function led to community. The new theory guaranteed togetherness. It guaranteed it in the abstract: Wittgenstein never identified or named any of the 'forms of life', the cultures which are to replace the semantic atoms or substances of the *Tractatus*. He never pointed to any actual historically existing culture, such as Kakania. Examples continued to be conspicuous by their absence. They remained nameless and unspecified, whether they were the ultimate items of the world, the 'things' of the *Tractatus*, or the 'forms of life' of the *Philosophical Investigations*. In the end, culture was treated as ultimate, as a kind of new ultimate visual field. So the solitude of the visual field (co-extensive with both self and world) is replaced by the solitude of culture . . .

There always has to be an ultimate base. It must be more than theoretical or tentative; it must represent a better and indubitable kind of truth. In the *Tractatus*, logical form, and the mystical, must be shown and not asserted, and are thus placed beyond either support or contestation. Wittgenstein appeared to have a psychic need for more-than-theoretical, more-than-contingent visions; he did not waste his thought on the contingent or temporary. Later, 'forms of life' acquired the same status. The deep structure of his thought remains the same. The oddest example is his mystical-ethical intuition, beyond articulation, therefore identical for all mankind. The entire history of contested and formulated ethical visions (precepts and rationales) goes by the board, and is dismissed from the life of mankind!

As for the fusion of the ethical and the aesthetic, it has a true Schopenhauerian ring and at the same time reflects, presumably, Viennese aestheticism. Aesthetics was really more important than ethics. At the very least, it may not be given a lower status.

21 Pariah communalism

When a minority is an object of discrimination and contempt, this is most frequently explained and justified by attributing some moral inferiority to the group in question. Its members are lazy, feckless, addicted to thieving, generally endowed with criminal tendencies, dirty, given to unsavoury sexual habits, drunkenness, and so forth. The attribution may of course be totally unfair and unjustified. Alternatively, it may be, as it were, enforced or imposed, by a kind of circular self-confirming procedure. An easily identifiable sub-population credited with strong criminal proclivities may find it difficult to secure ordinary employment and may in fact be forced into criminal activities. It is difficult to escape the consequences of social stereotyping, and determined attempts to do so quite often lead only to a strengthened imposition of the initial attribution.

But, leaving aside the fairness or otherwise of the attribution, this 'normal' condition of discrimination has a certain manifest logic. The minority in question is bad in terms of the recognised values of the dominant 'host' or majority society; if the attribution of the said inferiority is justified – and who knows, in some cases, it may be – discrimination does thereby acquire a kind of justification. That kind of situation – without prejudice to the question concerning whether the ascription of the relevant deficiency is in fact justified – constitutes what may be called the standard or simplest version of discrimination.

There is however a rather more interesting and complicated variant of minority persecution. This arises when, by the standards of at least some of the recognised and deeply respected values of the dominant host society, the unpopular minority is not inferior at all but, rather, conspicuously superior. The values of Habsburg society in the nineteenth century were no doubt diverse, complex, ambiguous and ambivalent: given the diversity and complexity of the society in question, one would hardly expect anything else. Nevertheless, there were some definite limits to this complexity and there can hardly be any doubt but that brilliant originality in the sciences and the arts, entrepreneurial dynamism, and proven high competence in the liberal professions were greatly appreciated.

If members of any of the numerous other ethnic groups in the Empire displayed any such abilities, let alone a combination of them, without any shadow of doubt such achievements would be loudly acclaimed and invoked as evidence of the merits, the talented and socially useful quality, of the ethnic group in question. Possessors of such attributes would be proudly claimed for their group of origin and, if their origins were ambiguous, there might even be acrimonious disputes concerning precisely which group was to be credited with the person and achievements in question.

But now something odd and unusual happens. The contempt for and discrimination against a given despised minority cannot easily be justified in terms of its vices, its failure to live up to the valued norms of the host society: on the contrary, by those very standards, surprisingly, the minority shines! What's to be done? Well, there are a few makeshift devices which can be adopted, and are. It can be claimed that the minority in question is not *really* creative at all: its members are merely expert at emulating real creativity, they steal the ideas of others, they lay claim to a spurious originality, etc. Hitler did indeed say something of the kind about the Jews. Or again it may said, and frequently is said, that the professional successes of the minority in question are due to its mafia-like organisation: they are all members of an efficient network, a pervasive mutual aid society, and so become beneficiaries of the hidden system of links, whilst their rivals are systematically hampered by exclusion from the secret brotherhood. These aspersions are common. The trouble is, they do not really convince. It is only too obvious that, far from being somehow at an advantage in virtue of their background, the members of the pariah minority are at a disadvantage, all of which makes their conspicuous and sustained success all the more enviable and infuriating. For instance, an anti-semitic publication which appeared in the Soviet Union during the Perestroika period asked with acerbity: how is it that a group accounting for 0.69 per cent of the total population also accounts for something like half the doctorates?

There is now a kind of contradiction in the value system of the general culture. On the one hand, given the deeply felt and engrained stereotyping of the society, members of the pariah group are bad, without any shadow of doubt. On the other hand, their achievements of a certain kind, notably in sciences and arts and scholarship, but also in industry and economic activities, are known to be outstanding. If the pariah group shines in these fields, it would seem that, confusingly, something is both good and bad, and this would seem to present a problem.

One way out would be to decide to abandon and disavow the prejudice against the pariah group, to declare it to be, indeed, a prejudice, and to practise – in the most conspicuous example of this kind – a new philosemitism. Some have indeed trodden this path, but not so very many. Others have trodden it, but with ambivalence and irony: praise is accompanied by a deprecating smile.

But there is a much more interesting way out, and one which is of great relevance both to the understanding of the sensibility of modern Europe, and for our argument. The way out of the contradiction is to say and, above all, to *feel* that the virtues in question are not really virtues after all or, at any rate, they are not unconditionally, not in *any* hands. They are, true enough, virtues normally, when part of the endowment of ordinary people; but, when found in such over-concentrated hands, well then, things are a bit different, and we must think again.

All this would seem an absurd argument, a blatant case of discrimination. What is sauce for the goose is sauce for the gander. How on earth can the Ruritanians have the nerve to scream with delight because one of their number manages to get a bit of international recognition in physics, but remain strangely cool when three Ruritanian Jews get similar or greater recognition? Is this not absurd?

Well, no, not altogether. If this unsymmetrical, discriminatory procedure came on its own, perhaps it could indeed be held up to ridicule for its blatant, brazen lack of equity. But there does happen to be a kind of ideological background, present so to speak independently, and endowed with its own persuasiveness, which bestows a measure of credibility on what would otherwise seem absurd. In the end it is absurd, but the considerations which attempt to mitigate the absurdity, to justify it, tell us a good deal about our world.

The Enlightenment was followed by romanticism, which was a powerful reaction to it, or against it. The Enlightenment had preached the authority of reason, whatever that might be: for practical purposes, Reason was not too far removed from the highly trained, specialised, explicit, well-informed thought processes of intellectuals. Reason was what intellectuals practise and unreason marked the thought processes of the masses. To some extent at least, the reign of reason was to be the reign of the clever. The enemy was seen to be the conservative stupidity and credulity of the populace: the *philosophes* were indeed liable to feel despair when they contemplated the daunting task of enlightening the masses. They preached rationality, but despaired when they contemplated its reception by the vulgar.

Romanticism inverted all this, at first timidly, and later with some arrogance. There was deep wisdom in what at first sight might seem the blind prejudice and conservatism of the *Volk* and the *narod*. The abstract, cold, universalistic reason of the intellectuals did not possess a monopoly of wisdom, and perhaps it did not possess wisdom at all. Rather, it exemplified a disease of the spirit. The diversity of folk reactions deserves at least some respect and in the more extreme formulations of romanticism, it and only it deserved to be treated as sound. The deep intimations of the people were healthy, the ratiocinations of uprooted cosmopolitans were not.

This, so to speak, communalistic argument against abstract, cold, socially disembodied reason in due course received powerful new support from biology. *Man the ape* joined *man the peasant* in the clamour of denigration of pure reason. Our true vitality and satisfaction does not lie in ratiocination, but it is linked to the Dark Gods. Sexuality, violence, arbitrary loyalty – whether to charismatic leader, gene pool or territory (*Blut und Boden*) – these are what really give us satisfaction, identity, and fulfilment; universal unselective love of all mankind is the expression or the cause, or both, of psychic disease and weakness. Romantic literature had been saying something of the kind for some time, but now it seemed that science in the form of Darwin had come to underwrite the very same conclusion. It was only left to Sigmund Freud to show, or claim to show, the precise mechanisms by which the severe abstract super-ego deceives us and helps make us both ill and unhappy. So-called reason and conscience, especially guilt for aggression – Schopenhauer and Nietzsche had said as much earlier without, admittedly, the authority of clinical experience – was but the pursuit of instinctual ends by other, and particularly pathogenic, means. These ideas and attitudes were there anyway, pervasive and influential. Many men, under their influence, would have felt ashamed to allow cold, barren reason dictate their affective life or their musical taste. There was no clear reason why one should not also extend this style to one's political life. And indeed many people did.

Given this pervasive and influential background picture, the idea that what would otherwise be praiseworthy intellectual achievement becomes something quite other, something negative and shameful, when practised by a population with no peasant roots, ceases to be something absurd and acquires a kind of plausibility. What is interesting and extremely important is that the picture is internalised and accepted not only by the favoured majority which is meant to benefit from this attribution of roots and the stress on their importance, but also, and perhaps with quite special intensity, by the minority against whom it is directed and whose achievements it is meant to discredit. It does, in fact, become a standard thread in the texture of Jewish self-hatred. In the context of the general situation of the Habsburg Empire, roots become all the rage. Some liberals, it is true, stand their ground, decry the cult of the closed society, and reaffirm the merits of openness, and its links with cultural and economic creativity. Others, if deprived of peasant ancestry of their own, try to borrow that of their neighbours in defiance of the commandment – Thou shalt not covet thy neighbour's *Gemeinschaft*! (In fact, there was in any case a god-awful mess-up in this business of the authenticity of cultural roots. The Magyar national poet was actually a Slav, the Croat national hero was at first a would-be Magyar, the founders of the most important Czech patriotic and gymnastic organisation – *mens patriotica in corpore sana* – were Germans, the founder of Zionism started life as an assimilationist . . .) Alternatively, drawing on the pervasive socialist-populist ideology, an ethnic group devoid of its own rural base can invent its own peasants in the form of members of communistic agricultural collectives, who then outdo peasants proper in martial virtues. All these options are there, and all of them found some adepts at least.

What matters for our purposes is this. What would be a virtue for a universalistically oriented, liberal mind can turn into a vice if it fails to have communal or ethnic 'roots'. A bit of intelligence or creativity is all very well and can be tolerated provided it is well rooted in a community; but if not . . . Roots, it would seem, are everything. *Gefühl ist Alles*, said Goethe. But feeling is authentic only if rooted in a genuine community. Otherwise it is but volatile, superficial affectation, emulation without real understanding, inspired by the hope of securing admission, or worse. Roots and roots alone make for authenticity. Universality is the opposite of rootedness. If you are rooted in universal rationality you are rooted nowhere. And in all probability is is just because you were rooted nowhere that you turned to the cult of universal reason. We can see right through you.

On the one hand, roots alone validate and legitimate everything and, on the other, rootlessness is the ultimate sin. Groups endowed with a territorial and peasant base clearly do have roots; but those which spring only from loyalty to a book, and are linked not to land but to cerebral activities, in a sense constitute a kind of anti-humanity, the very reverse of what mankind is or should be. These formulations are perhaps a little extreme, or at any rate a little blunt: but they are not too far removed, if indeed removed at all, from the vision which romanticism had diffused and nationalism adopted, and which pervaded the atmosphere of the world that concerns us. And if it be granted that this kind of vision was indeed pervasive, one can see how the paradox with which we began could be resolved in a surprising manner: the fact that the pariah group has virtues could be handled, not by removing the stigma from the pariahs, but by stigmatising the erstwhile virtues because they are not hallowed by ethnic-communal 'roots'.

All this becomes highly relevant when we try to understand the emergence of a philosophy which asserts that no rational, intellectual reason can possibly be found for any human practice, but that its justification can only be found by its place in a 'form of life', in other words, a culture. The author of the philosophy might just as well have said: roots are everything. Roots against abstract intelligence: justification by communal existence against justification by appeal to abstract and universal reason. The logic of the shame at one's own intellectual achievement – surprising, but somehow understandable, as we have shown, in a given context – is close to the shift of sovereignty from reason to custom.

The *Tractatus* had portrayed the human condition, cognitively, morally, semantically – in the spirit of an uncompromising, extreme, virtually comic universalism and individualism. Not only science but the mystical as well were described as ineluctably identical in all men. Culture, religion, gender, none of these, or any other specific characterisation, make any difference to anything that really matters in our life. We are all alike, the differences belong to a zone of the insignificant.

And just these differences lay at the heart of Wittgenstein's later, 'mature' philosophy. The isomorphism of these two movements of mind entitles one, at the very least, to suspect that one of them inspired the other. Wittgenstein's development cannot possibly be explained as the desire to perpetuate the social criticism of Kraus or the linguistic criticism of Mauthner, but to do so by more rigorous means. Such a motive could never have led Wittgenstein to a position which positively outlaws the very idea of social criticism by making every culture sovereign, self-validating, ultimate. From this viewpoint, he would have had either to endorse Kakania, as one further example of a self-validating form of life amongst others, or to declare it a non-culture, some kind of monstrosity – but he never to my knowledge actually said anything of the kind. If he had really sought, as Janik and Toulimin suggest, to escape from being a Viennese Jew by crediting himself with being an invisible transcendental ego, at the limit of the world but not of it or in it, then he would never have had cause to move beyond the *Tractatus*: internal emigration was already fully arranged and guaranteed within that work. No need to proceed to anything else, least of all to a philosophy which firmly and unambiguously proscribes all such inner exile, replacing it by compulsory citizenship in a speech community . . .

No: what does make sense is that, having worked out one philosophy in terms of abstract and universal reason and having found that it led to intolerable solitude, he replaced it by another philosophy, inspired by the one thing which, in the pervasive atmosphere of Kakania, was widely recognised to be the alternative to reason: namely, roots. Roots, not logical form, dictate our speech and confer our identity on us and limit our world. He renamed it 'a form of life'.

22 Iron cage Kafka-style

Wittgenstein's early vision is indeed one further working out of what may be called Descartes' problem: what is the world like, if the individual is to construct it himself, relying exclusively on elements he has himself assembled and tested? As Wittgenstein himself very aptly put it, in answer to this question, solipsism and realism converge, the world is the self and the self is the world. No transcendence is conceivable.

Given that there have been so many exercises in answering this question, just what is it that makes Wittgenstein's own little attempt of any interest? What is different about it? There are two things. One is the distinctive literary style: this unquestionably belongs to *fin-de-siècle* modernism. One might say that the other participants in the great epistemological tradition of Western philosophy worked in that field in order to explore the limits of human knowledge. That was their principal aim, and if they were a little unhappy about what they found – Hume and Kant certainly had their uneasy moments – that was the by-product of their endeavour, not its objective. With Wittgenstein, one is not quite so sure. When he constructs that icy silent world with its pointless and disconnected facts, it is of course partly because his premises dictate the conclusions he reaches . . . partly. Yet, he clearly gets a certain kick out of being the messenger of doom, and makes sure he rams home the message by every literary device at his disposal and he is no mean writer. There have seldom been such literary fireworks in philosophy. After *Thus spake Zarathustra*, Jacob Burckhardt ironically asked Nietzsche whether he also meant to turn his hand to opera. To me, it is astonishing that the *Tractatus* has not been set to, say, atonal music (leaving aside Russell's suggestion that proposition 7 can, in the original German, be sung to the tune of 'Good King Wenceslas'). No, there can be no doubt but that Wittgenstein used the work so as to indulge, and give dramatic literary expression to, his own anguish, his *Weltschmerz*.

The other distinctive feature of his early work, in the context of the greater philosophical genre of which it is a part, is its intimate relation to the problems of logic as they stood during the early decades of this century, and his employment both of logical notation and the ideas which underlie it. For instance, the author of the *Tractatus* tells us firmly that God does not reveal himself in this world. This is a sad, important and contentious claim, which has of course been bitterly disputed by various religious traditions which uphold a contrary view. What is somewhat unusual about this austere religious transcendentalism of Wittgenstein's is the manner in which it is reached: in that work, it is made into a corollary of the calculus of propositions, which decrees that all atomic propositions are independent of each other (whereas non-atomic ones are functions of atomic ones), which in turn implies that none of them is pre-eminent or affects the others. Ontologically, so to speak, the world is utterly levelled out, and no transcendent penetration of mundane reality is possible. Perhaps so: but it is curious that a neutral calculus should have such tremendous, shattering consequences, destroying the hopes of so many believers . . .

The use of logic is also part of the stylistic effect. The interspersing, within one work claiming organic unity, of aphorisms about the human condition and technical bits of logic, is a stylistic device very similar to the juxtaposition in the poetry of T. S. Eliot of what had traditionally been considered both poetic and highly unpoetic elements. The *Tractatus* unquestionably belongs on the same shelf as *Four Quartets*. Nothing that is worth saying can be said and what *can* be said is not worth hearing . . .

Imagine the conversation of a few Viennese characters, in the Café Central, on the assumption that the *Tractatus* is a correct account of the human condition:

CHARACTER A: High up on the left hand of my visual field, I note a fact in which a 9-value predicate links the appropriate number of things . . . I don't think I have had this one before, I'd like a snapshot for my collection.

B: I have a much more interesting one right in the middle of my field, a variable with 127 things attached – it has a lot of tentacles, holding those things. I've counted them.

C (to A): Don't you believe him. I have known him for years, he is invariably given to exaggerating the complexity of his facts, just to make himself interesting.

D (to C): I don't think he is deliberately lying, he just drinks too much and then imagines things.

B: (furiously, to both C and D): What you have both said is extremely offensive and I have no option but to call you out! My seconds will call on you. That is, assuming you have honour: my fraternity has decreed that Jews have none and we may not duel with them. Is either of you at least half Aryan? That is all one can hope for in Vienna these days.

A: Gentlemen, gentlemen, please calm down. May I remind you first of all that duelling is forbidden by law and, secondly, death not being an event in life, it is totally pointless anyway.

The above conversation is not copied out of *Die lätzten Tage der Menscheit* or *Der Weg ins Freie* or *Der Mensch ohne Eigenschaften* or even *Radetzky Marsch*. It is all my own work and it is copyright.

Part III

Malinowski

23   The birth of modern social anthropology

Some subjects or disciplines emerge in a slow and complicated way, and it is not possible to say exactly when or where they originated. But this is not so in social anthropology as taught and practised in the intellectual sterling zone, in what had been the British Empire and what continues to be, in the intellectual and academic spheres, its zone of influence. The United States and the continent of Europe are a different matter. This, however, does not affect our argument, though the relation to Eastern Europe plays its part in the story.

Within the British Empire and its successor states (and more important perhaps: its successor universities), the beginning of it all is clear, distinct and visible. There are traditional and founded religions, traditional and founded states, and, evidently, traditional and founded disciplines. Social anthropology is a founded discipline with a clear point of origin, from which all, or very nearly all, then follows. It has a Founder who set it up.

The baseline of social anthropology is the replacement of Sir James Frazer by Bronislaw Malinowski as *the* paradigmatic anthropologist. It is all a little like the foundation of the English state itself. The English kingdom effectively begins with William the Conqueror. Before him there is a kind of haze, in which nebulous figures with funny names such as Ethelred appear, without real continuity or any clear order, or much conviction. The status of figures such as Alfred or Arthur – fact or romance? – is none too clear. Undoubtedly something must have been going on in those ill-documented days, and specialists are familiar with it, but it does not add up to a clear and continuous story, internalised by present members of the English community and providing them with a kind of orientation. After William, on the other hand, the sequence is clear and without gaps: the story has its morals and antagonisms, everyone has his sympathies and antipathies, and the affinities between past and present alignments become visible. It becomes a living past, linked emotionally to the present.

British social anthropology is rather similar. Bronislaw Malinowski is the William the Conqueror of the subject. His victory set up the regime which, give or take a bit of turbulence or a few modifications now and then, has persisted ever since and whose legitimacy is not seriously contested. Frazer, on the other hand, was Harold, the only member of the previous dynasty who, thanks precisely to being its terminal point, has a clear and unambiguous place in folk memory and who contributes to the story. There are other pre-Bronislaw figures who are of genuine importance, and who are even objects of very serious attention: but it is less than clear just how (if at all) they relate to each other. They emerge from the swirling mists of time, but the clouds never disperse sufficiently for a clear and coherent canvass to become manifest, and to imprint itself on the mind. Before the First World War there was no anthropological profession. Individual scholars pursued their interests, and some even secured university employment, but there was nothing by way of a sustained professional community. All this was due to change with Malinowski. He marks the beginning of firm institutionalisation as well as the start of a continuous intellectual story.

The difference between Frazer and Malinowski did not lie only in the framework which surrounded them and the institutions which sustained them or which they lacked. There was also a clear, neat, and dramatic difference in their doctrines, ideas, style, and general approach. The contrast is marked and illuminating. The move from Frazer to Malinowski constitutes a complete break, a *coupure*.

Frazer exemplifies, almost to perfection and with elegant simplicity, the preoccupations, ideas, and opportunities which had, in the nineteenth century, engendered the subject of anthropology in the first place. The coming and acceptance of Darwinism had made it manifest that mankind had a history over and above the document-based record which preoccupies conventional historians. The evolutionary aspect of Darwinism, the stress on continuity of development, made it at the very least plausible to suspect that surviving pre-literate peoples might illustrate the condition of primitive peoples of the past, whose social organisation was otherwise barely accessible. The hope of establishing an evolutionary account of human development was tempting, and of course it would have philosophical and political implications: the pattern of evolution would provide a charter for power ranking in a world pervaded by a new type of empire, territorially discontinuous, where the power-holders seemed to be at a different 'stage' of social development from those they ruled. In brief, Darwinism had bestowed more past on humanity than men had previously suspected or bargained for, and the newly acquired past was full of the most potent suggestiveness. Contemporary ethnography, brought in *en passant* by missionaries, colonial administrators, and travellers (or, in Russia, by forcibly exiled political prisoners) provided at the very least a hope of access to a time machine, which would facilitate inspection of an otherwise lost past. This newly acquired plethora of past called out for a more systematic investigation: ethnography was there to satisfy the need. Anthropology became the Remembrance of Things Collectively Past. It would only be a matter of time before the satisfaction of this need became professionalised.

It should be stressed that this was how things were, all in all, in Western Europe. In other parts of Europe it was different. A British anthropologist was a man who, under the impact of Darwinism, was eager to use surviving 'savages' as evidence concerning the past of all humanity. By contrast, a Central European ethnographer was a man who, under the impact of nationalism and populism, was eagerly exploring and codifying a peasant culture in the hope of preserving and protecting it, above all from encroachment by rival nationalisms. (A Russian ethnographer was a man filling in time because the Tsar had sent him to Siberia.)

But to return to Western Europe: two items provided the main elements in Frazer's general approach to this problem. First of all, he was an evolutionist in the basic formulation of his problem: his central question was, by what path did mankind arrive at its present condition? Evolutionism is more a state of mind, a tendency to ask genetic questions, than a positive doctrine; and in this sense, Frazer was, very profoundly, an evolutionist. Secondly, he was an avid user of the new time machine made available in the by now rather rich and rapidly growing mass of ethnographic literature. He mastered an incredible amount of it and reproduced it, in elegant, somewhat mellifluous Augustan prose, in his widely known (though, in its unabridged version, seldom read) masterpiece, *The Golden Bough*.

In method, Frazer was an indefatigable magpie of genius. He gathered all the material he could find and he found a very great deal. The fact that he had to use the material he found in the writings of others meant that he could not probe further for the context of the information which came his way: he had to use it as it was. The use of such material committed him, at least by implication, to a denial of the relevance of context: he had at the very least to behave as if one could use the information that a given tribe believed this or practised that, without necessarily possessing other information concerning its form of life. The belief, the ritual, or the institution had to be used as a kind of acceptable atomic datum, significant and usable in itself, which could then make its contribution to the construction or validation of a theory, notwithstanding the fact that it floated in a context-free vacuum.

There were other important features of Frazer's intellectual style. He was a classicist, but a classicist with a difference. Classicists are, generally speaking, intellectual snobs: what attracts them in the classical world is its excellence – one might say, its miraculous excellence. They are attracted by its outstanding achievements. Frazer specialised in Pausanias, a kind of guide to late Greek culture who recorded local practices and beliefs. In other words, he focused not on the miraculous intellectual achievements of the Hellenes which distinguish them from almost anyone else but, on the contrary, on that superstitious underside of Hellenic culture which does not greatly distinguish the Greeks from anyone, if indeed it distinguishes them at all. This orientation already made Frazer into an anthropologist rather than a classicist, even when he was dealing with documentary material from a literate society.

In his philosophical orientation, which provided him with the ideas from which he constructed his theories, Frazer was an empiricist-associationist, an almost perfect disciple of David Hume. His conception of the working of the human mind was that of a kind of associative mechanism, which links one experienced element with another in virtue of their resemblance or their contiguity in experience, plus a few other similar simple relations. Whether he obtained this vision directly from reading David Hume or from some nineteenth-century follower of Hume is not entirely clear, but it hardly matters. The similarities between the two psychological visions is striking and obvious. Everything Frazer says about 'sympathetic magic' or 'homeopathic magic' – phrases he coined – might just as well have come straight from Hume. So if Frazer obtained his problem from the evolutionist post-Darwinian *Fragestellung*, and his data by the magpie method, then the tools for handling the data came from associationist-empiricist psychology.

There is one further feature of Frazer's intellectual procedure which deserves notice: what might be called the 'pluperfect method'. Like other evolutionists he used the past to explain the present: that seemed the natural way to carry on. But if something was found in the past for the emergence of which further evidence was lacking, Frazer's instinctive reaction was to seek something still further back in the past, which would in turn explain what required explanation. The official plot of the *Golden Bough* has precisely this form: a strange classical institution, the rule of succession for the priesthood at Nemi, by which the new priest must kill the old one in order to take office, is in the end explained by (speculative) practices which allegedly took place even further back in time. The supporting evidence sustaining this speculative theory was based on analogy with other similar practices found in the ethnographic record in other parts of the world. On the assumption (or was it the conclusion?) that the human mind works in similar ways everywhere, these analogies could support the hypothesis concerning the proto-history of Nemi, for which no direct evidence was available.

The official theory Frazer constructed was evolutionist in form and associationist in content. The book was meant not only to explain the grizzly events at Nemi, but to explain the intellectual development of mankind. He postulated a famous three-stage theory of the development of the human mind, which, on his view, passed through three successive conditions, that of Magic, of Religion, and of Science. In magic, man expected that like would cause like, or that associations as such were causally effective: man in fact behaved precisely as Hume's *Treatise* would lead one to expect, but at a rather low, uncritical level. Having noticed that things didn't always work, primitive man introduced the *Hilfhypothese* of animism, of spirits behind events, which controlled them and thereby accounted for the failure of crude, magical associa-tionism to deliver the goods. For Frazer, such animism was the essence of religion. When this failed in turn, man at long last turned to experimentally controlled associationism, to exploring just which associ-ations were genuinely effective and which were not, and differentiating between superficial similarities and genuine causal connections. Frazer did not suggest that any one of these successive principles or styles was exclusively present during any one historical period: it was a matter of relative predominance, not of exclusive presence.

There are many things wrong with this theory: for instance, its intellectualism. The theory, as formulated officially by Frazer in the passages in which he sums up his conclusion, seems to presuppose that when primitive man affirms a formula, which when translated seems to express a belief, or when he practises a rite accompanying some such formula, he is a *theoretician*, concerned with understanding, predicting and controlling nature, rather than being, say, a person reinforcing the social order of which he is part by reminding everyone, in a solemn manner, of the system of social relations of which they are a part. It all assumes, rather implausibly, that someone is keeping a tally of the successes and failures of magical and religious operations, and that such a record eventually induces mankind at large to change intellectual direction. None of this makes much sense. It may be said that Frazer's intellectualism is aided, or perhaps actually engendered, by his magpie method. The fact that the accounts he processes are presented out of context makes it hard to investigate what purpose the activities de-scribed really serve. Such descriptions encourage the naive, simple, and intellectualist assumption that the primitive shaman was really a fellow intellectual, an investigative scholar, but one who generally got it wrong.

In his actual practice Frazer was not always so naive, though his greater sophistication, when present, was in conflict with his formally propounded theories. For instance, when comparing the polytheism of classical antiquity with the doctrinal monotheism which followed it, he is, like Hume and Gibbon before him, full of admiration for the civic-minded, tolerant, this-worldly spirit of the ancients, compared with the egotistic and other-worldly orientation of the new faith. But such an account makes it obvious that the difference between the two types of religion lay, not in their theories of nature, but rather in their impact on social organisation and conduct. However, as stated, this insight, which certainly inspired his attitude to the two successive civilisations, is in no way incorporated into his main, officially proclaimed theory about the great stages of human thought. As far as the main theory goes, the difference between classical antiquity and Christianity is the difference between two theories of nature, one of them presumably with a much heavier load of magic, whereas the other systematises or centralises its animism into a single very dominant spirit.

Apart from the official evolutionist-associationist Frazer, and the less official classicist anti-monotheist, there is also a third Frazer, one wholly absent from his conscious mind, but nonetheless implicit in the manner in which he arranged his material. Frazer amasses a vast amount of material from all over the world and finds a great deal of similarity of pattern or structure in it all. Officially, in terms of his own theory, this must be due to the fact that, all over the world, the human mind works much the same, so that much the same associations turn up all over the place. This generic similarity then enables us to fill gaps where evidence is lacking, as in the pre-history of Nemi. Human associations of ideas must have worked much the same in very early Nemi as anywhere else, so we can reconstruct, Frazer thinks, that stage from what we know about the later Nemi practices.

But all this is highly implausible. Association is terribly volatile. If we really constructed our mental worlds by 'association', there would be far, far more diversity and chaos than in fact there is. This is the crucial, and conclusive, criticism which Emile Durkheim directs at the entire empiricist tradition, as an account of how we actually build up our worlds. Associations are born free but are everywhere in chains, and these chains need to be explained. The astonishing conceptual homo-geneity and discipline which we actually find in human cultures must have roots quite other than mere association.

Frazer neither saw nor faced this problem. But the astonishing homogeneity of pattern which he had dredged up in his rich material encouraged others to seek, and indeed to find, an explanation of that order. What they found was not to his liking and not at all in his style. This might be called the 'Jungian' reading of Frazer. If patterns of belief are so strikingly similar in so many societies, could it not be that all these ideas are dredged out of some common shared collective Unconscious? When T. S. Eliot uses Frazer in *The Waste Land*, it is in this spirit that he does so. Frazer was informed that Eliot made such use of him, but could make no sense of the poem, not surprisingly. His classical lucidity could not penetrate the newly fashionable deep obscurity.

Such, then, was Frazerian anthropology: a global picture of the intellectual evolution of the entire human race. The picture was illustrated, and supposedly established, by an enormous mass of material assembled from all places and times, but torn out of context. None of the material had been gathered by the author himself, and he was not expected to do so. His response to the question as to whether he had ever met a savage is often quoted: 'Heaven forbid!'

The background story which provides *The Golden Bough* with its official plot, the rule which allows anyone who kills the current incumbent of the priestly office to succeed him, is not devoid of a certain ironic relevance for the history of anthropology. The succession of the kingship or priesthood in the Sacred Grove of Anthropology passed from Frazer to Malinowski precisely in the manner in which things had once been acted out in Nemi. Intellectually speaking, Malinowski slew Frazer and thereby succeeded him.

Between the two wars Bronislaw Malinowski taught at the London School of Economics. He died in America during the Second World War. During his period in London he in effect created a new subject and profession, dominated it, and turned its practitioners into an astonishingly cohesive and effective guild. In the social sciences and the humanities, there can be few if any disciplines which are so homogeneous, so united in a shared intellectual and procedural paradigm, and so compact in social organisation as 'British' social anthropology. That this is so is, for better or worse, to a large extent the achievement of Bronislaw Malinowski.

In what sense was the discipline as practised by him and his followers a new subject, conspicuously different from the anthropology practised by Frazer? The 'functionalism' developed and practised by Malinowski differed from Frazerian anthropology in a number of important ways.

Anthropologists were now expected to carry out fieldwork. This, from now on, meant more than visiting an exotic location and interviewing informants through an interpreter. The anthropologist was now expected to go there for quite a long time, something preferably not too much short of a couple of years, learn the language and, above all, live immersed in the indigenous culture, in its style, in other words, to go native. So, in effect, East European populist ethnography, invented in the service of nationalism, which had practised 'going to the people' more as a moral and political, rather than methodological, principle was transplanted to Western colonial empires and placed at the service, not of romantic love of the national culture, but of science, of the theoretical understanding of the nature of human society. This is the essence of the Malinowskian 'functionalist' revolution.

When it came to interpreting the findings secured by this immersion, evolutionist speculations about the place of the current beliefs, rituals, etc., in some global scheme of development were to be strictly avoided. They came to be considered utterly unprofessional and were stigmatised as speculative history. Generalisations about the functional interdependence of cultural elements were to replace explanations in terms of evolutionary sequences.

But if that kind of theorising, hitherto simply taken for granted as the style appropriate to this field, was to be proscribed, what theorising was to be allowed and be appropriate? Answer: 'functionalist' theorising, which explains given beliefs or institutions by relating them either to the rest of the society and culture in question, or by relating them to 'human needs'. (This latter element in Malinowski's own variant of functionalism was the first to be largely abandoned by his school.)

Both the new style of research and the new style of explanation – and the two in any case dovetailed with each other – led to a strong sense of the unity and, so to speak, the reality of culture. In this way Frazerian anthropology was overturned at both its cardinal points. The deeply felt insistence on cultural context and unity damned the context-free magpie style of Frazer. The proscription of speculation about the past, and of explanations in terms of the past, damned the Frazerian evolutionist paradigm of explanation. Henceforth, anthropologists were to be, obligatorily, fieldworkers; and they were obliged to have an acute sense of social and cultural context and interdependence.

The profession so defined prospered marvellously. It was widely recognised and Chairs were created in many Universities. The Colonial Office came to use anthropologists not only for consultations, but also in training future colonial civil servants. Malinowski's seminar at the LSE was the recognised central shrine of the movement and in the early period it is doubtful whether anyone of importance in the profession failed to pass through it. Malinowski's charismatic personality on occasion excited hate as well as love, but it does not seem to have provoked indifference. The subject now had a new shape, a new vitality, a new sense of mission, and a new leader.

Radcliffe-Brown, who after a complex and peripatetic career came to occupy the Chair in Oxford (though Malinowski had aspired to it), also made an impact on the profession, so that there was a kind of double leadership. But Radcliffe-Brown's 'structural functionalism' did not radically change the picture. It stressed 'structure', in the fairly straightforward sense of social organisation, so that there was a more explicit stress on society as a system of interlocking units.

Since the time of these two founding fathers, the profession has, basically, remained what it had been in their time. There have been a number of attempted further revolutions or coups: the sacred grove at Nemi has not been untroubled. But not one of these attempted seizures has been successful or, at any rate, not one of them was even remotely as dramatically and conspicuously successful as Malinowski had been.

There has been the *structuralisme* of Lévi-Strauss, preoccupied not so much with the structure of society, as Radcliffe-Brown had been, but with the structure of culture, with the manner in which cultural themes, in mythology or gastronomy or kinship, are allegedly generated by an underlying core (inherent, according to variant formulations of the theory, either in the human mind as such or in a specific culture). This model had been inspired by certain analogies with phonetics, and probably suffers from the fact that society in many important respects does not resemble language. A little later there was the rather belated influence of Marxism arriving in a mainly Parisian form. It meant, as far as I can see, that some Marxists for once did some fieldwork and actually attended to reality, rather than that people concerned with the concrete reality of human societies benefited much from Marxist ideas. Later still, there was a heavy wave of so-called hermeneutic or interpretive anthropology, officially favouring the replacement of function and structure by *meaning*, and in practice encouraging a terrible outburst of self-preoccupation and subjectivism amongst its adepts, who believed that by these means they were somehow or other atoning for the sins of colonialism. If striving for lucid understanding of social structures accompanied colonialism, then an anguished introverted and largely unintelligible style was to mark the repudiation of domination. They dwelt lovingly on their epistemological *Angst*: never since the *Sorrows of Young Werther* had there been such poignant anguish. There was also, on the part of some other practitioners of the discipline, a return to asking historical, genetic and developmental questions – but no one particular style of doing so seems, at any rate so far, to have engendered anything resembling a new school.

It is probably true to say that the changes the discipline has undergone have been more under the impact of changed external circumstances than of internal ideas. The world has changed. The colonial system was eventually dismantled and consequently no longer provided an enormous reservoir of relatively insulated and protected, but safely accessible exotic cultures. The successor states were often committed to ideologies which prejudged the findings of ethnographic research, and which consequently were suspicious of external researchers, who might well find something quite different and report on it. Overall, the boundary between simpler and other societies became blurred and problematic. Roughly speaking, the profession came to see itself as a set of practitioners of micro-sociology with a bias towards fieldwork immersion, and the last shreds of defining anthropology as the study of simpler peoples were disappearing. But this later development of the subject is not so relevant to our argument.

25   How did Malinowski get there?

The view widely if tacitly held of Malinowski in the profession was that he arrived from outer space, and that his ideas emerged by a kind of conceptual parthenogenesis, without benefit or need of mundane parentage. This was a view which on the whole he seemed to welcome and encourage. His British or Imperial followers had little knowledge and indeed, so it would seem, little curiosity about his intellectual and other origins. Despite his very profound roots in Cracow and Zakopane, Malinowski eventually came to cut himself off from them. He had at first thought of buying a summer house in Zakopane in the Carpathians whilst continuing to profess in London, but in the end decided to buy one in Alto Adige in Italy instead, which his family still owns. The consequence was that his family grew up between the Italian-controlled South Tyrol and the English-speaking world, without much by way of contact with his own Polish roots. When his most leading disciples came to assemble the posthumous volume *Man and Culture*, under the editorship of Raymond Firth, his distinguished successor in the LSE chair of social anthropology, the work displayed little knowledge of Malinowski's Polish background and some profound misconceptions concerning its character. One had to wait till the centenary of Malinowski's birth in 1984 and the conferences occasioned by it, and above all the availability of the work of young Polish scholars, mainly in Cracow, before the really fascinating sources of his ideas and attitudes became clear (Ellen *et al.* 1988).

In many ways, Cracow was a suburb of Vienna in those pre-1914 days. I have heard it claimed that musical – and, presumably, well-off – inhabitants of Cracow might go to Vienna for a night at the opera, returning next day. Whether or not this is literally true, unquestionably anyone reading works of intellectual history about either place will come across references to many of the same names. It was all one intellectual continuum. Despite some interesting differences, the underlying polarity was the same as the one which haunted Wittgenstein's Vienna: positivism against romanticism. The positivism was much the same: the crucial name of Ernst Mach appears to dominate in both places. It is the romanticism which was different.

Vienna, for all the richness of its intellectual life, seems on the whole to have been spared Hegelianism. (Curiously, there is a Hegelstrasse in central Vienna.) It is not at all clear why this should be so: neither Catholicism nor a hierarchical and bureaucratic state structure, nor any other feature of Habsburg society one can think of, have in other places inhibited the spread of Hegelian ideas. But, whatever the explanation, it seems to be a fact: *Hegelianism in Vienna*, like *Democracy in Russia*, *Great English Dishes*, or *Victories of the Czechoslovak Army*, would make an exceedingly short book.

Now in Poland it was rather different. Hegelian historiosophy was a definite element in the cultural ferment, though it did have to compete with a strong positivistic trend. In a way this is rather odd, as the Polish attitude to Hegel could hardly be anything other than ambivalent, at best. Hegel had taught that nations truly enter history only by acquiring their own state and that stateless nations were not fully part of history; moreover, that what happened in history was part of a pre-ordained and rational plan, so that what happened, was right. The real, in the celebrated phrase, was the rational. Now the Poles had but recently, at the end of the eighteenth century, lost their own state when it was carved up by their three neighbours, one of whom Hegel had credited with being the expression of reason on earth. By an elementary syliogism, one could conclude that Polish political aspirations were neither real nor rational, which can hardly have been a welcome message in Poland.

None the less, Polish intellectuals were intensely interested in Hegel's ideas. Polish romanticism could bring a special twist to the Hegelian attitude to history, by seeing the fate of Poland, as it then was, as a very special case of vindication by history: Poland's place was established not by its triumphs but by its *suffering*. It was a kind of proof by redemption, expiation and atonement. This, so to speak, negative or inverse Hegelianism fitted in well with the general pessimism of the *fin de siècle*. Hegelian ideas were an excellent way of assimilating and conveying the idea of culture as being more than merely a summation of what people do, by being, rather, a spirit which pervades and guides them, giving purpose, direction and meaning to their lives. All the Hegelian talk about an Absolute Spirit, a kind of puppet master of history, makes sense if one interprets it as meaning that cultural, trans-personal ideas and values guide men, that they are carried by collectivities and change over time, and that cultural permeation and internal transformation are the real plot of history, actual events being but their outward manifestation. Romanticism, including Hegelianism, was a good preparation for cultural anthropology.

Austrian Poland was by far the freest part of Poland, and Cracow was its capital. Its informal summer capital was Zakopane, a mountain resort on the northern slopes of the Tatras, which are the highest part of the Carpathian range, separating Poland from the lands drained by the Danube. In Cracow and Zakopane young Malinowski was exposed to the full force of that intellectual and emotional turbulence which characterised Polish life of the period, as much as it marked Vienna. The claim that he was directly influenced by Hegelian ideas has been challenged by Andrzej Paluch (1981: 284 n8), but it hardly matters: the ideas were so much in the air that, directly or otherwise, he could not but be familiar with them. Wittgenstein may well never have read Herder (in all probability, he hadn't) and perhaps Malinowski did not meditate on Hegel: but neither could escape the influence of ideas which permeated the intellectual and moral climate of the time.

Both Malinowski's life situation and his temperament were significantly different from Wittgenstein's. Wittgenstein was the son of an enormously rich man, and he never seemed, in any ordinary way, either to be ambitious or to need to be so. Not so Malinowski. He was, it is true, of gentle birth (gentry, *szlachta*) on both sides. But it appears that his father, who did rise to be professor at the Jagiellonian University, had lost his lands and his mother had never had any. Malinowski's father died whilst Bronislaw was still young, and it does seem that the widow's financial situation was not all that easy. In brief, all in all, young Bronislaw Malinowski did have his way to make in the world, whereas Ludwig Wittgenstein did not. Wittgenstein needed only to cope with whatever inner anguish the relation of thought to the world, or the validity of mathematics, or the place of values in life, or anything else, engendered within him. On the other hand, Malinowski had no identity problem: he knew what he was, a member of the Polish gentry, and this was a prestigious thing to be. Wittgenstein, as a member of a converted Jewish family, belonged to a class of people doomed to be haunted by the problem of cultural identity: that problem pervaded their world. The Jagiellonian University in Cracow was predominantly Polish and proud of it. The intellectual world of Vienna did not know what it was; it was at best ambivalent about its frequently Jewish roots, and was troubled by it all.

One might add that, though Malinowski was, like Wittgenstein, a charismatic personality, in many ways he was far more conventional than Wittgenstein. There was none of that ferocious narrowness of interest which characterised Wittgenstein. In subjects which concerned him Malinowski read broadly and systematically, and it can on the whole be assumed that he was familiar with the ideas and literature current in the field. Moreover, and not only because he was a professional social scientist, one can assume him to have been familiar with the social issues of the time. None of these assumptions could ever be made concerning Wittgenstein.

Where Wittgenstein faced a philosophical problem and, in all probability, a personal identity problem, but perhaps no other, Malinowski faced a philosophical problem, a career problem, and finally a problem, not perhaps of personal identity, but rather of political orientation. (Just because his personal identity was comfortable, he could allow himself doubts and indulge in rational thought about the political role of nations in general and his own nation in particular.) The career problem and the philosophical one – which could also be called a problem of method in anthropology – must be considered jointly.

26 Whither anthropology? Or: whither Bronislaw?

Malinowski's early courses at the University in Cracow were at least as much in mathematics and natural sciences as in philosophy. Ill health, which did indeed haunt him all his life, is the reason he gives for not taking that direction professionally. His doctoral dissertation, 'On the Principle of the Economy of Thought', was completed by 1906 and received *sub auspiciis Imperatoris* in 1908 (Malinowski 1993: 89–115). It examined the arguments of Mach and Avenarius on the idea of the economy of effort in thought and it contains ideas destined to be crucial for his later development. Achieving what was required with minimal effort: as good a definition of *functional* effectiveness as you might wish. The application of this idea to society was to have a great future and constitute the basis of his reputation. What was it that turned him towards anthropology, where he found such a fertile field of application for the idea?

He himself tells us, in an oft-quoted passage, that it was reading Frazer's *Golden Bough* which converted him to the subject, by showing him that here there was a worthy field, to which one could well dedicate oneself (Malinowski 1948: 93–4). Did he see, at the same time, that this was an area ripe for a revolution? We have seen already that the Frazerian mix of evolutionist question and magpie data was, in due course, wholly inverted and abrogated by him, in an impressively coherent way. But where exactly did he find the tools for so doing?

The polarisation of Polish culture between positivist and romantic (at the time known as (literary) 'modernist') trends was, as indicated, somewhat different from the polarisation that prevailed in Vienna. In Vienna, the liberals, long after their flirtation with nationalism in 1848 which had ended in shared disaster, were centrist, confronting the *Völkisch* nationalism of the ethnic minorities and also, in the end, of the dominant ethnic group itself. (Something strangely similar, interestingly enough, was destined to happen a century later, when in the course of the break-up of the Soviet empire, the Russians themselves joined the ranks of ethnic discontent against the centre.) In Cracow and Lemberg, positivism was strong, but it is not clear that it had quite the same centrist, anti-ethnic connotations as it had in Vienna. In any case, it had a powerful influence on the young Malinowski. The most vivid and conclusive evidence is Malinowski's doctoral dissertation, mentioned above. Andrzej Flis has clearly specified the nature of Mach's influence on Malinowski (Flis 1988: 115–18, 123). Mach, as Malinowski notes, stood at the confluence of two currents: on the one hand, the collapse of materialism and its replacement by empiricism (observation, not matter, is primary) and, on the other, the impact of Darwinism, the importance of functional adaptation as a means to survival. These two elements led logically enough to the Machian version of radical empiricism in which the activities of our mind which go beyond observation are explained and justified, not by custom (as in Hume) or by an invariant inner compulsion (Kant), but by variable adaptation of the organism. This idea needed only to be extended to entire communities to yield what was to become 'functionalism'.

In Mach two themes were conspicuous, destined to play a crucial role in the construction of Malinowski's approach. One was radical empiricism, the distrust of the invention of entities beyond experience. This led to his preference for constructs *made up of* observables over entities *inferred from* observables. The other element was a kind of biologically inspired functionalism. Why should we construct anything out of and beyond the experiential sphere at all? And, given the fact that what we construct is not uniquely determined by the data, why should we choose to construct this rather than that? This is one of the crucial questions empiricism has to face: given that data, like patriotism, are not enough, since our world seems doomed to go beyond them, how do we justify that something *extra* in which we inevitably indulge, and how do we justify our choice from the range of available extras?

The answer to this question, in Malinowski's mind, is already contained in the very title of his dissertation. Of possible alternatives it is the most economical which must serve. Simplicity, convenience for the organism, is the principle which properly guides our cognitive choices. The underlying strategy is decided by the needs of the organism. It is the service of mundane needs which explains and justifies transmundane invention!

This combination of extreme empiricism and biological functionalism is what Malinowski found in Mach, who influenced him so powerfully, as he had influenced so many others. There can hardly be any doubt now, after the patient work of Andzej Flis and others, that this is where Malinowski found these ideas. Speculating about the underlying inspiration of Malinowski, before the Polish work on Malinowski's youth existed or was available, Edmund Leach, in his contribution to *Man and Culture*, suggested William James as the origin of these ideas, adding that James was fashionable in London at the time Malinowski arrived there, and so Malinowski could hardly have avoided coming across his work (Leach 1957: 121). Leach then quotes from Bryce Gallie's book, *Peirce and Pragmatism* (1952), where William James' position is summarised as follows: 'from the plausible thesis that certain biological interests underlie . . . all our thinking, he [James] passed to the more exciting . . . thesis that the sole function of thought is to satisfy certain interests of the organism, and that truth consists of such thinking as satisfies these interests' (Gallie 1952: 25).

This is indeed a good summary of the central intuition of Jamesian pragmatism, and Leach's guess concerning the origins of Malinowski's functionalism was not at all a bad one. An excellent piece of speculative history, one might say. But in this case, the speculation is quite unnecessary. Those very ideas were also available in Mach – without the name 'pragmatism', of course – and we know that they preoccupied the young Malinowski who, when he arrived in London, had no need to read James to learn about them. Perhaps he did so, but it hardly matters: he was already, through his well-documented and thorough study of Mach, in full possession of these ideas. Had Leach carried out fieldwork on the culture of Malinowski's youth, instead of indulging in speculative history, he would have found the correct answer . . .

Empiricism and biological functionalism explain a good deal of Malinowski, but they certainly do not explain it all. They are necessary, but not sufficient. If empiricism plus Darwin had been all there was to it, Malinowski might well have become another Edward Westermarck, an important figure with whom he worked in London and who had preceded him on what might be called the empiricist pilgrimage from Eastern Europe to the Homeland of Empiricism. Westermarck was a Finnish Swede, or Swedish Finn, who found East European Hegelianism, romanticism and nationalism less than congenial, and preferred to move to London, where he was indeed an important member of the generation which prepared the ground for the new subject of social anthropology.

It is an interesting question: why did Westermarck not become the person Malinowski in fact became, the founder of empiricist fieldwork-based social anthropology? He was an empiricist, and had come to England because he was attracted by this aspect of the British intellectual tradition. He was a fieldworker and did a very great deal of fieldwork in Morocco, and continued to do it much longer than Malinowski. However, he persisted, for all his empiricism and practice of fieldwork, in manifesting those two crucial Frazerian traits, the magpie method and the evolutionary or genetic *Fragestellung*. Though he culled a vast amount of ethnographic information in Morocco, it comes assembled as a list or collection of bits and pieces, rather than as a unitary canvass. As for his theorising, he is remembered and used to this day for his theories of the evolution of marriage and of morality, and in particular for his theory of the origin of the incest taboo.

The reason, in my view, why Westermarck failed to do what Malinowski was to do shortly afterwards, was that, although Westermarck did indeed reject East European romanticism (as, up to a point, did Malinowski), he *only* rejected it. He did not at the same time incorporate it, which is precisely what Malinowski did. One might add that Westermarck, as a Finnish citizen of Swedish mother tongue (thereby more or less excluded from Finnish ethnographic romanticism), had more cause than Malinowski ('gentry on both sides' as he is reputed to have observed) to opt out of that romanticism. Malinowski's reasons must have been more subtle (gratitude to the Emperor-King who had so signally honoured his doctoral dissertation?). Whatever they were, they led Malinowski *both* to reject *and* to use East European romanticism; and it was partial rejection, partial use and incorporation, which endowed his position with its uniqueness, its originality, and its freshness, and enabled him to supplant Frazer and become the new priest-king of the sacred grove of anthropology.

What were those features of East European romanticism which he retained? What matters most in that tradition, for the present purposes, is the East and Central European style of ethnography, as developed in the nineteenth century and as practised by some scholars to this very day. The aim of populist or nationalist ethnography is not, as was the case amongst West European scholars, to use 'simpler' populations to answer questions about the early condition of mankind. The village schoolteachers who painfully recorded customs, songs, sayings, dances, and stories, did not do so in the hope that their findings would in due course decide some question about early forms of marriage, religion or the state; they barely knew about these questions and did not care a great deal about the answer. They cared about the 'rebirth' (in fact, frequently, just *birth*) of their nation, or the nation they were helping to create. (Admittedly, it is true that on occasion, the other motive or use of data was also present: Russian peasant forms of ownership and Yugoslav forms of kinship have played a significant role in discussions concerning early social forms. But this was not the dominant motive.)

So the main driving inspiration was different. The aim was to record, codify, and protect the national culture, or its peasant variant, either because the peasant version was held to be the purest and most valuable form of it or because, in some cases, it was the *only* available form of it. Some 'un-historical' or 'small' nations simply did not possess an aristocratic or urban version of their own culture at all. If that culture was to be maintained, and eventually to become the basis of a new national state, and to provide the medium for a national educational system, it simply had to be extracted and distilled from peasant customs. Sometimes a region would be specially selected as embodying the national culture: during the national revival the folklore of south-western Bohemia and south-eastern Moravia somehow acquired the standing of being paradigmatically Czech. But if this culture was to be codified and protected and taken over by a national educational and bureaucratic system, it had to be presented as a *unity*, and not as a thing of shreds and patches. This theme is absent in Westermarck who was, as noted, a bit of a shreds-and-patches merchant in his ethnography. In Malinowski the 'culture as unity' theme is not just conspicuously present, but marvellously well fused with the empiricism: the duty of thorough, immersive fieldwork is not merely the categorical imperative of the movement, it is justified by the need for genuine and thorough observation, the rejection of (un-empiricist, shameful) use of inference to the unobservable (in this case, the *past*). Isolated traits or practices can be observed in a short and limited time: to secure the *feel* of a culture requires intimacy and perseverance. So, implicit in Malinowski's empiricism, or the method chosen to implement it, is the recognition that culture is a complex, holistic thing, requiring participation, not mere snapshots, for its observation. So radical empiricism and cultural holism were blended. Westermarck had only employed one of these two elements.

The various nationalisms were, of course, inevitably often in conflict. The boundaries of dialects are unclear and complex, populations are intermixed, and there simply were not, in Eastern Europe, clear and distinct ethnic frontiers. Inevitably many territories and populations were contested and claimed by two or more rival nationalisms. So nationalist ethnography was concerned not merely with codifying peasant custom, linguistic and other, so as to use it as the base for a new national culture which was in the process of construction, but also to establish that a given dialect really was a version of Ruritanian, and not, as was shamefully and meretriciously claimed by jealous and unscrupulous Bragadoccian politicians and intellectuals (whose opportunist scholarship was matched only by their lack of political conscience), a dialect of Middle Bragadoccian. Any fool who looks at the phoneme pattern of this dialect, or at its characteristic verb forms, or at the beautiful themes which pervade the local folktales, can tell at a glance, without any shadow of doubt, that this is a form of Middle Ruritanian: indeed, in its touching archaisms it is one of the most moving forms of Ruritanian! (A certain literary scholar, visiting a village outside his national boundaries but still speaking a variant of his own tongue, was moved to tears by this throwback to the eighteenth-century form of his own language: but the peasants in question, insufficiently 'awakened', firmly refused to campaign for a return to the homeland. They wanted the boundary to stay as it was, and the ethnographic researcher was honest enough to record the fact.) To return to our main theme: Bragadoccian nationalism is as utterly unscrupulous in its scholarship as it is in its expansionist designs, being in part motivated by the strategic importance of the district in which this dialect is found. The scholars who act as its mouthpiece will not be restrained by shame from making claims, however absurd, as long as they can hope to advance their nefarious ends. It is this which makes it so important that those preposterous claims be refuted publicly and clearly, by well-documented ethnography. This is why ethnography matters so much in Eastern Europe, and this is the *way* in which it matters.

Ethnography in this style is carried out, not with theoretical, detached curiosity about some aspect of the society of early man: it is carried out, above all, with love, and furthermore, with an intimate awareness of the nuances of local idiom, and with a sense of the overall unity of the culture, and with a desire to preserve it. One of the most famous episodes in this kind of romantic populist world was the occasion when two young Polish intellectuals decided to carry this 'going to the people' to its full conclusion and actually married two village maidens, so as to round off their intimacy with folk culture. The spirit of observer participation, later to be formalised by Malinowski as fieldwork method, could hardly go further. Whether, abstractly and doctrinally speaking, Malinowski obtained his holistic idea from Hegelianism, or whether he obtained it from the modernist literary movement, hardly matters. Malinowski could not but have failed to be utterly familiar with the spirit of this kind of culture-loving, culture-preserving fieldwork, which used the local idiom, not so much from methodological purity, but from sheer love. His father had been a professional dialectologist, and his own frequent residences in Zakopane familiarised him with that most romantic of local groups, the Górale (mountaineers, highlanders).

Reflecting on his fieldwork in the Trobriands, Malinowski admitted that he resented alien cultural intrusions such as a piece of calico cloth or a Christian belief (Malinowski 1935, I: 481). In effect, Malinowski behaved, and felt, in the Trobriands rather as his ethnographer compatriots had behaved and felt in the Carpathians. More important, he used the same method. The central idea of the approach was that culture was a unity, an interconnected whole, and had to be seen as such. The magpie method of using isolated beliefs and looking at their internal logic was out.

But not only did he exclude magpie atomism; he equally excluded, and this is perhaps the most famous aspect of his anthropological revolution, the invocation of the past: the explanation of present practice in terms of supposed earlier conditions. Here his main argument was methodological and an application of Mach-style severe empiricism: do not invent entities which will then, in circular fashion, serve you as explanations! In a society without records, invoking the past is most liable to be circular. Frazer ended by explaining the strange ritual or rule of succession at Nemi as a survival of an even stranger and more ancient one – but the main evidence for the existence of the explanans was the explanandum! Malinowski's methodological revolution firmly proscribed the Frazerian pluperfect method of explanation.

This is, as it were, the negative aspect of Malinowski's rejection of genetic or evolutionary questions and explanations in anthropology. Do not invoke what you do not know about! In a sense, anthropologists had done nothing else: they had used simpler societies as surrogate time machines, and the spirit of looking yet further back pervaded their thought world so much that when something did not make sense in this putative report from the human past, they looked towards a still more remote past. If it wasn't there to be found, they were easily tempted into inventing it. Now, they were not to do it at all. If Malinowski was to slay and replace Frazer, here was a dramatic inversion indeed. The cult of fieldwork and explaining the present had a multiple vindication: empiricist abstention from the invocation of unobservables, and a both functionalist and romantic sense of the unity and interdependence of culture.

Thus Malinowski's methodological inversion was rich indeed. Mach, like his follower Russell, had commended not merely the avoidance of unobservables, but also their replacement by constructions out of observables. Our thought and language are full of what at least seem to be references to things which cannot immediately be identified with unambiguous bits of experience, so to speak. The radical empiricist finds himself in a bit of a dilemma: if he insists on the uncompromising execution of his programme – out with all unobservables! – he may find himself with an intolerably impoverished and unrecognisable world, and one which simply cannot function. But there is a way out, and we have already seen what it is: theoretical constructs are to be allowed, said Mach, provided they serve the needs of the organism. Function, usefulness, economy of effort, replace the transcendent as the legitimator of trespassing beyond the strict bounds of experience. Usefulness replaces the Beyond as the ground of a fuller, more tolerable world.

So history may be out, but there is still the indisputable fact that many societies are preoccupied with the past and say quite a lot about it. Is one simply to ignore this? Here we come to the positive side of the functionalism which Malinowski inherited from Mach and adapted to anthropology. Beliefs about the past are indeed relevant and important, not as evidence about the past, but in virtue of their *present function*, their *role*, their *use* (to use the term Wittgenstein was to employ for a similar purpose) in contemporary society: usually that use is to be found in the validation of current practices. This is the most characteristic Malinowskian doctrine concerning the role of history and myths and legends: they are 'charters' of contemporary institutions.

Thus Malinowski's ahistoricism has first of all a negative aspect: the rejection of the invocation of an invented, speculative past in the hope of explaining some puzzling aspect of the present; and second, a positive aspect: the 'functionalist' doctrine that everything existing in the present – including assertions about the past (and they perhaps most of all) – has a function, a role, a usefulness, *in the present*. The two aspects of the doctrine complement each other and each can find its intellectual roots in Mach. At the same time, the positive aspect of the ahistorism, the insistence on the functional interdependence of the present, fits in exceedingly well with the romantic vision of culture as a self-sustaining, coherent unity, and indeed the ultimate form of human fulfilment. This view, as stated, Malinowski could just as well have obtained from the Hegelians or from the literary modernists, or, most directly, from the actual practice of nationalist ethnography which pervaded the atmosphere in Zakopane.

If carefully scrutinised, however, the various elements in this functionalism were not always in full harmony with each other. If the past is to be eschewed whenever absence of documents makes assertions about it speculative, what is to be done in societies in which documents *are* available? Does a different method apply to them? If it is the speculativeness, the absence of documentary evidence, which matters, then the method should cease to be binding when documents do exist – but this is in conflict with the functionalist insistence on explaining the present *by* the present, a consideration which, if it applies at all, applies *anyway*. The functional interdependence, the mutual support of institutions, seems to imply that there must be stability, at any rate unless there is some disturbance coming from the outside. But to credit a society with stability is to make a tacit affirmation about its past – that it was the same as the present, which after all is what stability *means*. But does this mean that functionalists, far from avoiding speculative history, merely indulge, on the quiet, in a different kind of speculation – namely, the attribution of stability instead of evolutionary change to the past? All these questions were to arise in due course, but they did not, initially, inhibit the enthusiastic reception and implementation of the functionalist revelation.

What Malinowski had done was remarkable. He had taken elements from both sides of the great divide which had polarised intellectual life, in Europe in general and in Poland in particular, and had concocted a totally original cocktail. The elements were, all of them, old but the combination was wholly new. He had taken the romantic sense of the unity of culture, but weaned it from its long-standing partner, the romantic sense of the partnership of past and present. The unity of culture here and now was now no longer linked to the Burkean companionship of the dead, the living, and the as-yet-unborn. Malinowski endowed the holistic sense of the unity of culture with a new and severely empiricist rationale, and exiled the past in the name of severe empiricist standards. The Malinowskian past was not an inference, it was a social function *in the observable present*.

At the same time, Malinowski adopted synchronicism, normally a positivist attitude (positivists are allergic to historical romanticism, and gladly leave nostalgia for mediaeval idylls to others); for him this meant an insistence that any situation must be understood in terms of the contemporary balance of forces. However, he linked this to a most unpositivist sense of the unity of culture. He was an empiricist organicist, a positivist romantic, and a synchronic holist. All these alignments were new: European thought was used to romantics who also revered history, the Hegels and the Burkes, and it was used to empiricists who had scant respect for it: but here was someone who had altogether reshuffled the cards and had come out with a coherent hand that no one had ever played before.

It was a hand which enabled him to do a number of things. This set of ideas, to formulate it in a way he might have chosen himself, provided a magnificent *charter* for the new style of fieldwork which he initiated: sustained observation and description of a given culture, based on immersion and intimate familiarity, tracing all its inner connections, but eschewing speculations about the past. Under his leadership and inspiration the quantity and quality of ethnography provided during the last decades of colonialism rose enormously. Moreover, the fieldwork became comparable, being carried out by men (and women) who had undergone similar training under his auspices. It goes without saying that it enabled him to take over the profession – in a sense, actually to *create* it – and to become its leader. In a physical sense, Frazer continued to live and he only died a year before Malinowski, only just enabling Malinowski to make a kind of oration honouring his predecessor as the last and greatest of the old kind – leaving it to be clearly understood who was the greatest of the new dispensation.

But Malinowski's anti-historicism is not restricted in its methodological application to the study of simpler, document-less societies. Eastern and Central Europe, as well as being the zone of nationalist ethnography, of the loving and indeed passionate recording and preservation of folk culture, was also the zone of nationalist historiography, of the sustained use of the past for the expression and fortification of contemporary sentiment. Nowhere is this more visible than in Malinowski's own home city of Cracow. Quite literally, not an hour passes without one being reminded of the past and its significance. Every hour, on the hour, the trumpeter sounds the bugle from the top of the highest tower in the old town square; and the sound is then very abruptly broken off at a certain point, commemorating the occasion when the watchman on the tower alerted the city to the arrival of Tartar hordes, only to have his throat pierced by a Mongol arrow – but he did not sacrifice himself in vain, for his warning was heard and alerted the citizens. So every hour, on the hour, the Polish citizens are reminded – as if this were necessary – that their civilisation is in danger from savages from the east. Vigilance and heroism are needed to ward off the danger.

As indicated, Poles who flirted with Hegelian-style reverence for history had a bit of a hard time: should they accept history as having granted Poland a very special status through its expiatory suffering, or should they strive to correct the verdict of history by restoring the Polish state? On this issue, Malinowski and Witkiewicz, the writer and painter, probably his deepest and most significant friend, in practice and no doubt in theory took different lines, and they parted after a quarrel which has never been properly documented in 1914. Witkacy (as he was known) left to fight in an elite Tsarist regiment and Malinowski to carry out the fieldwork which was to make him famous.

Malinowski was deeply appreciative of the quality of Habsburg rule in Cracow and Galicia, and he had an unusually clear perception of the nature of the ethnic-political problem in Central and Eastern Europe. Changes in boundaries or the establishment of new political units could only, given the complexity of the ethnic map, change the identity of dominant and dominated groups, but could not, on its own, solve much. All this, and perhaps other considerations, prevented him from being a political nationalist. All the same, he obviously was a cultural one. Above all, he had a vivid sense of the crucial nationalist premise: that men live their lives through a culture and can hardly find fulfilment in any other way. So the particular philosophico-methodological cocktail which enabled him to displace Frazer and define a new anthropology, at the same time also provided him with a charter for his own personal and political position.

It is relevant here to return to the difference in the way in which the deep pervasive polarity was felt in Vienna and in Cracow. The influx of nationalities into the expanding imperial capital meant that by the end almost everyone went over to a *Völkisch*-national position. The only liberals, or very nearly, were those of Jewish background or with Jewish links, i.e. the cosmopolitans. They could choose, in their public persona, to be proud of their universalistic liberalism and spurn the ethnic totem poles as shameful atavisms – such is the stance of Popper's *Open Society* – or they could sardonically indulge their self-hatred and damn themselves for their lack of roots. It hardly mattered: as Arthur Schnitzler remarked about a similar dilemma faced by the same category of people, you could be pushy or shy, but you could not win. So a man might well be driven to want to be a transcendental ego, at the limits of the world but not of it, in order to escape being a Viennese Jew.

In Cracow it was all somewhat different. The overwhelming majority of the intellectuals were Polish, which was a good and prestigious thing to be, and they did not have trouble with their own personal identity. Assimilated Jews amongst the Polish intelligentsia, such as Gumplowicz, were few in number. The Jews from the *Städtl* did not, on the whole, try to enter the ranks of the Polish gentry, though Sir Lewis Namier's family became landowners and converted. Instead, they made straight for Vienna and entered German rather than Polish culture. The fact that German is closer to Yiddish than Polish was probably a less important consideration than the fact that, if you must assimilate anyway, you might as well go straight for the capital and the top culture and a world language, rather than another minor culture with its own problems. But by so making for the centre, they created problems for their predecessors, the earlier entrants into Viennese high culture and society. The constant influx of new *Ostjuden* could not but remind both the host culture and those already acclimatised, the well-established Jewish bourgeoisie, of their own ambiguous status.

The members of the Polish-speaking intelligentsia in Cracow and

Galicia may not have had worries about their own individual identity. What they were less clear about, on the other hand, was what was to be done about their *collective* identity: how to link their philosophy to their politics. Unlike the top Viennese intelligentsia, they were not pushed into passionate pro-centrism by fear of the virulent chauvinist ethnics. The centre might allow them to dominate Galicia, but they would do the same in an independent Poland. They may have been grateful to the centre for its tolerant, indeed supportive cultural policy – this was certainly Malinowski's feeling – but at the same time they could hope that, if the Empire broke up, Poland would re-emerge in consequence, as indeed it did.

There are other differences between Malinowski and Wittgenstein. Malinowski did study Mach intensively, but he did not extract from him the doctrine of the vanishing self (which re-emerges in Wittgenstein's *Tractatus* with such emphasis). Mach's gift to Malinowski was the doctrine of the functionality of thought and language, something Wittgenstein did not bother with till much later during his 'second' philosophic phase: even then he probably took this idea directly from the general intellectual atmosphere, rather than from Mach.

Wittgenstein was a reasonably typical member of the Viennese intelligentsia. I am not suggesting that everyone in this class resembled him, but alienated intellectuals seeking escape through very pure thought were there to be found. By contrast, Malinowski's attitude was really quite unusual amongst, so to speak, his own people. His reaction to the Polish question, and in general to ethnic issues, *is* untypical: it is to be found in his remarkable freedom from *political* nationalism, combined with an acute sense of and love of *culture*. In Vienna, the cosmopolitan liberals did not make a fuss of ethnic culture(s), but preferred an international civilisation; those who did make a fuss of ethnic culture also displayed a corresponding nationalist attitude in politics.

So, in Malinowski's case, radical empiricism was not used to extricate the ego from the world; but rather it was used to amputate the politically loaded history from the sense of culture. A sense of culture was retained, the cult of history abandoned. Machian radical empiricism could, quite legitimately, be used for either purpose. Radical empiricism can be used as a corrosive acid, and turned either against an over-sold, manipulated, demanding past, or against an over-involved ego; either way the acid works. The past is reduced to the invocation and use of legend in the present; the ego is reduced into the focus of the visual field. Malinowski used the first of these options, but not the latter. Wittgenstein, in his youth, had used the latter but not the former.

So Malinowski reshuffled the two packs of cards traditionally displayed in Eastern Europe, and took what suited him from each pack. He did ethnography, as it was done in the Carpathians, on the Danube, in the Balkans or the Caucasus, but he did it in the Trobriands, and justified it, not by love of homeland, but by science and a radical empiricism. This enabled him to revolutionise anthropology. He transformed it from a time-machine into a history-exterminator. In a sense he created a new subject, and he certainly created a new profession, with its very severe rules – fieldwork as the *sine qua non* initiation rite – and with its clearly demarcated membership. At the very same time, he had solved his personal-political problem. The key device, the re-assemblage of romantic and positivist elements in the package, he then christened 'functionalism'. It helped make sense of his subsequent life, his career, and his professional-political orientation. One can only admire the elegance with which one set of ideas could be used for so many purposes, and endowed with so much coherence.

The discipline initiated by Malinowski continued to exhibit the interesting mix of elements which he had bestowed on it. It was, at least until very recently, a firmly empirical science: its practitioners were expected to gather their data strenuously and carefully, and the level of ethnographic accuracy in this tradition was very high. At the same time, its members were expected to have a sense of the social interconnectedness of things; and, although it was not compulsory to come out with a functionalist conclusion demonstrating 'seamless unity', nevertheless, they were expected to look carefully into institutional interconnections. Indeed one attempt at securing originality within the tradition consisted precisely of stressing conflict rather than harmony; but as the conflict was then credited with making its oblique contribution to harmony after all, this in the end turned out simply to be functionalism by other means.

Malinowski's politics were interesting. They were not ever systematically worked out until a posthumous book, *Freedom and Civilisation*

(1944), if indeed they can be described as fully worked out even then. On the one hand, given the fact that the book was written during the Second World War, the author did of course have to attend to the general problem of post-war reconstruction, the establishment of a new world order, and so on. But as a distinguished, indeed the leading, social anthropologist, liable to be consulted by the authorities on problems concerning the future and administration of the colonial empire, he naturally also had to express his opinions on this burning issue.

His views on these two sets of questions form an interesting unity. The same central insights and intuitions pervade the argument. The book conveys a man's vision, not a catalogue of opinions. One would of course have expected no less from the man who had so ingeniously garnered themes from two previously rival, indeed bitterly opposed traditions, and turned them into a single coherent vision. I shall sum up his views in my own words, and perhaps a little more starkly and provocatively than he did, so as to bring out their point, their relevance, and the manner in which they stand in contrast to the conventional wisdom – but I trust without, for all that, misrepresenting them.

First of all, for all his organic sense of the unity of culture, Malinowski *was* a liberal. Liberalism, attachment to liberty, is not an monopoly of those committed to the view of man as an isolated atom and of society as a mere summation of such atoms or as a market of convenience. Malinowski was of course deeply imbued with the sense of the unity and reality of culture – this after all was the gift of Carpathian ethnography to the new British anthropological tradition – but this did not prevent him from valuing freedom. There had been other such organicist liberals, of course: T. H. Green, for instance, had used the metaphysics of Hegelianism to articulate a version of liberalism (and of the welfare state into the bargain). Anyway, liberty as defined by Malinowski is the expression of aims which have cultural roots, rather than the socially disembodied caprices of a culture-free individual, landing in society from outer space.

So, in his politics as articulated during the early 1940s, he clearly retains his sense of culture. It would however be absurd, in politics, to retain the synchronicism which was his hallmark in anthropological method. It would be absurd to turn it into a normative principle and claim, not only that societies perpetuate themselves, but that they ought to do so, that they ought to remain what they were and display stability. There are romantics who do feel this about simpler societies, but he was not of their number. Even in method, the Malinowski of the 1940s has come to feel some qualms about wishing away, or pretending away, that intrusive piece of calico or Christianity. He recognises the inevitability of change, and even stresses that the understanding of this new tremendous diffusion must be the task of anthropology. But what are his views on the desirable direction of change?

Malinowski was favourably impressed by the British practice of 'Indirect Rule' without in any way subscribing to the illusion that it *really* preserves indigenous institutions in their pristine form. He remained loyal to this idea even during the Second World War, as Janusz Mucha (1988) points out in his illuminating essay. This kind of attitude may have earned Malinowski the reputation amongst subsequent generations of anthropologists of having been mildly liberal by the standards of the time, but not really surmounting the assumptions or prejudices of the colonial era. But this assessment does not do full justice to his position. Let us go back to the fundamental issues concerning the evaluation of colonialism.

Anti-colonialists hold two positions:
(1) The asymmetry between coloniser and colonised is morally repellent.
(2) This being so, colonialism must be abolished.

Anti-colonialists do not normally distinguish or separate (1) and (2). To them they seem virtually identical. In any case, they seem so closely linked that to distinguish them would be pedantic and unnecessary.

This is a terrible mistake, not just in logic, but also in politics. The two propositions are not identical and the first does *not* entail the second. On the contrary, it is perfectly possible to embrace the moral truism (1) without, for all that, endorsing (2). And it was precisely something like this which was Malinowski's position. There happens to be another alternative attitude, one which does embrace (1), but uses it to proceed to quite a different conclusion:
(3) Therefore, *everyone* should be colonised!

Note that this eliminates the morally offensive asymmetry just as effectively as would the abolition of colonialism. If equality is your value, if political symmetry is your aim, than the universalisation of colonialism is just as good as its abolition. But is it feasible, and why should it be preferable?

Let us begin by asking – what is the essence of that Indirect Rule which Malinowski found so attractive? It is not really an ice box preserving the past. That cannot be done. So its charms must lie elsewhere. What are they?

The real essence of indirect rule is that it limits the political power of local rulers, whether genuinely taken over from the pristine past or created and invented by colonialism. What it really does is to encourage, foster, and sustain the cultural expression of the indigenous society, including its political hierarchy. The rajah, amir or sheikh is encouraged to keep up, indeed to enhance and develop, all the pomp and circumstance – but at the same time his power is markedly restrained. He is no longer allowed to do really dreadful things to his subjects (or at least not so much and not so publicly). In this way, the standards of humanity are raised. Also, he can no longer go to war against the neighbouring rajah, amir or sheikh . . . Political independence is limited, cultural exuberance and idiosyncrasy are enhanced and assured. More elephants and camels, less terror. *That* is the real heart of Indirect Rule.

Malinowski did not merely approve of Indirect Rule when it was practised under that name. He also recognised the merits of Habsburg rule in Cracow and Galicia. The Habsburgs allowed Polish culture to flourish in Galicia, but obviously set limits to Polish political assertion *vis-à-vis* other groups. Malinowski's positive recommendation for the post-war future was the creation of a more effective League of Nations to which individual nation-states would surrender much of their sovereignty, enough to render further wars or oppression difficult or even impossible, without however inhibiting their own cultural exuberance. And here one can, I think, see the underlying equation in his thought: Indirect Rule = Habsburg practices = League of Nations with teeth. That was what the Habsburgs had done in Cracow: they deprived Polish nationalism of its political power, or at least limited it, but certainly in no way inhibited cultural expression. (They did not prevent Polish gentry lording it over Ruthene peasants, but they did set limits to it.) And what would a really effective League of Nations, capable of preventing future wars, do? Precisely the same: limit the political power of nations, but permit, indeed enhance and encourage, the perpetuation of all those local cultures within which men found their fulfilment and their freedom.

The failure to implement some intuition similar to Malinowski's in 1918 had well-known consequences. The Versailles Settlement accentuated nationalism and eventually inflamed it to a point of frenzy. In the 1940s, when conditions permitted or indeed encouraged it, this led to genocide and subsequently, by way of retaliation, to massive forcible transplantations of populations, also accompanied by a measure of, as it were, incidental murder. Thereafter further indulgence in nationalist excess was inhibited, for about forty years, by the ruthless and determined imposition of a new ideology, which proved at least as capable of restraining nationalism as the old religious-dynastic system had been during the century between Vienna and Versailles. The strange, self-initiated dismantling of that system after 1985, culminating in the total un-shackling of Eastern Europe in 1989, has led to a situation similar to that which followed the dismantling of the Habsburg Empire. It may indeed have similar consequences and, in Yugoslavia, has already had them. Given the complexity of the ethnic map, the plurality of criteria applied – which leads to multiple mutually incompatible claims, each of which however seems overwhelmingly cogent to its own partisans – it would seem that some solution along the lines proposed by Malinowski is the only humane one, the only one with some prospect of implementation without major loss of life. Colonise simply everybody – i.e. deprive their political units of sovereignty – whilst allowing them absolute cultural freedom of expression, thereby incidentally depriving boundaries of some of their importance and symbolic potency. It is not easy for states to own territory jointly, but there is no reason whatsoever why more than one culture – each operating through its own TV network, educational system, etc. – should not function, and very effectively, on the same territory. Culture is not necessarily territorial, even though it imprints itself on the landscape. So the integral preservation of the cultural unity – indeed, its encouragement, support, provision with the required infrastructure – could perhaps be combined with a kind of defusing of the old blood-rousing issues. No longer will it matter quite so much whether the fatherland reaches the sacred river, or goes right up to the watershed on the mountain ridge on which our boys bled so bravely – because the manifestation of the beloved national culture in this zone, right up to the hallowed river or the blood-stained ridge, is ensured anyway, and the political institutions on the ground are reduced to mere administrative conveniences and so, as far as possible, emptied of their emotive potency. Whether or how such a programme can really be implemented and enforced on the warring ethnic factions is another question: but it is obvious that this is our only hope.

29 Malinowski's theory of language

Malinowski was right in politics: was he also right on language? Wittgenstein's later views on language and society are intimately blended and virtually identical. In fact Wittgenstein's theory of language, central to his philosophy, is but a coded theory of society: mankind lives in cultural communities or, in his words, 'forms of life', which are self-sustaining, self-legitimating, logically and normatively final. They can only be described, they cannot be justified or explained, for they constitute the terminal, ultimate point of any explication or validation. From time to time, men are tempted into seeking extra-cultural or transcultural grounds for their conceptual custom: this is *the* error in philosophy, the mistake which in fact engenders all (past, misguided) philosophy. Sound philosophy consists of curing men of the temptation to indulge in this mistake, and in leading them back to accepting their cultural/linguistic custom, so that sound philosophy does indeed 'leave everything as it is'. To put all this in an idiom he never used, because he never attended to socio-political issues (he was politically colour-blind and tone deaf): the nationalist-populists are right, the individualist-universalist liberals are wrong and exhibit *the* pathological condition of thought. In fact, of course, Wittgenstein had unwittingly imbibed this vision from the populists (many of whom were due to become fascists), for it totally pervaded the Viennese atmosphere. He reapplied it in a wholly different field (problems of the validity of mathematics and science) and sold it to a set of people who disliked the universalist vision for quite different reasons: they had no craving to idealise the Danubian (or even Home Counties, for that matter) village, it was just that they knew no maths, and were overjoyed when told that ordinary language, not logic and physics, was the key to the universe . . .

The real point is that the issue concerning the validation of linguistic habits is in effect the question concerning the validity and justification of social practices and customs, and the two issues become fused. Wittgenstein's egregious errors about society are expressed as errors about language, or the other way round. Malinowski's views tended to be correct on both topics, but not quite so intimately fused.

Malinowski had been quite clear, unlike those who enthusiastically accepted the European settlement of 1918, that setting up new states and re-drawing the boundaries did not solve anything. In these matters, the history of the past seventy years has vindicated Malinowski's political judgement. So Malinowski had been right in that sphere. But was he as perceptive on language? His views on language are not quite as central or pivotal to the exposition of his views as were those of his Viennese opposite number, and they have certainly not attracted comparable attention. But, in fact, the manner in which he did get it right is not accidental. It is connected with the overall contrast between the two positions.

Malinowski's views about language are found partly in his Appendix to *The Meaning of Meaning* by Ogden and Richards, first published in 1923. This, incidentally, creates an interesting historical link to Wittgenstein in as far as Ogden was also the translator of the *Tractatus*. The whole issue of the nature of language in simple and in sophisticated societies, and the problem of the relationship of language to reality, are obviously related to each other. In pre-literate societies it is particularly obvious that the 'meaning' of expressions is linked to the context in which they are used and indeed it is tempting to say that their meaning *is* their use; furthermore, words often have uses other than that of referring to 'things'. For instance, they may be used to create or confirm relationships between people. What is the relationship between this kind of employment of speech and its purely referential use (if such a pure use exists)? Can the recognition of the context-bound and use-related nature of speech be compatible with the view that (a) the essence of language is the same in all men and (b) that this essence is some kind of mirroring of reality? In brief, research into the working of 'primitive' life, thought, and language, was bound to raise much the same questions as had arisen in quite a different context in philosophy – and indeed they did arise.

The relationship between the two kinds of thought was due before long to be exploited by Wittgenstein to the full, in fact to provide him with the solution to his main problem and become the basis of his fame: but in the 1920s the connection had not yet aroused much comment in philosophy, if indeed it had attracted anyone's attention.

Malinowski's basic point in this Appendix is simple and plainly correct. The 'savage' use of speech is deeply implicated in the daily purposes of life and, in that sense, highly effective and functional. But its very merits at the same time render it unfit for scientific use. A certain detachment and standardisation are required there. Standardisation of conceptual currency, and detachment from over-involvement in the multiple purposes of daily life, does not constitute a sufficient formula for either defining or explaining science: but it is, no doubt, a significant element in any answer to the question concerning the nature of science and the explanation of its amazing power and success. The point is neither original nor difficult to grasp and Malinowski was never acclaimed as a genius for having made it: he did get it right, but this part of his work, at any rate, was not original and did not constitute any special achievement. As the question had been raised, it needed to be said and put on record, but it did not deserve any acclamation, and quite properly did not receive it.

Ironically, it was Wittgenstein who was acclaimed for getting this point completely wrong. When the truth is well known, and thus has become platitudinous, originality and *éclat* can presumably be secured only by getting it all egregiously wrong, which is precisely what Wittgenstein did. Wittgenstein's great discovery in his second or later period, and its essence from the viewpoint of the new method he introduced into philosophy, was precisely to insist on focusing and treating as ultimate the involvement of speech in all the multiple purposes and complexities of daily life. *That* language is use-bound and context-linked is not in doubt; it is perfectly correct and it is also in no way an original perception. That the pursuit of extra-cultural norms of scientific or moral validity is simply a misguided by-product of the failure to see this, is totally false. It is also original. So, in the Wittgensteinian mix, there are both true and original elements . . . but, alas, that which is true is old and that which is new is false.

Malinowski's theory can be conveyed by a set of quotations from his Supplement 1, 'The Problem of Meaning in Primitive Languages', in *The Meaning of Meaning*. In their preface to the first edition, Ogden and Richards note:

To Dr Malinowski the authors owe a very special debt. His return to England as their work was passing through the press enabled them to enjoy the advantage of his many years of reflection as a field-worker in Ethnology . . . (Ogden and Richards 1960 [1923]: ix)

Malinowski himself says, in his Supplement (in the initial summary of contents):

Language, in its primitive function, to be regarded as a *mode of action*, rather than as a *countersign of thought*. (Malinowski 1960 [1923]: 296; emphasis in the original)

In the expository text itself he writes:

What I have tried to make clear by analysis of a primitive linguistic text is that language is essentially rooted in the reality of the culture, the tribal life and customs of a people, and that it cannot be explained without constant reference to these broader contexts of verbal utterance. (*ibid*.: 305)

A statement, spoken in real life, is never detached from the situation in which it has been uttered. (*ibid*.: 307)

. . . the meaning of a word must always be gathered, not from a passive contemplation of this word, but from an analysis of its functions, with reference to the given culture. (*ibid*.: 309)

Malinowski gives as good a formulation of the 'meaning is use' principle as you could wish to find:

These conclusions have been reached on an example in which language is used by people engaged in practical work, in which utterances are embedded in action. (*ibid*.: 312)

It is perfectly obvious that, in connection with 'simpler' peoples and their use of language, Malinowski already possessed the functional, culture-bound theory of language, later to be acclaimed as the terminal revelation in philosophy. One should add that he was also in full possession of what was later called the theory of the 'performative' use of language, except that he called it 'phatic':

There can be no doubt that we have here a new type of linguistic use – *phatic communion* I am tempted to call it . . . – a type of speech in which ties of union are created by a mere exchange of words . . . Are words in Phatic Communion used primarily to convey meaning . . . ? Certainly not! They fulfil a social function and that is their principal aim . . . Once more language appears to us in this function not as an instrument of reflection but as a mode of action. (*ibid*.: 315; emphasis in original)

Malinowski stresses that this is characteristic of primitive thought and speech ('I wanted to emphasize that such and no other is the nature of *primitive* thought', *ibid*.: 315; original emphasis), but that this trait is also found elsewhere (' . . . our discussion could have been equally well conducted on a modern example': p. 315). However, whilst the action-linked, context-embedded style is to be found everywhere, there is another style which is rarer:

It is only in certain very special uses among a civilized community and only in its highest uses that language is employed to frame and express thoughts . . . In works of science and philosophy, highly developed types of speech are used to control ideas and to make them the common property of civilized mankind (*ibid*.: 316)

He notes what is indeed a crucial characteristic of this distinctive style: it strives to be context-free, to be addressed to-whom-it-may-concern, rather than to a listener already tied to the speaker by a specific context which enters into the significance of the utterance: 'To take the clearest case, that of a modern scientific book, the writer of it sets out to address every individual reader who will peruse the book and has the necessary scientific training' (*ibid*.: 306).

Let us consider the point or points on which Malinowski here agrees with what was due later to become the centre of Wittgenstein's philosophy, which at the time Malinowski wrote was as yet unformulated and indeed unthought. In fact, the nearly contemporaneous *Tractatus* vigorously contradicted these ideas. One might say that Malinowski formulated the key idea of *Philosophical Investigations*, almost in Wittgenstein's own words, at a time when the latter was still sunk in the darkness of the *Tractatus*! Malinowski emphatically agrees with the later Wittgenstein that to treat this 'highly developed' scientific/referential style of language as a model for *all* language is a terrible mistake. This is certainly correct and here the two authors concur.

There is a further interesting point of convergence. Malinowski, like Wittgenstein, formulates a linguo-genetic theory of philosophy:

Meaning, the real 'essence' of a word, achieves thus Real Existence in Plato's realm of Ideas; and it becomes the Universal, actually existing, of mediaeval Realists. The misuse of words, based always on a false analysis of their Semantic function, leads to all the ontological morass in philosophy . . . (*ibid*.: 308)

Malinowski's version of the linguistic theory of philosophy is historically much richer than Wittgenstein's, with its awareness of Platonic and Scholastic philosophy, but otherwise the similarity is striking, and one can only ask oneself why the philosophers had to wait for Wittgenstein, when it was all there, ready, in Malinowski. The answer must be that Wittgenstein invented his tribes while Malinowski studied them, and Malinowski would have sent them into the field, whereas in post-war Oxford the study of the context-bound active use of language could be carried out, far more cheaply and comfortably, on Saturday mornings.

But there are interesting differences. In his characterisation of that other, *non*-primitive style of thought, Malinowski focusses on what it achieves, rather than on the means by which it is achieved: 'The manner in which I am using [language] now, in writing these words . . . is a very far-fetched and derivative function of language. In this, language becomes a condensed piece of reflection, a record of fact or thought' (*ibid*.: 312). He concentrates on the achievement, the recording of facts or thought, without specifying the manner of its achievement: he avoids the Wittgensteinian doctrine that thought or language operate by mirroring the structure of reality. The method by which action-free thought can come into existence and say something about reality is left open. One might say that it all hinges on the two senses of the word 'reflection': Wittgenstein was concerned with it in the sense of 'echo' or 'mirror' and Malinowski in the sense of deep, detached, ruminative thought.

But more important than this difference is that Malinowski emphatically recognised that there was indeed a profound and important difference between the two styles. He is of course primarily stressing that the abstract-detached style of thought must not be used as a model for language (here the two thinkers agree), that indeed it is a rarity. But: the abstract mode does exist, it is distinct, it is important, even if generalising it leads us into total misconstruing of savage thought and language. By contrast, poor Wittgenstein, having first maintained that the abstract, context-free thought and use of language was absolutely universal, only hidden under the misleading intricacies of ordinary language and signalling wildly to be let out, later went over to the opposite extreme and said it never existed at all, that the striving for it was pathological and needed curing . . .

This is the really important point, the one which separates the two thinkers, and where Malinowski is right and Wittgenstein catastrophically wrong. Both styles exist, each is important, and neither can be reduced to the other. The irreducibility of the savage to the rational/universal is agreed by both sides and not in dispute. What is important and contentious is the reduction of the rational to the functional.

30   Malinowski's later mistake

Here we must regretfully admit and report that later in his life, Malinowski moved away from his views as outlined in his contribution to *The Meaning of Meaning*. My view is that the opinion expressed by Malinowski in that work is basically correct: there is a profound, fundamental, immensely important difference between the functional, culturally embedded use of language, and the, as it were, disembodied, abstract investigation of the world, which stands in contrast to it. Certainly, Malinowski failed to give any deep account of the nature of non-savage, genuine thought. He had indeed failed to take even the initial and most elementary steps in such a direction. There was no call upon him to do so: he was an anthropologist, and was content with affirming, correctly, that savage thought cannot be understood by projecting onto it abstract scholarly reasoning. But, in his first important essay on this topic, he did at least uphold the recognition that this crucial difference was there, whether or not he personally advanced our understanding of the rational option. His contribution to our comprehension of the culturally embedded, practice-linked option was achievement enough.

In a subsequent work, however, he moved away from this position. From the viewpoint of the history of thought or, rather, the history of the intellectual climate, what is really interesting is that he underwent a development exceedingly similar in its internal logic to that experienced by Wittgenstein. The movement was not nearly so violent in his case: his initial position, certainly, was in the first place not remotely as extreme as that of Wittgenstein in the *Tractatus*: context-bound speech was not ignored (anything but), it was not denied, it was just that abstract thought was *also* allowed to exist. In his later work, *Coral Gardens and their Magic* (1935), he changed his mind. At first, the change is moderate:

The pragmatic relevance of words is greatest when these words are uttered actually within the situation to which they belong . . . It is in such situations that words acquire their meaning . . . [I]t is the function, the active and effective

151

influence of a word within a given context which constitutes its meaning . . .
(Malinowski 1935, II: 52)

These statements, though forceful, might still just about be squared
with the earlier position. Even if words *acquire* their meaning in this way,
it might perhaps be modified later. Use and context are not yet
sovereign. Use ('function') in, as it were, its home context is what
constitutes meaning. It follows from this that use is sovereign and
cannot be corrected from the outside, but this implication is not highlighted, if indeed it is noticed, and it is not, so to speak, enforced.
Malinowski is quite aware of the type of situation in which this sovereignty might be impugned and he leaves the matter open. He does not
assert the sovereignty of use against the critic, he treats the linguo-
conservative and the critic as equal, and he personally identifies with the
latter: '[T]ake certain utterances in the Holy Mass . . . .here words
produce an actual change in a universe which, though mystical and
imaginary to us agnostics, is none the less real to the believer' (*ibid.*: 55).

What is crucially important here is that Malinowski, though legitimating the believer through a theory of meaning, does not disqualify,
intellectually disfranchise, his opponent, the agnostic. He indulges in no
discussion as to whether there is a rational way of deciding between the
two viewpoints. Holy Mass is, unquestionably, a part of a 'form of life',
but the attempts by agnostics or others to transcend the alleged
authority of forms of life is not derided, as in due course it was by
Wittgenstein.

But Malinowski goes much further in a later passage:

it seems to me that, even in the most abstract and theoretical aspects of human
thought and verbal usage, the real understanding of words is always ultimately
derived from active experience of those aspects of reality to which the words
belong . . . In short, there is no science whose conceptual, hence verbal, outfit is
not ultimately derived from the practical handling of matter. I am laying
considerable stress on this because, in one of my previous writings, I opposed
civilised and scientific to primitive speech, and argued as if the theoretical uses
of words in modern philosophic and scientific writing were completely detached
from their pragmatic sources. This was an error, and a serious error at that.
Between the savage use of words and the most abstract and theoretical one there
is only a difference of degree. (*ibid.*: 58)

The 'previous writing' to which he refers is identified in a footnote as the
Appendix to *The Meaning of Meaning*.

The passage, alas, is not unambiguous. What is meant by detaching
science *completely* from its pragmatic sources? No doubt, abstract
thought has its *origins* in pragmatic thought: *Am Anfang war die Tat*,
Goethe's Faust was right on that point. What is at issue is not the origins

of abstract thought (we can happily allow it humble, savage, pragmatic ancestry, which no doubt it has), but its eventual liberation from the criteria, the standards of primitive thinking, and the attainment of other, culture-transcending criteria. Is context-free, culturally transcendent thought possible or is it not? *That* is the big question. Does that 'difference in degree' allow this difference or does it not? He does not tell us. It is possible that he did not fully appreciate the weight of the question. He certainly did not face it squarely.

The big, really important philosophical divide is between those who insist on the pragmatic nature of language, not in answer to questions about *origins* – which hardly matter – but in answer to questions concerning the *validity* of reasoning and standards. The example he chooses, the Holy Mass, is excellent. If cultural context and use *is* meaning, then not only is transubstantiation 'real to the believer', but it is simply *real*; there is no other reality, other than that which a culture endows to utterances which have a place in its practices – for to affirm such a further reality is to invoke transcultural criteria of reality. For instance, radical empiricists believe that experimental testing constitutes a court above individual cultures, and can tell them which of their beliefs are legitimate and which of them are mere phantasies, however much they may be embedded in daily life . . . But if such culturally transcendent criteria are denied, there is no further room for any 'agnostic': he becomes simply a person committing the philosophic error of supposing that there are criteria of legitimate meaning which transcend all culture. Malinowski did not go this far, he allowed the agnostic his position and indeed declared it to be his own. But the denial of such a possibility is of course the step which Wittgenstein did take. It accounts for much of his popularity. It makes it oh so easy for anyone to believe whatever he wishes: 'my cultural meanings right or wrong'; the cleverest philosophy has shown us, they can say, that culture is God and hermeneutics is its prophet.

It is not fully clear how far Malinowski went along such a path. The evidence is contradictory. On the one hand, he does say that even abstract thought cannot sever its links with practical involvement. One passage makes this sound quite innocuous, a mere insistence on testing: 'The chemist or the physicist understands the meaning of his most abstract concepts ultimately on the basis of his acquintance with chemical and physical processes in the laboratory' (*ibid.*: 358). This sentence could come from some positivist manifesto. It could be read as affirming, in the spirit of Ernst Mach, some kind of operationalism: the linkage of concepts to the operations involved in their testing. What is at issue is whether cultural practice validates concepts and whether all cultural systems are equally valid, or whether, on the contrary, it *is* possible to judge rationally between them. On this point the evidence concerning Malinowski is less than conclusive. I prefer the earlier Malinowski, who firmly upheld the distinction between the two types of thought which he subsequently disavowed.

It is, however, very interesting that obviously he went through a development very analogous to Wittgenstein's, even if this change was less extreme and attracted incomparably less attention. Perhaps this was the intellectual undercurrent of the time, and there may be other examples (e.g. Heidegger's development on the basis of the teaching of Husserl).

31   The (un)originality of Malinowski and Wittgenstein

The similarities between Malinowski's and Wittgenstein's view of language are striking and important and the question naturally arises whether Wittgenstein borrowed, consciously or otherwise, from Malinowski. If he did, he certainly did not acknowledge it. Malinowski was unquestionably the first to publish the action-involved, culture-embedded view of language, and he did so at the very time when Wittgenstein was still committed to the 'mirror' or 'brass-rubbing' theory of language, and the total irrelevance of culture to the real function of thought and language. Moreover, in 1923 Malinowski published his ideas as an Appendix to *The Meaning of Meaning*, co-authored by C. K. Ogden, who was at the same time Wittgenstein's translator.

An interesting and highly authoritative contribution to this question appears in the form of a letter from Sir Raymond Firth to the *Times Literary Supplement*, dated 17 March 1995. Firth was Malinowski's pupil, colleague, and successor, as well as editor of the posthumous Festschrift to Malinowski (*Man and Culture*) in which his erstwhile pupils collectively expressed their intellectual and other indebtedness to him. Firth was close to Malinowski intellectually, personally and professionally, and his views therefore deserve the utmost respect. Firth tells us that Wittgenstein did receive a copy of *The Meaning of Meaning* (containing the relevant Appendix by Malinowski) 'soon after it appeared, and characteristically seemed very dismissive of it. He may not even have glanced at Malinowski's essay . . . any resemblance in their views may be accidental' (Firth 1995).

Perhaps we shall never find out whether or not Wittgenstein was aware of Malinowski's views. In my opinion it does not matter, because *neither* of them initiated the idea in question. The romantic view of language, linking it to action and culture, so utterly pervaded the intellectual climate in which both men grew up that both of them, inevitably, 'took it from stock' when it suited them. Whether they also noticed each other hardly matters: they could, and no doubt did, equally well obtain the idea from countless other fellow citizens of their world.

The idea itself was in no way original, though its employment may have been. Malinowski used the idea to forge a theory of primitive language and a method in social anthropology. One way of summing up his advance on Frazer would be this: he noticed that Frazer credited the savage with a mind constructed on the principles of David Hume, and he pointed out that this could not be true because the savage was a social agent, not a solitary theorist. So Malinowski applied the idea in an area where it works. Wittgenstein used it to handle problems of philosophy – the question of the validity of our convictions – where it most definitely does not work.

Firth mentions the possibility that Wittgenstein could have obtained the idea from Piero Sraffa, whose influence he did acknowledge. The evidence is reported among others by Ray Monk in his biography of Wittgenstein. Sraffa, criticising Wittgenstein's then view that the structure of language and thought mirrored each other, made an obscene Neapolitan gesture, which certainly conveys (an offensive) 'meaning', and challenged Wittgenstein to describe the structure of that significant gesture (Monk 1990: 260–1).

The story is both amusing and illuminating. It does convey, in a nutshell, the difference between the two theories of meaning, and the kind of evidence that can be invoked in support of the cultural rather than referential theory. But it is exceedingly unlikely that the entire later philosophy of Wittgenstein was born of a single gesture of Sraffa's. More important, the explanation is redundant, given the pervasiveness of the romantic theory of language: Wittgenstein had no need to wait for Sraffa's gesture . . . The idea that Wittgenstein, in *Philosophical Investigations,* 'propounded a wholly novel philosophy of language' (Hacker 1995: 9) is absurd. That allegedly novel philosophy was a commonplace in the climate in which both Malinowski and Wittgenstein grew up.

Part IV

Influences

32   The impact and diffusion of
Wittgenstein's ideas

Wittgenstein's ideas (i.e. those connected with his 'later' philosophy) spread in a number of waves or currents, which it is useful to distinguish. These need to be given names. Three of them in particular are of interest. The names I shall give them are code terms and are to be used without prejudice: the ideas of these trends overlap, and the stress suggested by the name of any one of them may refer to something which is not necessarily absent in the other trends. The names to be used are:

(1) Philistinical exorcism;
(2) Relativistic idealism;
(3) Expiatory hermeneutics.

The first two are explored in this section and the next; for the third, see section 34 below.

Wittgenstein used the 'cultural practical involvement' theory of language to escape from the dreary solitude of the world of the *Tractatus* – there being nothing else. All worlds were solitary and similar, for there could be no other kind. As this depressing vision was a consequence of a theory of language, if that theory came to be seen to be deeply misguided, and the only alternative theory gave us a, relatively speaking, much cosier world of the closed speech community with its 'form of life' – well then, this escape was warmly welcome. The *déraciné* and despised Viennese Jew escaped on the shoulders of the Transcendental Ego and his escape ladder (language): or, alternatively, you can say that the Transcendental Ego, equipped with ladder but with nowhere to go, was shown by the Viennese Jew that there were all these *gemütlich* communities to which one could escape, if only one could get to them. Of the two prisoners, one had a ladder and the other knew of the safe houses: either on his own was helpless; together they could, and did, make their escape.

This, in essence, is Wittgenstein's story. He was both Transcendental Ego and Viennese Jew. From solitary confinement to gregarious confinement: an improvement of a kind, perhaps. From a philosophy which denies the existence of culture to one which affirms that there is nothing else. As it happens, Wittgenstein never specified just *which* cosy closed community he wished to join, now that the sentence of solitary confinement in the Tractatus Tower had been squashed by the demonstration that the tower in question was founded on a misguided theory of language. He never said that he now chose to become a Tyrolean or a Hanak or a Góral . . . Characteristically, he never even offered concrete examples of forms of life (invented tribes, at most), let alone choosing one for his own habitation. The fact that his own personal experience of an Austrian village in the capacity of local schoolmaster was far from happy, may be significant. So in effect he preached a kind of omnibus populism, in the abstract, which taught that language and thought could only be understood as part and parcel of the ongoing concrete life of such a community, and that (old) philosophy was a pathological deviation from such earth-bound custom, without however singling out any one of these ultimate and sovereign forms of life for his attention, loyalty or habitation.

All this was due to be changed by the first set of 'companions of the prophet'. Initially, there was a small, carefully vetted, conventicle of devotees in Cambridge, in the years preceding the Second World War. These were so few in number and so secretive that they were barely noticed in the outside world, even if global events had not claimed most of the available attention. But the movement grew in size and did attract much attention after the war, when its centre of gravity shifted to Oxford, and when it came to be known under various names, such as Linguistic or Oxford Philosophy.

The central doctrine was still the same: the correct method in philosophy was to give an accurate and patient account of the actual use of language, because this will (milder and more cautious, insurance-conscious version: it *may*) eliminate the problem by showing it to be spurious, arising from a misunderstanding of language rather than some genuine difficulty. Characteristically, the very word 'problem' gave way to the term 'puzzle'. The underlying argument justifying this total change of strategy was Wittgenstein's switch from language as brass-rubbing in logical notation to language as a heterogeneous set of concrete and social functions. The hypothesis – and it was not treated as a hypothesis, but as a manifest illumination and as a definition both of philosophy and of that new enlightenment which distinguished the adherents of the school from unfortunates not sharing this vision – was that intractable problems about the human condition, society, knowledge and so on, were only intractable because they were not problems at all. They were pseudo-problems, to which no answers were possible, and which had to be *dissolved*, never *solved*, by careful attention to the actual, *ordinary* use of language. At the end of philosophical inquiry there would never be a theory, but only the restoration of common sense. As Wittgenstein himself had put it, if there were theories in philosophy everyone would agree with them; or: philosophy leaves everything as it is; or: in philosophy one can only describe, not explain. With the passage of time, now that the movement is more or less dead, it is difficult to recreate the atmosphere of total confidence and dogmatism which pervaded the participants. This, they *knew*, was the end of philosophy: a new era, or a new subject, was beginning. Bliss was it in that dawn to be alive, and they thoroughly enjoyed their bliss.

There is an interesting difference between Wittgenstein's own and his followers' use of the same idea. Wittgenstein preached relativistic populism *in the abstract*, in general, without favouring any particular single cultural cocoon. By contrast, his followers *did*. In practice, the deployment of the technique aimed not merely at obviating alleged pseudo-problems (engendered, on Wittgenstein's account, by the chimaera of a unique universally valid way of referring to the world, which in turn could only engender one kind of – rather tedious – world), but also at positively vindicating their own 'common sense'. This was one of the most curious self-vindications ever attempted in the history of thought. Major premise: all cultural cocoons, all forms of life, are valid and self-sufficient, and Wittgenstein has shown this to be the case. Minor premise, never spelt out or discussed, but operationally taken for granted: only our cocoon is of any interest, the others, for practical purposes, do not exist.

In this curious way, Wittgenstein's populist escape from the iron cage, conceived as the result of a painful encounter with the icy cold disenchantment of the consistent Cartesian world, with that re-valuation of all values imposed by the severe critical examination of what he could possibly know, was consumed, in the Oxford of around 1950 or so, as the unbelievably complacent doctrine that the world is as common sense proclaims it to be. The most acute point of conflict between science and common sense is of course the problem of determinism: our normal conceptualisation of our conduct allows us to possess free will and the capacity of choice, whereas both the procedures and the findings of science suggest that (a) the 'inner' conceptualisation or characterisation of conduct is unreliable, incomplete and incoherent, and (b) that there are good grounds for suspecting that causal laws operate in the area of human activity, even when they are not known. This is an extremely serious problem and it was characteristic of the leaders of the movement that they derided it as a pseudo-problem.

The position of the movement can be stated in (at least) two alternative ways:

(1) The meanings of the words we employ is determined by their *use*. Those abstract and intractable problems known as 'philosophy' arise because we have made a mistake about the real use/meaning of a given term or group of terms, and handle them as if they belonged to quite a different category of uses. If we examine them carefully and correct the mistake we have made, we shall (weaker, cautious variant: we may) find that the problem does not arise at all: there is no case to answer.

(2) Because, as stated in the first formulation, these problems arise from a misunderstanding of the nature of language, and can be corrected by a proper observation of how the relevant terms are actually used, it follows that all the ideological conflicts and transformations which make up the intellectual history of mankind were really sound and fury, signifying nothing. The switch from customary religious to revealed doctrine, from magic-oriented religion to morality-stressing faith, from the authority of sacred personnel to the authority of scripture, from the authority of any revelation to that of reason and evidence, from the innovation of tradition to the calculation of consequences . . . all this was quite unnecessary. If only the participants had anticipated Wittgenstein, they could have saved themselves a lot of bother, not to mention bloodshed. Philosophy leaves everything as it is. Nothing can or need be changed by thought.

Positions (1) and (2) are formally equivalent. The difference between them is only that something which is entailed by (1) is actually spelt out in (2), thereby rendering the absurdity and offensiveness of the entire position manifest. (1) was how the position was generally (and *ad nauseam*) expounded, though usually at much greater length and with greater portentousness. (2) was the real or relevant meaning, but it was ignored by most of the participants of the movement because the historic context of modern thought, the enormous transformation wrought by the coming of modernity and the problems involved in the confrontation of rival 'forms of life', was something which had no reality for them. In their own abbreviated formulation, the position can be made to sound modest, sober, and undeserving of condemnation. It provokes justified irritation because, of course, in its unstated but unambiguously implied corollary, it simply condemns and ignores everything that is important in the history of human intellectual life.

Conflicts about basic moral or conceptual alternatives are, by that position, confined to the irrational, unarguable realm of conceptual custom. Some kind of irrationalist conventionalism or traditionalism is the only possible logical consequence. The great change in human history, in the course of which morality and the nature of the world were both taken away from tradition and revelation, and handed over to egalitarian reasoning, is either denied or condemned, or both. Of course, users of the system were not obliged to be consistent and could reincorporate a bit of science, or rational discussion of morality, into that very custom which is to be 'left as it was' by philosophy. Wittgenstein himself did not soften his position in this underhand way; he was clear that these matters were beyond reason.

33 The first wave of Wittgenstein's influence

The first and most important and obvious thing about the Wittgenstein-ian movement in the fifteen years after the war was that it was revelational, charismatic, and absolutist. This is something people reading about it, or reading its product in cold blood, with hindsight, may fail to appreciate or may fail to appreciate adequately. The *atmosphere* may no longer be discernible between the lines, after such a passage of time. It may have, as it were, evaporated. But it was not so at the time. In the discussions of the time, it was simply *known* by the participants that all this was true, that although perhaps they might commit errors of detail in implementing the key ideas of the new revelation, those ideas themselves were beyond the reach of any possible doubt. And the new movement was not seen as simply *a* movement amongst others, having to stake its claims, and to defend them and wait for the verdict. It simply was not like that all. The movement, as it saw itself, simply replaced and displaced all past philosophy. Philosophy had come to an end, or was just about to do so when this movement had done its job, and a new era had begun. The root of all past philosophy had been laid bare by Wittgenstein and all that remained to be done was to implement and diffuse his insights.

Wittgenstein himself had always held his views in this brazen, dogmatic spirit: even if his views changed, the fact that they were incontrovertible and beyond challenge evidently did not. It had always been his view that those who failed to agree with him should not be argued with, but be *cured*, by the application of the appropriate therapeutic method which he had devised. Language could only work *one* way, and (misguided) philosophy arose because people did not see this, and his job, and that of his followers, was to set them right by careful description of how language did work. By this kind of careful attention to the real role of various expressions, the temptation to erect general philosophical theories would be exorcised. Common sense would then be a kind of residual legatee. Wittgenstein said all this in so many words: in philosophy there are no theories, or if there were, everyone would agree with them. In effect, there is only the re-endorsement of common sense, the affirmations built into the ongoing life of a culture. We have seen how he reached this position, given his premises. But why should this position have appealed to his new and rapidly multiplying followers?

The peculiar position of Britain in general, and of the educational system in particular, and of Oxford and philosophy within it, must be considered before this question can be answered. Now the Kakania against the background of which Wittgenstein emerged may have been racked with anguish and doubt. This was not, to put it mildly, the atmosphere of post-war Oxford, and least of all that of its enormous, as these things go, philosophical profession.

Perhaps a word should be said about this size, because it is rather relevant. In Cambridge, philosophy is taught more or less on its own, and it is consequently a relatively small and specialised school. In Oxford philosophy is not taught on its own, but as part of certain degrees which are meant to constitute a generic, unspecialised (and hence all the more prestigious) preparation for life, public service, or business. The other constituents of these general degrees were, in the past, classical philology and history, and, more recently, economics and politics. This meant that the number of philosophy teachers was very large, and the catchment area for their students very large indeed. Within the courses they were studying, philosophy might well be the most exciting thing going or, at any rate, something one could *argue* about. In the period in question, politics was quite exceptionally dull, and economics was becoming increasingly technical. Classical philology doesn't really offer too much scope for discussion and not everyone is interested in classical history. So, in this situation, the large mass of Oxford students who did not come to the university with a view to specific professional training, but rather wanted to be, so to speak, 'finished', were led towards philosophy, and philosophy acquired a position in intellectual life which was not otherwise called for by the logic of the situation. One thing was sure, few were led to philosophy by anguish. It was a kind of inverse Kakania.

The movement had actually begun in a closed, restricted, and virtually secret coterie around Wittgenstein in Cambridge in the late 1930s. Entry to Wittgenstein's seminar was restricted at the master's whim, and the ideas circulated in privately copied typescripts which Wittgenstein himself refused to have published. This esotericism greatly enhanced the appeal of the ideas, which were treated as a major revelation by the adepts. Wittgenstein had a great flair for publicity whilst claiming and appearing to flee and avoid it. It is this feature perhaps which once led Elie Kedourie to comment on the similarity between Wittgenstein and T. E. Lawrence.

By around 1950 the movement had spread from being a Cambridge-based clique to becoming the dominant force in the teaching of philosophy, above all in Oxford, and was indeed at times referred to as 'Oxford philosophy'. In the British academic world, Oxford is to the teaching of philosophy what Detroit once was to the motorcar industry. As noted, a high proportion of those going to the university with no very specific academic interest did a fair amount of philosophy and, within this broad category, the ablest ones were encouraged to specialise in it. On top of that, Oxford was successful during the post-war period in organising postgraduate training, which very successfully attracted philosophy graduates from other universities, contemplating or decided upon a professional commitment to the subject and eager to slot themselves into what at the time seemed to be the permanent new revelation in the field, teaching a definitive and rather attractive (user-friendly) technique. The path to philosophical illumination was to be sought by attention to ordinary speech and the use of its idioms in the context of real life: all past philosophy was mistaken, and the mistake had been the supposition that valid reasoning has some basis other than linguistic custom (which equals 'culture', though this word was not used).

This, above all, was how the Wittgensteinian ideas were presented and marketed at the time. A certain programme was implicit in Wittgenstein's ideas and was indeed explicitly recommended by him as the only possible way of proceeding in these matters. Cultures/languages being self-validating, they could neither have nor did they in any way require vindication other than their own existence. This was the central, culture-populist idea. But the question still arises: why is it that men think that their practices do need justification, why do they seek such justifications, why is there an entire subject devoted largely to the pursuit, discussion and evaluation of such justifications? How could this entirely pointless activity emerge, and even make successful claims on the resources of universities, have degrees conferred in the name of the mastery of its secrets, and so forth? How could this be?

Wittgenstein did have an answer to this question and this answer probably constituted the most preposterous part of his entire philosophy, but it was taken with utmost seriousness for all that. The answer ran as follows: men seek to validate their practices, to 'prove' that the principles underlying some aspect of our use of language must be what they are, because they are prey to a deeply misguided theory of language. They had assumed that language consists of one homogeneous activity, that all use of language is justified in a single way by some kind of standard relationship to reality. The specification of that relationship then constitutes a vindication of the use of language. (Thus empiricists, for instance, supposed that all language, if legitimate at all, consists of references to isolable bits of experience. For Platonists, the relation was a reflection of transcendent entities.) Demolish that illusion, show that language consists of a wide variety of diverse activities, each self-justifying, and the temptation to seek for general justifications, or indeed for any justification, will thereby be exorcised. Problems will not be answered, but be shown not to arise in the first place. Wittgenstein recommended such exorcism as the only valid or possible method in philosophy. It would make men attend to the actual use of expressions, see their logic and point, and thereby be freed from the noxious, pointless pursuit of validations. As already noted, this feature always stayed with him: he refused to treat critics as equals. They were not to be argued with, they were to be cured of their delusion. This recipe for handling dissent is found both in the *Tractatus* and in the *Philosophical Investigations*.

The implementation of this programme required philosophical thinkers, when faced with a problem, under no circumstances to take the problem at face value by seeking and arguing for a solution or an answer. To do anything of the kind was to show oneself philosophically utterly misguided, deeply incompetent and unenlightened and, in fact, to be guilty of that pervasive and pernicious error which had engendered all past and misguided philosophy, now due to come to an end thanks to Wittgenstein's insights. The correct strategy and procedure was quite other: it was to attend, very carefully, to the actual pattern of use of the expressions related to the alleged problem and, by perceiving their real functioning – as opposed to expecting them to conform to a general supposed pattern of language-use – to be liberated from the temptation even to ask the question. Questions must be eliminated, not answered. Problems must be dissolved in this manner and they can never have 'solutions' or answers. There is no question to answer, only an unanswerable disquiet to be cured.

The theory was that no philosophical problem is ever genuine; it is always a pseudo-problem, arising from a misunderstanding of language, and it is due for dissolution in the light of the proper understanding of the use of the expressions in question. There was to be no theorising whatsoever in philosophy, only the description of uses of expression and their role and context in life. For this reason, the philosophy in question was also often known at the time as 'Linguistic Philosophy'. It was not a philosophy of or about language: it was a theory of the non-existence of philosophy, the problems of which were merely mirages of questions, engendered by a misunderstanding of the real nature of language, and themselves being a case of the faulty functioning of language. It was a linguistic theory against philosophy, more than a philosophical theory of language.

The argument is both strange and totally invalid. Important philosophical questions concerning the validity of various procedures – our rules of scientific inference, of moral evaluation, of what you will – are genuinely problematic, and no amount of attention to actual usage will either solve or dissolve them.

Wittgensteinianism had two aspects, a positive and a negative one. The positive one consisted of the doctrine that cultures were logically terminal and self-justifying, and no other kind of justification was either possible or necessary. The negative aspect of the doctrine was the claim that if requests for validation nevertheless arose, they are to be handled by careful attention to the actual deployment of language in the relevant sphere and this would result in a kind of voluntary abandonment of the question, and a contented return to the authority of actual usage, i.e. the acceptance of the rules actually built into our language/culture. In fact, this programme was of course never successfully carried out, though the enthusiastic adherents of the movement for a time persuaded themselves that if only they persisted, any moment now, it would work. As with other true believers, the day when prophecy failed was indefinitely postponed.

The positive aspect of the doctrine raises very deep problems; the negative aspect, the prediction of dissolution by careful description of actual linguistic practice, is simply false.

Why were those who embraced this doctrine so astonishingly complacent? There were both good reasons and bad. The Habsburg Empire had fought and lost a war. The British Empire had fought a war against a very formidable enemy, a war which had at one time looked utterly hopeless, and it had won. It had maintained liberty at a time when most of the continent of Europe had cravenly surrendered, and its stand made the eventual defeat of tyranny possible. But far more than this: having won, it voluntarily dismantled imperial dominion, without being forced to do so, as less enlightened European countries were, by humiliating defeats in colonial wars. Internally, a welfare state was being set up which promised to diminish the poverty and inequality which had been the shame of an advanced industrial country. Unemployment was confidently expected to yield to the techniques of Keynesianism. Liberty, social justice, greater equality, a voluntary and at least relatively peaceful replacement of empire by a consensual Commonwealth, were all being achieved. There was a remarkable degree of consensus both concerning these values and even about the manner of their implementation. Though some of these expectations were in the end not fulfilled completely, nevertheless this spirit, which inspired them, was admirable. There was as yet no suspicion of the persistent failure of the economy to keep up with other countries; there was no notion that Keynes might lead to stagflation, which was to undermine confidence later on. If this was a period of complacency, it was one which was understandable and, in the light of the situation as it was then, it was far from unjustified.

Whether complacency was quite as justified within philosophy, or whether it was forced to endow complacency with such a bizarre philosophical underwriting, is another matter. Perhaps it would have been better to use that peaceful time to re-think the newly emerging world, rather than inhibit serious thought by declaring all deep questioning to be pathological, and to turn dreadful intellectual philistinism into a norm of health.

The position of the professional philosophers was curious. What were they to teach? It is a praiseworthy element of the local tradition that it required that some definite position be taught, that the teacher should not content himself with simply teaching the history of the subject. But what?

Traditional metaphysics was *passé*, and really went against the naturalistic mood of the time. There had indeed been a Hegelian vogue in Oxford, but by then it was virtually dead. One could, of course, turn towards some version of radical empiricism, and see philosophy as primarily the theory of science. This was the path of Russell and this had been the path of the Vienna Circle. But there was a snag. The scholars recruited into philosophy at the time were almost exclusively drawn from the humanities, in a peculiar educational system which imposed a parting of the ways between science and letters very early, about the age of fourteen or fifteen. The consequence was that almost all of them knew virtually no science or mathematics. At the same time, they were very much at home with the customs of words, for various reasons. For one thing, classical philology was an important part of the training of many of them. For another, the custom is that at High Table in an Oxford college, one does not discuss 'shop' or women. On the other hand, a discussion of the nuances of meaning is utterly acceptable. They knew no science and could not cope with mathematical logic, and here there was a philosopher who seemed at home in both but who told them that the key to all mysteries, or pseudo-mysteries, was familiarity with the actual employment of words! They could hardly believe their luck, they had had no idea they were sitting on a philosophical goldmine.

Moreover, they had been recruited into philosophy more by the vagaries of the educational machine than by inner perturbation. They were strongly inclined to believe that the world must be as it seemed to them (any alternative suggestion was really rather offensive), and they were averse to the idea that modern advances of knowledge impose a dramatic and perhaps painful need for revision on us. Their work situation reinforced this complacency: to urge religious belief, or doubt, on their pupils would have, by then, been a solecism. Professionalism and personal gossip were deemed bad taste: but words and their use, that was in order. So the skill was there, and a philosophy which taught that this was also *the* correct method in handling deep questions was most welcome.

Other aspects of their work and life situation made this clientele susceptible to the new philosophy. Colleges have chapels and are, nominally, religious institutions, but in practice it would unquestionably be improper for a philosophy teacher to use his teaching position either to favour, or indeed to criticise, religion. All religions, and none, were tolerated, and a position which affirms that philosophy is inherently neutral *vis-à-vis* religion, though absurd in the light of the real history of European thought, simply confirmed intimations deeply rooted in the actual work situation of the don. He had not much taste for metaphysics, and was now told that this was good; he had no access to science, and was told that this need not worry him. He was disinclined to examine the existential premises of his words, and this inhibition too, he was now told, was inscribed into the very nature of his subject. His *Lebenswelt* was restored *and* endowed with authority, his common sense was credited with being the best and only possible (hence guaranteed best) guide to the world. All this had come from a man who had made contributions to the arcane world of mathematical logic, and who had experimented with the idea of reforming philosophy in the image of logic. If he said it was no good, he ought to know. He had now seen the error of his youthful ways. He said that the only way forward was to observe the customs of words. Well it so happens that we are terribly good at that and like doing it, better than anything else. In part it was less than clear that there was anything else they *could* do. The convergence between the Wittgensteinian message and local taste was amazing. His motives and background may have been wholly different, but no matter. The man ever haunted by deep and obscure anxieties provided a philosophy for those who had none, to the point where it was somewhat comic that they should engage in philosophy at all. The message and the audience were made for each other, and the enthusiasm of the reception of the message at the time knew no bounds.

The philosophy of science towards which they might have turned in fact devalued the world of common sense. Either it was a realistic version, in which case it said that tables were not really tables but masses of whirling particles, which merely looked like tables because of the crudity of our sense organs. Alternatively, it said that tables were not really tables, but merely logical conventions for referring to classes of actual and possible sensations. Either way, the ordinary world was devalued and undermined, and the same went for all other aspects of it. But now at last here there was a dreadfully clever philosophy, excogitated by a logical whizzkid who knew all the tricks on the other side, which established generically that all these re-valuations and de-valuations were no good, that if one really knew what was happening in these arguments, one would know that common sense always, always wins! If you really understand the nature of meaning, you know that the ordinary world is ever-valid. Tables were tables, and that goes for everything. Everything is what it is and not another thing. The news was almost too good to be true. It was hard to say whether one should be more pleased by the *conclusion*, the vindication of an unmysterious world, or by the *method* of its vindication, the examination of the nuances of usages, which was a well-established hobby among the recipients of this revelation, and one in which they felt themselves to be champions. So it was taken as definitely true, the latest and also final revelation. It fitted in, only too well, with local preconceptions and preferences.

There is a problem in Wittgenstein's endorsement of one's own common sense and its vision of the world. The snag is very simple. The Wittgensteinian argument, which unreservedly endorses one's own world, is alas entirely symmetrical, and applicable *generally*: it does just as much for every and any other cultural world. So, if my own world contains as part of itself – as most of the ideologies of the literate world civilisations do – a claim for its own unique validity, absolutising its own gods and anathematising those of others, then an immediate contradiction arises. Every 'form of life' is ultimate, logically terminal, self-validating: but what if it damns *other* forms of life? Either the damnation is valid, and then other forms are not valid after all; or it is not valid, and the supposedly self-justifying vision contains at least one major error . . . How did the enthusiastic followers cope with this?

There were two ways, the majority way and the minority way. Take the minority first. This position was first, and very forcefully, formulated by Peter Winch (in *The Idea of a Social Science*). It consists of *accepting* this symmetrical, universally relativist corollary: yes, indeed, all social visions are equal, all of them are valid by their own lights, and there can be no other. The absolutism found *within* some visions is disavowed: it is claimed either that it is not really there (against all evidence), or that it had no business to be there, constituted a kind of mistake, and should be excised. The trouble with this kind of benign universally symmetrical relativism is that it might conceivably make sense in a world which did indeed consist of culturally self-contained islands. Our world, on the other hand, consists of an enormous number of unstable and, above all, overlapping cultural zones, and the conflicts or options within them cannot possibly be resolved by inviting those who face such options to consult, each of them, only the oracles of their own culture – because their cultures are endowed with multiple competing oracles. In fact, they do not in any sense *have* a 'single' culture.

However, this way out was chosen only by a minority. It is marked at least by a praiseworthy recognition of the reality of the problem, and also, alas, by a wholly unrealistic, literally meaningless recipe for solving it. 'Respect your culture' or 'your culture, right or wrong' have no meaning, because there is simply *no* way of implementing it as a recipe, in a situation in which there are no given cultural boundaries, but where these are themselves in dispute.

What was far more characteristic of the period, however, was the majority reaction, which consisted very simply of ignoring the problem. The adherents of this philosophy were delighted to have their own life-world, their own 'common sense', endorsed by what they held to be deep philosophical reasoning: by one simple argument, all attempts at devaluing that lived world, whether by scepticism, metaphysics, or by according higher status to the world revealed by science – all this was dismissed. Their own dignity and authority as fully paid-up members of the commonsensical, not to say philistinical, world was thereby vindicated and underwritten. In their complacency, they had always been rather inclined to think that the world must be as they saw it, and now the latest and most refined philosophy confirmed that this was indeed so. Those who had challenged any of this were unmasked as conceptually pathological and destined, not for counter-argument, but for the insult of a *cure*.

The fact that the same argument would equally apply to the Bushman, or medieval, or Buddhist, or any other, world view, is something which simply was not considered. The question was never at the centre of discussion and barely at its periphery. One or two thinkers touched on the problem of why *our* common sense should be so privileged: J.L. Austin briefly flirted with a natural selection argument, without really following it up or really taking it seriously; Peter Strawson suggested that the basic categorical apparatus of our thought changed so very slowly – like a slowly moving glacier which can be mapped as a fixed object without invalidating the map, as you might say – that cultural diversity need not really trouble us much. It is most doubtful whether this is remotely true: the common-sense vision of the human body, of nature, of matter, may well have changed radically in recent centuries. In any case, the philosophers of this persuasion did not seriously pursue the question. Basically, they were happy to find a waterproof vindication of their own common sense and they simply did not think about other systems of common sense.

After about 1960, the entire movement gradually dissolved. The habit of communicating with one's own culture as the only possible source and repository of conceptual propriety, of analysing its actual linguistic customary law, its habit-based concepts, with a view to obviating any temptation to stand outside language and seek other authorities – all that was gradually abandoned. Some claim this faith was never actually held. Others, more honest, are a bit sheepish about it. As it was meant to be a *practice* rather than a theory, leaving no formal record, it has a kind of in-built self-destruct mechanism. It can, it seems, disavow its own existence. It was part of its doctrine that it had no doctrine, that it was *only* to be practised; so when the practice failed, it could be claimed that there had never been any doctrine (though this is patently dishonest).

But in as far as this device is employed, it also means that nothing is learnt through or from its failure. The movement was not replaced by another one reacting to its own weaknesses but, rather, by a kind of characterless eclecticism. A few continued to practise what we have called the minority view, i.e. conscious general relativism based on the terminal, ultimate status of culture. Some reverted to the earlier logical technicism, without evidently heeding the arguments against it which had been very nearly the only single valid element in the late-Wittgensteinian revelation, and without any coherent rationale for so doing. And some took up a newly fashionable applied moral philosophy, somewhat hanging in thin air, which, it is claimed, has its roots in the acuteness of political crises and of their moral aspect during the period of the Vietnam war and subsequently.

34 The belated convergence of philosophy and anthropology

By about the 1980s there was a curious and partial convergence of the two traditions that have concerned this book. The philosophical line which sprang from Wittgenstein and his absolutisation of culture under the name 'form of life' flowed together with the tradition springing from that other and more overtly loyal subject of Franz Josef. Wittgenstein, you might say, had in his own life re-lived human history, *in reverse*. He had first worked out the only possible epistemology and ontology of the solitary individual living within a cultureless *Gesellschaft*, and had then switched to a closed community in which people only speak and think as a team. He reinvented the theory of *Gemeinschaft* in a linguistic idiom. His life went contrary to the main current of humanity . . . Malinowski, on other hand, always recognised the co-existence of the two styles of thought, and moved only mildly in the same direction as Wittgenstein, from treating the two styles as equal, to stressing the communalistic one as more fundamental (though not, it would seem, as exclusively sovereign).

At the time when the two traditions were both being formed in England, they interacted very little, despite the interesting overlap in personnel, notably in C. K. Ogden. But, in subsequent generations, the two currents were due to meet. By then, of course, neither tradition was pure. Late Wittgensteinianism had by now become *vieux jeu* in philosophy. Everyone knew the opening moves and counter-moves and it was not easy to claim superior insight and standing in virtue of this familiarity: it was too well diffused. So the style migrated to neighbouring fields such as literary studies, anthropology, and the humanities generally. In anthropology, Malinowski was likewise *vieux jeu*, except of course in Poland where he was rediscovered, partly as an extremely attractive and useful means of needling the Communist authorities of the time.

The confluence of the two streams occurred, amongst other places, in the wider world of Anglophone anthropology, a discipline which, though by and large conforming to Malinowskian norms and principles, also included the vast American anthropological profession, which had never been as fully dominated by Malinowski as the British Commonwealth. A certain subjectivism, an exaggerated preoccupation with 'meaning' and hermeneutics, characterises this movement; or, perhaps one should call it a style or mood. In part, it reached anthropology from literary studies, and more generally that part of the 'humanities' which had never even aspired to constitute a 'social science' (let alone, like Radcliffe-Brown, to emulate natural science). It had various names: first, in its milder form, it was called 'interpretive anthropology', whilst the later, more virulent version liked to be known as 'postmodernism'.

The central idea seems to have been a shift away from either 'structure' or 'function', to *meaning*. The move was justified both by methodological and by political considerations, and the two were, it appears, intimately connected. One of the men who influenced the movement profoundly, though he dissociated himself from its more extreme versions (and vice versa), was Clifford Geertz. He argued that there was a connection between the lucid objectivity (or semblance thereof) aspired to, and insouciantly practised, by the British school (offspring of Malinowski all of them, though some also came to loathe him) and that effortless domination which the British exercised over the Empire on which the sun never set, during those golden, and, all in all, very peaceful final decades of the colonial system. At any rate, they were peaceful for anthropology: a vast amount of successful and excellent fieldwork was carried out, and not a single one of the researchers who went out to do it amongst the 'savages' came to any harm. Later, things were to change.

Geertz directed his attention quite particularly at Evans-Pritchard (Geertz 1988: ch. 3). For all the protestations of recognising cultural-conceptual diversity, for all the insistence that fieldwork is only complete when one came to handle effectively what had initially been alien and unintelligible local concepts (claims which Evans-Pritchard made with emphasis, and which might just as well have come from some manifesto of 'interpretive anthropology') – that lucidity, that clarity, which was the mark of a gentleman, was in the end both a mark and a tool of domination. By contrast, Geertz commended a style which was to be, so to speak, more romantic and less classical (though these were not his words), more subjective, more tormented, more 'epistemologically hypochondriac' (his own ironic characterisation, *ibid.*: 71), more haunted by the difficulty of reaching from one culture, one set of ideas, to another.

In part the transition was also justified by the fact that, in the meantime, the world had become a more complicated place: boundaries between cultures had become more fluid, and some cultures, both erstwhile dominant and erstwhile dominated ones, had lost both their inner unity and their confidence. The underlying argument, whatever its merit, is slightly odd in as far as, if taken at face value, it would imply that classical, clarity-seeking, objectivity-aspiring anthropology would be in order at one stage of world history, when things were still relatively tidy, whilst hermeneutic subjectivism would take over during the more turbulent sequel. The ability to perceive this change would seem to suggest that firm objective knowledge is available after all, and thus be in contradiction with the imposition of subjective torment or tormented subjectivity. Can these methods really be so tied to periods? Are the characteristics of periods knowable, whilst knowledge itself is suspended within some periods in clouds of interpretative unknowing?

The hermeneuts felt superior to their predecessors not only methodologically, but also, and perhaps above all, morally. It was their moral superiority, they seemed to convey, that led them to their sharper insights, just as it was the moral offensiveness of their predecessors which blinded them to deep hermeneutic truths. All that clarity and objectivity and confidence, were they not a sign of a certain – shall we say – shallowness? Did it not spring from the fact that those practitioners of Malinowskian anthropology did not fully appreciate just how very difficult it is to capture the spirit of another culture? Had they known this, they would have been more anguished, and had they only been anguished enough, it would have come out in more turbulent, romantic, muddled, unintelligible and, above all, narcissistic prose. But now we have learnt better. No one could possibly accuse *us* of clarity, let alone objectivity. A tortuous style is a sign of inner torment, which in turn is a mark of depth and respect for 'the Other'. Never since *The Sorrows of Young Werther* was there such deep and well advertised anguish, though the literary style did not quite rival Goethe.

The argument seems to be – Descartes led to Kipling. We repudiate Kipling, so we must repudiate Descartes as well. The expiation of colonialism and of the domination of the world must include the repudiation of clarity, for that had been but the tool, or the mask, of domination. Instead, we demonstrate our commitment to the equality of men and cultures by our preoccupation with our own selves and our own cultural blinkers, a preoccupation so intense that it prevents us on occasion even from trying to reach out to that external object which we are supposed to be investigating. But our failure to reach it, our preoccupation with our own conceptual navel, is only the index of our methodological sophistication and our political purity. There are some practical advantages to be secured by this method: the investigation of one's inner anguish in face of the unaccountability of the other does not require a permit from the Ministry of the Interior, or the cooperation of the local Party Secretary.

In its final and wilder version, this movement constitutes a kind of hysteria of subjectivism, which does indeed have parallels with the wilder forms of ultra-modern art, where more and more conventions are abandoned or inverted and the resulting arbitrary output marketed with the challenge that anyone who fails to be impressed, thereby proves himself to be philistinical, shallow and incapable of appreciating true depth and originality. It is a fad, and as academic fads go, it is bound to have a limited time span: obsolescence is built into it.

But it does represent, in the end, a kind of convergence of the two currents which have concerned us. It is only a partial convergence: by now, the streams are no longer pure. Wittgenstein, with his carte blanche, joker-card mysticism and hermeneuticism, is only one of the authorities or fountainheads invoked by the ultra-hermeneut mood. They are operating within a profession which admittedly retains the profile which Malinowski gave it, though it no longer reveres him, and which has multiple ancestors. But, for all that, the two rivers, though by now fed by so many other streams, have come together in the end. The profession whose outline has been influenced by Malinowski, more than by any other single person, is now deeply influenced by a mystique of meaning which, in its turn, owes much to Wittgenstein.

Part V

Conclusions

35   The truth of the matter

Our beginning lay in the two visions of knowledge, and indeed of man, society, everything. This polarity, and the tension between its two poles, is one of the deepest and most pervasive themes in modern thought. On the one hand, there is atomistic individualism, which sees the individual building his cognitive world (and indeed any other) by orderly, step-by-step, individual effort, possibly maintaining cooperative relationships with others similarly engaged, but without this fundamentally affecting the nature of the enterprise, which in the end is solitary. The individual and his judgement are in the end sovereign and in assessing claims, he practises atomism; he subdivides cultural package-deals so as to assess their merits. Self-sufficiency and atomism are his deepest principles.

On the other hand, there is romantic organicism, which sees the community, or the ongoing tradition as the real unit, transcending the individual, who only finds the possibility of fulfilment and creativity and thought, even or especially of identity itself, within that community.

Each of these visions has been articulated in many fields other than that of knowledge, even if knowledge is possibly the most important. For instance, each of the two poles has its own conception of economic life. In modern times, political attitudes have most often been classified in terms of their stance on this issue. The individualist sees the polity as a contractual, functional convenience, a device of the participants in the pursuit of mutual advantage, and one to be subjected to cost-benefit accountancy and required to pay its way. The holist sees life as participation in a collectivity, which alone gives life its meaning. It alone engenders the values which confer merit on life, and it cannot be judged by some others.

Each of these visions incorporates or expresses a distinctive vision of the nature of man: is he of his very essence a social animal, finding fulfilment only through community, through participation in a distinctive culture? Or is he, on the contrary, basically an individualist, who enters communities only in a contractual spirit, expects them to provide services, but does not allow them to dominate him, either conceptually or politically?

Each of these outlooks in effect puts itself forward as the norm both of what human beings are really like and of what they ought to be like. They claim to tell us what they are like when they are true to themselves, and not under the sway of some alien, distorting influence. Each of them sees its rival as the expression or embodiment of pathology, as a deformation of the natural and appropriate order. Each possesses its own rhetoric and idiom, within which it is easy to make its own claims seem overwhelmingly strong, obvious, self-evident, and those of the opposition, patently absurd, question-begging, self-serving, if not positively vicious.

How on earth are we to choose between them? A difficult, not to say daunting task, if this indeed were what we had to do. As it happens, we do not need to do so, or at any rate, not in any overall and stark and uncompromising manner. Not only do we not need to do so: we simply cannot, and we are not even in a position to do so. Our real situation is not endowed with such stark simplicity. It may have seemed so in Kakania in, say, 1905: the human condition only came in two sizes and everyone had to make his possibly anguished choice as to which one he would put on. But all that is so no longer: happily, the world has changed. Our real situation and its options are somewhat different and more complex. Or rather, we have come to understand our world a little better than when its nature was disputed by two parties, each claiming a monopoly of truth for itself and, more significantly, tacitly united in supposing that there is no third option (the assumption which proved so crucial for Wittgenstein's development, by providing him with the premiss that if individualism is false, then communalism *must* be correct).

Each of these two grand options, as presented by their adherents, constitutes a grave misrepresentation of our real situation.

Consider individualism first. The Crusoe tradition, which begins with Descartes, finds its supreme expression in Hume and Kant, and is reformulated again in the second positivism and the neo-liberalism of recent times, offers the story of how a brave and independent individual builds up his world, cognitively, economically, and so forth. All this simply will not do either as an actual descriptive or as an explanatory account. This simply is not what actually happens, nor how it possibly could have happened.

This lack of realism, whether as description, or as a serious specification of underlying mechanisms, does not mean that the Crusoe model is unimportant or worthless. It is not. It is enormously important and meritorious, as a kind of normative charter or model of how one particular tradition, namely our own, critically reconstructs and purges its own cognitive and productive worlds. It constitutes an *ethic of cognition*: all cognitive claims are subjected to scrutiny in the course of which they are broken up into their constituent parts and individuals are free to judge as individuals: there are no cognitive hierarchies or authorities. This is the unwritten Constitutional Law of the Republic of the Mind, and its implementation has transformed the world. Its codification has been the mainstream of philosophy since Descartes and, far from 'leaving everything as it is', it has totally transformed the world, both in content and in the spirit in which it is seen.

This normative function is its real role: it is not good history or description. People were not atoms to begin with, nor did they from the very start atomise their perceptual world. They begin as docile members of communities, and their perceptions begin as *Gestalten*. But it was when they began to think as individuals, and to break up their world, as an intellectual exercise, that they also burst through the erstwhile limits on cognition and production. It was then that the great scientific and economic revolutions took place. It was then that cognitive and productive growth, which are *essential* not contingent elements of our world, became possible. The separation of issues and data, the imposition of a standard and symmetrical descriptive idiom, the exclusion of claims to special and privileged status (either for sacred data, or for sacred sources of information) – all this is almost certainly an important element in any genuine understanding of the distinctive world to which we belong. These features are also embodied, and erroneously presented as inherently human and as defining humanity, in the kind of model of man we find in Hume or Kant. As an account of how men actually grow up and function, or as a universal account of humanity, that model does not have much merit; but as the underscoring of those features which have made one tradition very distinctive, and uniquely successful cognitively and economically, it is supremely important. *That* is its real status. It happens to be the charter of one very distinctive, indeed unique, tradition, and not, as it would present itself, a portrait of man as such.

So rationalistic individualism is *a* tradition amongst others, and not the transcendence of all and any tradition by heroic individuals. Its self-portrait in the works of Hume and Kant, its programmatic anticipatory outline in Descartes, and their lesser followers during the positivist revival, is a kind of symbolic highlighting of its style of thought, of what makes it distinctive and great – the equalisation of all evidence, the symmetrical view of the world, the atomisation of evidence – and not, in any sense, a genetic account of how its members actually emerge into adulthood. But although it is *a* tradition, a social ethos with its organisational underpinning, like all the others, it is still wrong to say that it is *just* like the others. It is unique and distinctive, above all in its unbelievably great cognitive and technological power, which has totally transformed the world. It has conquered. There are also spheres in which it may well be markedly inferior: it cannot, from within its own resources and in accordance with its own central principles, engender those other valued aspects of a culture, such as a gratifying sense of belonging, or the integration of the social and natural orders, or providing a basis for obligation and cooperation, or a source of symbolism and sacraments for rites of passage, or consolation for tragedy. Its defectiveness in these respects is as distinctive and conspicuous as is its superiority in the spheres of cognition and production.

This Crusoe tradition in philosophy, from Descartes through Hume and Kant to, say, Carnap and the *Tractatus*, performed a valuable service in formulating a myth, which highlighted the values and the principles of this tradition. But it *was* but a myth, useful in the way that myths are – it provided an easily graspable, suggestive, powerful image. It highlighted the principles by which we think, though not the devious paths by which we reached our condition. But we must understand that it was but a myth, not to be taken literally, at face value. That much, at any rate, one must learn from the work of Max Weber. He it was who highlighted that the Protestant individualist tradition was a historic phenomenon like others, even if in a sense unique, both in its roots and in its consequences. It is a very great pity that Weber took Benjamin Franklin, rather than Immanuel Kant, as his model of the personality which emerged in this tradition. It would have made it all much plainer, all the more so as Kant had so brilliantly described the inner mechanics of this type of personality (under the illusion that he was analysing human reason as such).

Consider the rival position, romantic communalism, the doctrine that knowledge, and virtually everything else, is a team game, so that the isolated individual is a pathological abstraction. (In the days when the neo-Hegelians, who held a variant of this view, constituted an influential movement in Britain, they acquired the habit of using the term *abstraction* as a term of abuse, signifying *the* intellectual sin. It constituted the ever-ready, easy-to-use diagnosis of their opponents, rather similar to the assumption-of-linguistic-homogeneity view of their opponents on the part of Wittgensteinians.) This position too is a fraud. For one thing, no one can ever credit himself to be a practitioner of this faith truly: the real traditionalist, as the Muslim thinker al-Ghazzali observed, does not know himself to be a traditionalist. He who understands the notion, can no longer fully exemplify it. He has eaten of the tree of knowledge. In explaining the limits of his alleged position, he constantly transcends it and thereby contradicts it: Wittgenstein did this throughout his life.

In the nineteenth century, when this romanticism became very widespread, it was also quite specially fraudulent. The peasants who were meant to exemplify the organic way of life would have had no understanding of the idea and it would have bewildered them, if the attempt had been made to explain it. The enthusiastic consumers of the idea of ethnic *Gemeinschaft* were those who found themselves in a *Gesellschaft* which, owing to the exigencies of a modern economy, *had* to organise itself around one standardised high culture or another. Rival cultures, struggling for the control of the commanding bureaucratic heights of a given society, did so in the language of communal ethnicity, which was totally alien to the actual reality of the situation. *Gemeinschaft* was now the ideology of a particular kind of *Gesellschaft*, namely, the modern chauvinistic nation-state. There are of course many definitions of 'romanticism', a genuinely protean notion, but one that is particularly appropriate here would run as follows: romanticism is the re-affirmation of agrarian values (aggressiveness, valour, sense of rank, uncritical fidelity to political and religious leadership, conduct inspired by precedent and affect rather than reason) in post-agrarian contexts in which these values have lost their old function, though they may have acquired new ones.

Fraudulent in this way, the cult of *Gemeinschaft* was also deeply misguided in denying the universal diffusion, authority, and applicability of one particular cognitive style, namely culture-transcending science. This was of course part of its attraction: it appealed to those who hated the disenchanting vision, and naively thought they could escape it, and who welcomed a philosophy which claimed to show that such an escape was feasible and justified. The tolerant, symmetrical versions of the organic vision – so seemingly attractive in their willingness to grant *every* culture its own place in the sun, the legitimacy of its own values and vision – in fact inverted the reality of the situation. The truth of the matter is, for better or worse, deeply unsymmetrical. Relativism is an absurdity. It simply is not the case that all cognitive styles are equal. We might or might not wish it to be so, but it simply is not the case. The technological superiority of one cognitive style has transformed the world and the rules of the social game. Any philosophy based on the contrary assumption is preposterous as a guide to the world in which we actually live.

So here again, we may make a partial use of the myth, which certainly does highlight some points of importance, but we must beware of swallowing it whole. What is perfectly true is that society is not a mere assemblage of self-created individuals, entering into contractual relations but otherwise remaining self-sufficient. On the contrary, life is lived in terms of shared ideas, concepts and values which are not created by individuals, who at best bring in an innovation here and there. Shared culture can alone endow life with order and meaning. That much is true. But beware of certain mistakes which this picture tends to bring with itself.

There is within this vision a persistent tendency towards a certain kind of noxious idealism, the view that culture, i.e. the set of ideas shared by a community, is the main or the only agency of social order and control. It ignores the importance of physical and economic coercion in society, and the manner in which these can decide internal cultural options. It tends, as stated, to be far too egalitarian as between cultures, and to obscure the cognitive or technical superiority of some over others. In connection with this, it has a terrible list towards narcissism: it likes the idea that norms are internal to cultures – this is part and parcel of that inter-cultural egalitarianism which gives so much pleasure and grounds for self-congratulation on the part of the adherents of the position – and hence denies what is perhaps the most important fact in the history of mankind: transcendence. Truth is not cultural, but trans-cultural. In many spheres, men have indeed failed to transcend their culture, but this is a contingent weakness, not a necessary and inherent aspect of the human condition, which is what the romantics of organic immanentism would have us believe.

The asymmetry of cognitive and technical power, the sheer fact of cognitive transcendence (however it may come to be explained), the failure of transcendence or consensus in other spheres – these are *the* key facts of our shared human and social condition.

What follows is that any uncritical presentation of either the Crusoe or the communalistic model of the human condition will not do. Neither solitary do-it-yourself world-creation, nor on the other hand the presentation of the world as a Carpathian village green, with all knowledge assimilated to an initiation to the village dance, does justice to our real condition. Our world is basically one in which communities resembling that Carpathian village are being rapidly replaced by a new order, which is far from properly understood, but one which is dependent on sustained cognitive and economic growth. This in turn depends on at least the partial presence of a scientific culture which comports itself, in general outline, along the lines of the Crusoe model. It exemplifies principles which that model mistakenly attributed to the human mind as such.

That is our condition and our world. After Max Weber it ought to be absolutely obvious that it can only be understood in terms of the transition from one kind of society to a fundamentally different kind. Consequently any philosopher who absolutises *either* one of the two models, whether it be Crusoe or the ultimate conceptual sovereignty of the village green, is committing a howler. Many thinkers have committed one or the other of these two howlers. Wittgenstein has the unenviable distinction of committing both of them in the course of a single life, in an exaggerated form, and in reverse order. What he achieved, on each occasion, was in effect an unintended parody. On both occasions, he also did it with great and highly characteristic dogmatism. This rather curious accomplishment has earned him the distinction of probably being the most influential thinker of the century.

Malinowski never attained comparable fame, though he too for a time dominated a discipline. Actually, within anthropology, though this is not so loudly proclaimed, his hold over the discipline is rather stabler than Wittgenstein's in his. He recognised that two types of social and conceptual order were involved and absolutised neither of them, let alone both in succession (though one must regretfully admit that in later life he seemed tempted to accord action-based communalism more authority than it deserves). But his in the main moderate and sober recognition of the truth of the matter did not have the same rousing appeal as did the wild exaggeration of two absurdities by the other migrant and fellow subject of Franz Josef. Malinowski knew full well that men lived within communities, and that those communities and the ideas they carried gave meaning to their lives and had to be understood from within: this is the old wisdom of the romantic tradition. Neither of the two men can claim to be its discoverer. But Malinowski knew and explicitly recognised (especially in the first formulation of his position on thought and language) that when it comes to serious cognition, detachment from, not a return to, communal involvement is required. The social involvement of language and ideas is valuable for understanding the actual life of communities, but it may not be used – and this was Wittgenstein's most preposterous belief – to solve the problem of the validity of our cognition. Cultures are not terminal. The possibility of transcendence of cultural limits is a fact; it is the single most important fact about human life.

In addition to not extending his sense of the reality of culture to treating it as the terminator of the problem of knowledge, Malinowski also understood the distinction between culture and power. His cultural pluralist nationalism, and his political internationalism, so very much ahead of his time, and so relevant to ours, makes this obvious. He wanted cultures to be protected, but polities to be restrained by higher authority. Wittgenstein never remotely faced this or similar problems. His absolutisation of cultures never led him to look at concrete cases and ask whether this, that or the other named, historically and geographically identified culture was to be treated as ultimate and given the kind of terminal status he attributed to 'forms of life'. Was it Kakania? If not, then who? Nor did he consider the disastrous political implications of his omnibus absolutisation of culture, of 'forms of life'. Were they to be politically, as well as conceptually, sovereign?

The son of minor gentry, sunk into genteel near-poverty (no land left) but sustained by academic respectability, got it right, all in all. The offspring of mixed Austrian-Jewish industrial magnates got it egregiously wrong. The thought of both of them can best be interpreted as the fruit of the deepest and most pervasive tension of this society, between individualism and communalism. Neither of these visions will do: we are not, in fact, self-sufficient individuals, nor do we possess self-contained and self-authenticating communities. Mankind has shifted, and is continuing to shift, from relatively self-contained communities to a wider community endowed with powerful knowledge, which works more or less in terms of norms conveyed by the individualist model. It is only by understanding this transition that we can come to terms with our condition. Absolutising either end of the old polarity will not do.

The central problem facing contemporary societies, or group of problems, arises not from the existence of either of these social types in
themselves, but from the tensions generated by the shift from one to the
other and by their coexistence within what are, by other and obvious
criteria, single societies. Once upon a time mankind lived, by and large,
in closed intimate communities, governed by practices simultaneously
geared both to maintaining internal order and adjusting to nature (with
the former consideration, however, predominating). The criteria
adapted for judging the acceptability of practices – morally, technically,
ritually, grammatically, sartorially, what you will – were, so to speak,
self-validating, traditional. They were not systematised; no attempt was
to deduce them either from some supposedly self-evident general
premise or from some single authoritative revelation. So, by and large,
such communities conformed to the model elaborated by the organic or
romantic theorists.

Then, one day, a new style of cognition emerged, which separated the
referential inquiry into nature from the concern with internal social
harmony and which, by means which are still only partly understood,
succeeded in acquiring astonishingly accurate, general, and consensus-
securing understanding of the environment. Those who questioned the
authority of the new science were in the end effectively silenced by the
unbelievable power of the technology based on it, which completely
transformed the human condition. It also transformed human society,
replacing societies made up 90 per cent or more of peasants – agricultural workers living close to destitution and surviving precariously by the
sweat of their brows – by relatively affluent societies made up of literate
specialists moving fairly freely between a variety of occupations. The
new style of knowledge spread rapidly, being adopted and adapted by a
variety of cultures and social organisations, more easily and quickly by
some than by others. How did the new style work? The answer given is
known as philosophy or, at any rate, makes up an important part of that
ill-defined subject. The best known answer is contained in the empiricist

tradition, and consists of a kind of Crusoe-like fictitious story about how a single individual amasses and digests and organises his data, and ends up with the marvellous knowledge which in fact we possess. The most famous and distinguished versions of this story can be found, in the eighteenth century, in Hume's *Treatise* and Kant's first *Critique*, and again in our time in the work of men such as Mach, Russell, and Carnap. One particular version, curious and unusual in style, content, and context, is to be found in Wittgenstein's *Tractatus*.

The real intellectual problems that modern society faces consist, in very large part, of the relationship between the two styles, between universalism-atomism, which helps explain the success of the new science and thereby itself acquires a certain authority, further reinforced by the superiority of the market form of production over centralised and socially oriented ways of running the economy, and, on the other hand, by the yearning for 'meaning', social coherence, the fusion of value and fact, the absorption of the individual in a supportive and loving community, which in turn blends into the natural background. These are the terms of reference for our problems. Anyone who simply proposes one of them and ignores or dismisses the other, has little to tell us. That might have been possible once, but it is so no longer.

The error of treating one or the other of these models as sufficient on its own is a howler, which really ought no longer to be tolerated. Just how we should use them both is an exceedingly difficult matter. The individualism probably gives us a correct answer to the question of how valid and powerful knowledge really works and, in matters of cognition, deserves a kind of normative authority. But it cannot conceivably fill our life. Individuals as such have virtually no aims or needs, over and above the crudest biological requirements. What gives them their fulfilment, their satisfactions, are the values instilled by contingent and variable cultures. A satisfactory life is one which is provided with the means of playing out a part in a culture/play, a part agreeable to the actor. This fact is obscured in our society by the egalitarian levelling out of roles that has allowed people to pursue recognition mainly through the acquisition of goods. This creates the illusion that those goods are, in themselves, desired and satisfying.

The culture-plays and their systems of roles may, once upon a time, have absolutised themselves or imposed themselves firmly on individuals: this is no longer so. Our attitude to cultures is ironic. We do not accept any absolutist claims they may make, we put them on as we put on clothes, and feel free to vary our sartorial styles. The cognitive claims found within them we treat with reserve, in the knowledge that in matters of cognition, one particular intellectual style is sovereign. It has proved its superiority by the incredible power of the technology it has engendered. However, it is not all-powerful: for reasons which are not fully clear, attempts to extend that style into the sphere of social and human phenomena have not been markedly successful. Complexity, free-will, feed-back, the fact that the phenomena are themselves constituted by the meanings of the participants – these (probably overlapping) causes have been invoked to explain this failure. No one really knows whether this failure is one of principle – the task being inherently impossible – or whether it may in time be remedied.

Either way, we must for the time being live with this failure, whether it be temporary or permanent. The fact that neither our values nor our life-style nor our understanding of our social environment can be fully linked, or linked at all, to the best and most respected type of understanding of our natural environment constitutes a problem. We have to live with this problem, whether or not a theoretical and cogent solution exists: any society, any individual even, implicitly makes use of some compromise in this matter, whether he can articulate and defend it or not. But a philosopher who absolutises, in succession, each of the polar extremes, and pretends, each time, that this revelation is beyond doubt and free of tension, totally misrepresents our condition. He lived out the two options in reverse order, and decreed that the romantic one constituted normality, and the universalistic one was a disease of language. He projected his own rather bizarre development onto the history of thought . . .

The truth is exactly the opposite. Organic, self-contained social and conceptual cocoons cannot cope with either their internal or external conflicts. The notion of a culture-transcending truth emerges partly to cope with the resulting problems, partly to help explain the culture-transcending achievements of science. Whether or to what extent this individualist rationalism can cope with those genuine problems, is an open question. But one thing is certain: it cannot be dismissed as a misunderstanding of language. It is, on the contrary, a most central and immensely important part of *our* culture.

Bibliography

Ackerman, R. 1987. *J. G. Frazer: His Life and Work*. Cambridge: Cambridge University Press.

Baker, S. 1973. 'Witkiewicz and Malinowski: The Pure Form of Magic, Science and Religion', *Polish Review* 18: 77–93.

Beller, S. 1989. *Vienna and the Jews, 1867–1938: A Cultural History*. Cambridge: Cambridge University Press.

Davis, J. 1991. 'An Interview with Ernest Gellner', *Current Anthropology* 32: 63–72.

Ellen, R., E. Gellner, G. Kubica, and J. Mucha (eds.) 1988. *Malinowski Between two Worlds: The Polish Roots of an Anthropological Tradition*. Cambridge: Cambridge University Press.

Firth, R. 1957. 'Ethnographic Analysis and Language with Reference to Malinowski's Views', in R. Firth (ed.). 1957

   1995. 'Wittgenstein', letter to *The Times Literary Supplement*, 17 March 1995, p. 15.

Firth, R. (ed.) 1957. *Man and Culture: An Evaluation of the Work of Bronislaw Malinowski*. London: Routledge & Kegan Paul.

Flis, A. 1988. 'Cracow Philosophy at the Beginning of the Twentieth Century and Malinowski's Scientific Ideas', in Ellen *et al.* (eds) 1998.

Frazer, J. G. 1990. *The Golden Bough: A Study in Magic and Religion* (3rd edn). London: St Martin's Press.

Gallie, B. 1952. *Peirce and Pragmatism*. London: Penguin.

Geertz, C. 1988. *Works and Lives: The Anthropologist as Author*. Cambridge: Polity.

Gerould, D. 1981. *Witkacy: Stanislaw Ignacy Witkiewicz as an Imaginative Writer*. Seattle and London: University of Washington Press.

Hacker, P. M. S. 1995. 'Thought, Language and Reality', review of *Wittgensteinian Philosophical Occasions, 1912–1951*, eds. J. Klugge and A. Nordmann, *The Times Literary Supplement*, 17 February 1995, pp. 8–9.

Hroch, M. 1985. *Social Preconditions of National Revival in Europe*. Cambridge: Cambridge University Press.

Hume, D. 1888 (1789). *A Treatise of Human Nature*, ed. L. A. Selby-Bigge. Oxford: Clarendon Press.

James, W. 1990 (1907). *Pragmatism*. New York: Dover.

Janik, A. and S. Toulmin 1973. *Wittgenstein's Vienna*. New York: Simon and Schuster.

Kant, I. 1968 (1929). *Critique of Pure Reason*, trans N. Kemp Smith. London: Macmillan.

Leach, E. R. 1957. 'The Epistemological Background to Malinowski's Empiricism', in R. Firth (ed.) 1957.

McCagg, W.O. Jr. 1989. *The History of the Hapsburg Jews, 1670–1918*. Bloomington: Indian University Press.

Macfarlane, A. 1978. *The Origins of English Individualism*. Oxford: Blackwell.

McGuinness, B. 1988. *Wittgenstein, A Life: Young Ludwig 1889–1921*. London: Duckworth.

Mach, E. 1959. *The Analysis of Sensations and the Relation of the Physical to the Psychical*, trans. C. M. Williams. New York: Dover.

Malcolm, N. 1958. *Ludwig Wittgenstein: A Memoir*. London: Oxford University Press.

Malinowski, B. 1935. *Coral Gardens and their Magic: A Study of the Method of Tilling the Soil and of Agricultural Rites in the Trobriand Islands*, 2 vols. London: George Allen & Unwin.

1947. *Freedom and Civilization*. London: George Allen & Unwin.

1948. *Magic, Science and Religion and Other Essays*. Boston: Beacon Press.

1960 (1923). 'The Problem of Meaning in Primitive Language', supplement 1 in Ogden and Richards, pp. 296–336.

1960a (1944). *A Scientific Theory of Culture and Other Essays*. New York: Oxford University Press.

1961 (1945). *The Dynamics of Culture Change: An Inquiry into Race Relations in Africa*. New Haven: Yale University Press.

1993. *The Early Writings of Bronislaw Malinowski*, eds. R. J. Thornton and P. Skalnik, trans. L. Krzyzanowski. Cambridge: Cambridge University Press.

Monk, K. 1990. *Ludwig Wittgenstein: The Duty of Genius*. London: Jonathan Cape.

Mucha, J. 1988. 'Malinowski and the Problems of Contemporary Civilisation' in Ellen *et al.* (eds.) 1988.

Ogden, C. K. and I. A. Richards 1960 (1923). *The Meaning of Meaning: A Study of the Influence of Language upon Thought and of the Science of Symbolism*. London: Routledge & Kegan Paul.

Oxaal, I., M. Pollak and G. Botz (ds.) 1987. *Jews, Antisemitism and Culture in Vienna*. London and New York: Routledge & Kegan Paul.

Paluch, A. 1981. 'The Polish Background to Malinowski's Work', *Man* (ns) 16: 276–85.

Popper, K. 1962 (1945). *The Open Society and its Enemies*. London: Routledge.

Russell, B. *See* Whitehead.

Schorske, C. E. 1981. *Fin-de-Siècle Vienna: Politics and Culture*. New York: Vintage Books.

Stern, J. P. (ed.) 1980. *The World of Franz Kafka*. London: Weidenfeld and Nicolson.

Symmons-Symonolewicz, C. 1959. 'Bronislaw Malinowski: Formative Influences and Theoretical Evolution' *Polish Review* 4 (4): 17–45.

Timms, E. 1986. *Karl Kraus, Apocalyptic Satirist: Culture and Catastrophe in Habsburg Vienna*. New Haven and London: Yale University Press.

Whitehead, A. N. and B. Russell 1910–12. *Principia Mathematica*. Cambridge: Cambridge University Press.

Winch, P. 1958. *The Idea of a Social Science and its Relation to Philosophy.* London: Routledge & Kegan Paul.

Wistrich, R.S. 1990. *The Jews of Vienna in the Age of Franz Joseph.* Oxford: Oxford University Press for Littman Library.

Wittgenstein, L. 1974 (1921). *Tractatus Logico-Philosophicus*, tr. D. F. Pears and B. F. McGuinness. London: Routledge.

1953. *Philosophical Investigations*, tr. G. E. M. Anscombe. Oxford: Blackwell.

Bibliographies of Ernest Gellner's writings on Wittgenstein, Malinowski, and nationalism

Compiled by I. C. Jarvie

These bibliographies were compiled from the master bibliography of Gellner's writings published in John A. Hall and I. C. Jarvie, eds., *The Social Philosophy of Ernest Gellner*, Amsterdam: Rodopi 1996. The date/letter identification system used there has been preserved. Reprints and translations are included.

ERNEST GELLNER'S WRITINGS ON WITTGENSTEIN

1951*c*. 'Use and Meaning', *Cambridge Journal* 4 (12): 753–61.

1951*d*. 'Analysis and Ontology', *Philosophical Quarterly* 1 (5): 408–15.

1951*e*. 'Knowing How and Validity', *Analysis* 12 (2): 25–35.

1954*a*. 'The Philosophy of Wittgenstein' (review of L. Wittgenstein, *Philosophical Investigations*), *The Tutor's Bulletin of Adult Education*, nods. 95 and 96: 20–4.

1957*h*. 'Reflections on Linguistic Philosophy I and II', *The Listener* 58 (8 and 15 August): 205–7, 237 and 240–1. (See also correspondence at pp. 354, 439–40.)

1957*i* 'Logical Positivism and After or: the Spurious Fox', *Universities Quarterly* 11 (4): 205–7, 237, and 240–1; also in *Universities and Left Review*, Winter (Winter): 67–73.

1957*j*. 'Professor Toulmin's Return to Aristotle', *Universities Quarterly* 11 (4): 369–72; also in *Universities and Left Review*, 1958 (Summer): 73–4.

1957*m*. 'Contemporary Thought and Politics' (article-review on P. Laslett and W.G. Runciman, eds., *Philosophy, Politics and Society*), *Philosophy* 32 (123): 336–57.

1958*e*. 'Time and Theory in Social Anthropology', *Mind* (n.s.) 67 (2): 182–202.

1958*f*. 'The Devil in Modern Philosophy', *The Hibbert Journal*, 56 (April): 251–5.

1958*g*. 'Reply to Mr. MacIntyre', *Universities and Left Review* (Summer): 73–4.

1959*c*. 'Am Anfang war das Wort', *Studium Generale* 12 (9): 611–14.

1959*d*. *Words and Things, A Critical Account of Linguistic Philosophy and a Study in Ideology*. London: Gollancz; Boston: Beacon.

(See also the correspondence in *The Times*, 5 November, p. 13 (Bertrand Russell); 9 November, p. 11 (Gilbert Ryle); 10 November, p. 13 (Conrad Dehn, G. R. G. Mure); 11 November, p. 11 (Ernest Gellner, Leslie Farrer); 13 November, p. 13 (John Wisdom); 14 November, p. 7 (B. F. McGuiness); 16 November, p. 13 (J. N. Wright, Kevin Holland); 17 November, p. 13 (Joan Robinson, Arnold Kaufman); 18 November, p. 13 (T. P. Creed); 19 November, p. 13 (J. W. N. Watkins); 20 November, p. 13

195

(John G. Vance); 21 November, p. 7 (Alec Kassman, E. H. Thompson); 23 November, p. 13 (R. Meager, Alan Donagan); 24 November, p. 13 (Bertrand Russell and leading article.)

1959e. 'Patterns of Fact-and-Choice' (review of A. J. Ayer (ed.), *Logical Positivism*), *The Guardian*, 4 December, p. 12.

1960d. Review of Peter Winch, *The Idea of a Social Science*, *British Journal of Sociology* 11 (2): 170–2.

1961c. *Parole e Cose* (Italian translation of 1959d), Milan: Il Saggiatore.

1962b. 'Concepts and Society', *Transactions of the Fifth World Congress of Sociology (Washington)*, Louvain, vol. 1, pp. 153–83. Reprinted in B. Wilson (ed.), *Rationality*. Oxford: Basil Blackwell 1970, pp. 18–49; and in D. Emmett and A. MacIntyre (eds.), *Sociological Theory and Philosophical Analysis*. London: Macmillan 1970, pp. 115–49.

1962c. *Palabras y Cosas* (Spanish translation of 1959d), Madrid: Editorial Tecnos, S. A.

1962d. *Slova i Vieshchi* (Russian translation of 1959d), Moscow: Publishing House of Foreign Literature.

1963h. 'Ayer's Epistle to the Russians', *Ratio* 5 (2): 168–80. Spanish translation in Rafael Beneyto (ed.), *Filosofio y Ciencia*. Valencia: Universidad de Valencia, 1975.

1964h. 'The Crisis in the Humanities and the Mainstream of Philosophy', in J. H. Plumb (ed.), *Crisis in the Humanities*. Harmondsworth: Penguin, pp. 45–81.

1965a. *Thought and Change*. London: Weidenfeld and Nicolson; Chicago: University of Chicago Press (with the imprint 1964).

1968a. 'The Entry of the Philosophers', *The Times Literary Supplement*, no. 3449, 5 April, pp. 347–9. See also correspondence at pp. 427, 457, 514.

1968d. 'The New Idealism', in I. Lakatos and A. Musgrave (eds.), *Problems in the Philosophy of Science*. Amsterdam: North Holland, pp. 377–406 and 426–32; reprinted in Anthony Giddens (ed.), *Positivism and Sociology*. London: Heinemann 1974, pp. 129–56; in German in Hans Albert (ed.), *Theorie und Realität*, 2nd edition. Tübingen: Mohr, 1972, pp. 87–112.

1971h. 'Ernest Gellner on the Belief Machine' (review of Alasdair MacIntyre, *Against the Self-Images of the Age: Essays on Ideology and Philosophy*), *The Spectator* 227 (28 August): 307–8.

1971k. 'The Sacred Word' (review of Bryan Magee (ed.), *Modern British Philosophy*), *The Spectator* 227 (8 December): 888–9.

1972k. Review of Peter Laslett, W. G. Runciman and Quentin Skinner (eds.), *Philosophy, Politics and Society*, 4th Series, in *The Times Literary Supplement* 3694 (22 December): 1552.

1973g. *Cause and Meaning in the Social Sciences*, ed. I. C. Jarvie and Joseph Agassi. London: Routledge and Kegan Paul. Contains: 1956d, 1962b, 1962d, 1868d, 1968a, 1958e, 1967f, 1958h, 1965c, 1970f, 1957g, 1960c, 1963f, 1959b, 1958i. See also 1987a.

1974a. *Contemporary Thought and Politics*, ed. I. C. Jarvie and Joseph Agassi. London: Routledge and Kegan Paul. Contains: 1959a, 1969i, 1976c, 1957m, 1969g, 1969d, 1958d, 1967d, 1971e, 1958a, 1973e, 1971j, 1971b, 1966a.

1974*f*. 'The Phoney Revolution' (review of P. F. Strawson, *Freedom and Resentment and Other Essays*), *The Spectator* 231 (8 June): 708–9.

1974*g*. *The Devil in Modern Philosophy*, ed. I. C. Jarvie and Joseph Agassi. London: Routledge and Kegan Paul. Contains: 1958*f*, 1964*h*, 1973*f*, 1955*a*, 1957*l*, 1951*a*, 1955*b*, 1951*d*, 1956*b*, 1964*g*, 1973*d*, 1969*h*, 1963*h*, 1972*a*, 1971*h*, 1962*a*, 1961*f*, 1971*d*, 1972*c*, 1972*f*, 1969*e*.

1975*a*. *Legitimation of Belief*. Cambridge: Cambridge University Press.

1975*e*. 'A Wittgensteinian Philosophy of (or Against) the Social Sciences', *Philosophy of the Social Sciences* 5 (2): 173–99; reprinted in S. G. Shanker (ed.), *Ludwig Wittgenstein: Critical Assessments*. Vol. 4, London: Croom Helm, pp. 260–89.

1979*j*. *Words and Things*, 2nd edn. London: Routledge and Kegan Paul. (Reprint of 1959*d*, with the addition of 1979*k*.)

1979*k*. 'The Saltmines of Salzburg or Wittgensteinianism Reconsidered in Historical Context', a new introduction specially written for the 2nd edn of 1959*d*. Pp. 1–37 of 1979*j*.

1979*o*. 'Philosophy, the Social Context', in Bryan Magee (ed.), *Men of Ideas*. New York: Viking Press, pp. 286–99. (American edition of 1978*f*.)

1980*a*. *Spectacles and Predicaments, Essays in Social Theory*. Cambridge: Cambridge University Press. Contains: 1980*b*, 1976*e*, 1975*p*, 1975*e*, 1975*m*, 1977*i*, 1978*m*, 1974*c*, 1978*g*, 1976*h*, 1975*o*, 1975*h*, 1981*e*, 1978*c*, 1975*d*, 1979*h*, 1976*g*, 1979*a*, 1977*d*, 1975*l*.

1980*b*. Introduction to 1980*a*, pp. 1–9.

1982*c*. 'The Paradox in Paradigms' (review of Barry Barnes, *T. S. Kuhn and Social Science*), *The Times Literary Supplement* 4125 (23 April): 451–2.

1983*b*. 'Verbal Euthanasia' (review of A. J. Ayer, *Philosophy in the Twentieth Century*), *The American Scholar* 52 (2): 243–58.

1984*b*. 'The Gospel According to Saint Ludwig' (review of Saul Kripke, *Wittgenstein on Rules and Private Language*), *The American Scholar* 53 (2): 243–63.

1984*d*. *Slowa i Rzeczy*. Warsaw: Ksiazka Wiedza. (Polish translation of 1959*d*.)

1984*f*. 'Tractatus Sociologico-Philosophicus', in S. C. Brown (ed.), *Objectivity and Cultural Divergence*, Cambridge: Cambridge University Press, pp. 247–59; also in Erik Cohen, Moshe Lissek and Uri Almagar (eds.), *Essays in Honour of S. M. Eisenstadt*. Boulder and London: Westview Press, 1985, pp. 374–85; and in Italian in Massimo Piatelli Palmerini et al. (eds.), *Livelli di realita*, trans. Gianni Mancassole. Milan: Fettinelli, 198?, pp. 487–505.

1985*d*. *Relativism and the Social Sciences*. Cambridge: Cambridge University Press. Contains: 1985*e*, 1985*f*, 1981*f*, 1984*l*, 1981*g*, 1982*i*, 1984*b*.

1985*e*. 'Positivism Against Hegelianism', in 1985*d*, pp. 4–67.

1985*i*. 'Positively a Romanticist' (review of A. J. Ayer, *Wittgenstein*), *The Guardian*, 13 June, p. 22.

1986*f*. 'Three Contemporary Styles of Philosophy', in Stuart Shanker (ed.), *Philosophy in Britain Today*. London: Croom Helm, pp. 98–117.

1987*g*. *Culture, Identity, and Politics*. Cambridge: Cambridge University Press. Contains: 1979*m*, 1979*n*, 1980*l*, 1981*a*, 1982*h*, 1983*c*, 1984*c*, 1984*f*, 1985*b*, 1987*h*.

1989*q*. 'Tri savremene pristupe a filosofii' ('Three Contemporary Approaches in Philosophy'), *Ideje* (Belgrade) 3–4: 113–30. Serbo-Croat translation of 1986*f*.)

1991*d*. 'Two Escapes from History or the Hapsburg Impact on British Thought', in Alfred Bohnen and Alan Musgrave (eds.), *Wege der Vernunft, Festschrift zum siebzigsten Geburtstag von Hans Albert*. Tübingen: J. C. B. Mohr (Paul Siebeck), pp. 227–44.

1992*e*. *Reason and Culture, The Historic Role of Rationality and Rationalism*. Oxford: Blackwell.

1992*ai* Articles 'Linguistic Philosophy' (pp. 339–40), 'Nation' (pp. 402–03), 'Nationalism' (pp. 409–11), 'Psychoanalysis' (pp. 524–27), 'Unconscious' (pp. 682–83) in William Outhwaite, Tom Bottomore, E. Gellner, R. Nisbet and A. Touraine (eds.), *The Blackwell Dictionary of Twentieth-Century Social Thought*. Oxford: Blackwell.

ERNEST GELLNER'S WRITINGS ON MALINOWSKI

1958*h*. Review of R. Firth (ed.), *Man and Culture: An Evaluation of the Work of Bronislaw Malinowski*, *Universities Quarterly* 13 (1): 86–92.

1963*f*. 'Nature and Society in Social Anthropology', *Philosophy of Science* 30 (3): 236–51.

1964*a*. 'Foreword' to I. C. Jarvie, *The Revolution in Anthropology*. London: Routledge and Kegan Paul, pp. v-viii.

1967*f*. 'Sociology and Social Anthropology', *Transactions of the Sixth World Congress of Sociology (Evian) 1966*, Louvain, vol. 2, pp. 49–63.

1973*g*. *Cause and Meaning in the Social Sciences*, ed. I. C. Jarvie and Joseph Agassi. London: Routledge and Kegan Paul. Contains: 1956*d*, 1962*b*, 1962*d*, 1868*d*, 1968*a*, 1958*e*, 1967*f*, 1958*h*, 1965*c*, 1970*f*, 1957*g*, 1960*c*, 1963*f*, 1959*b*, 1958*i*. See also 1987*a*.

1981*l*. Introduction to E. E. Evans-Pritchard, *A History of Anthropological Thought*, edited by André Singer. London: Faber, pp. xiii-xxxvi.

1982*i*. 'No Haute Cuisine in Africa' (review of Jack Goody, *Cooking, Cuisine and Class*), *London Review of Books* 4 (16): 22–4.

1985*d*. *Relativism and the Social Sciences*. Cambridge: Cambridge University Press. Contains: 1985*e*, 1985*f*, 1981*f*, 1984*l*, 1981*g*, 1982*i*, 1984*b*.

1985*h*. 'Malinowski and the Dialectics of Past and Present', *The Times Literary Supplement* 4288 (7 June): 645–6.

1985*o*. 'Malinowski Go Home: Reflections on the Malinowski Centenary Conference', *Anthropology Today* 1 (5): 5.

1986*k*. 'Original Sin', *The Times Higher Education Supplement* 727 (10 October): 13.

1987*a*. *The Concept of Kinship*, paperback reprint of 1973*g* with 1986*k* as a new Introduction. Oxford: Blackwell.

1987*g*. *Culture, Identity, and Politics*. Cambridge: Cambridge University Press. Contains: 1979*m*, 1979*n*, 1980*l*, 1981*a*, 1982*h*, 1983*c*, 1984*c*, 1984*f*, 1985*b*, 1987*h*.

1987*h*. 'Zeno of Cracow', in 1987*g*, pp. 47–74.; also in 1988*q*.

1987n. 'The Political Thought of Bronislaw Malinowski', *Current Anthropology* 28 (4): 557–9.

1988a. 'Leaves from the Golden Bough' (review of Robert Ackerman, *J. G. Frazer, His Life and Work*), *The Times Higher Education Supplement* 793 (15 January): 18.

1988b. 'The Stakes in Anthropology', *The American Scholar* 57 (1): 17–30. (See also 1988n.) Reprinted in: Joe Liebowitz (ed.), *Advanced Reading*, Seoul 1989.

1988g. Review of Clifford Geertz, *Works and Lives: The Anthropologist as Author*, *The Times Higher Education Supplement* 807 (22 April): 26.

1988n. 'The Politics of Anthropology', *Government and Opposition* 23: 290–303. (Modified version of 1988b).

1988q. Edited with Roy Ellen, Grazyna Kubica and Janusz Mucha, *Malinowski Between Two Worlds: The Polish Roots of an Anthropological Tradition*. Cambridge: Cambridge University Press. Pp. 240. (Contains 1987h, pp. 164–94.)

1991d. 'Two Escapes from History or the Hapsburg Impact on British Thought', in Alfred Bohnen and Alan Musgrave (eds.). *Wege der Vernunft, Festschrift zum siebzigsten Geburtstag von Hans Albert*. Tübingen: J. C. B. Mohr (Paul Siebeck) pp. 227–44.

1994l. 'James Frazer and Cambridge Anthropology', in Richard Mason (ed.), *Cambridge Minds*. Cambridge: Cambridge University Press, pp. 204–17.

1995x. *Anthropology and Politics. Revolutions in the Sacred Grove*. Oxford: Blackwell. Contains: 1992k, 1988b, 1988v, 1989i, 1996a, 1985h, 1994l, 1990v, 1987k, 1993af, 1991z, 1991k, 1991c, 1994n, 1992q, 1995p.

1996g. 'Reply to Critics', in John A. Hall and Ian C. Jarvie (eds.). *The Social Philosophy of Ernest Gellner*. Amsterdam: Rodopi, pp. 623–86.

ERNEST GELLNER'S PRINCIPAL WRITINGS ON NATIONALISM

1954b. 'Reflections on Violence' (review-article on Stanislaw Andrzejewski, *Military Organization and Society*), *British Journal of Sociology* 5 (3): 267–71.

1957f. 'Independence in the Central High Atlas', *Middle East Journal* 1 (3): 236–52.

1957m. 'Contemporary Thought and Politics' (article-review on P. Laslett and W. G. Runciman (eds.). *Philosophy, Politics and Society*), *Philosophy* 32 (123): 336–57.

1960a. 'The Middle East Observed', *Political Studies* 8 (1): 66–70.

1961g. 'From Ibn Khaldun to Karl Marx' (review of Donald E. Ashford, *Political Change in Morocco*), *The Political Quarterly* 32 (4): 385–92.

1961h. 'The Struggle for Morocco's Past', *Middle East Journal* 15 (1): 79–90; reprinted in I. W. Zartman (ed.), *Man, State and Society in the Contemporary Maghrib*. New York: Praeger, 1973, pp. 37–49.

1961i. 'Morocco', in Colin Legum (ed.), *Africa, A Handbook of the Continent*. London: Anthony Blond, pp. 43–60.

1962e. 'Patterns of Rural Rebellion in Morocco: Tribes as Minorities', *European Journal of Sociology* 3 (2): 297–311; reprinted in 1973b, pp. 361–74.

1963a. 'Going Into Europe', *Encounter* 20 (January): 54–5.

1963c. Review of Rom Landau, *Morocco Independent*, *Middle East Journal* 17 (1 and 2): 174–5.

1963d. 'Sanctity, Puritanism, Secularisation and Nationalism in North Africa', *Archives de sociologie des religions* 15: 71–86; also in J. G. Peristiany (ed.), *Contributions to Mediterranean Sociology: Mediterranean Rural Communities and Social Change*. Acts of the Mediterranean Sociology Conference, July 1963, Paris: Mouton, 1965, pp. 31–48.

1965a *Thought and Change*. London: Weidenfeld and Nicolson; Chicago: University of Chicago Press (with the imprint 1964).

1965b. 'The Day the Pendulum Stood Still' (review of Sylvia G. Haim (ed.), *Arab Nationalism*), *New Society* 5 (15 April): 30–1.

1971f. 'Going Into Europe–Again?', *Encounter* 37 (August): 40–1.

1972b. Review of Elie Kedourie, *Nationalism in Asia and Africa*, in *British Journal of Sociology* 23 (1): 120–3.

1972d. (under the pseudonym 'Philip Peters') 'Algeria After Independence', *New Society* 20 (497): 9–11.

1973e. 'Scale and Nation', *Philosophy of the Social Sciences* 3(1): 1–17.

1974a. *Contemporary Thought and Politics*, ed. I. C. Jarvie and Joseph Agassi. London: Routledge and Kegan Paul. Contains: 1959a, 1969i, 1976c, 1957m, 1969g, 1969d, 1958d, 1967d, 1971e, 1958a, 1973e, 1971j, 1971b, 1966a.

1975b. 'Cohesion and Identity: The Maghreb from Ibn Khaldun to Emile Durkheim', *Government and Opposition* 10 (2): 203–18.

1975g 'Théorie du Nationalisme, Cohesion and Identity', in *Identité Culturelle et Conscience Nationale en Tunisie*, Université de Tunis, *Cahiers du CERES* [Centre d'Etudes et de Recherches Economiques et Sociales], Série Sociologique, 2, June, pp. 21–37. (Reprint of 1975b.)

1977l. Review of Eugene Kamenka (ed.), *Nationalism: The Nature and Evolution of an Idea*, and Anthony Smith (ed.), *Nationalist Movements*, in *British Journal of Sociology* 28 (4): 413–4.

1978a. 'Trousers in Tunisia' (review of L. Carl Brown, *The Tunisia of Ahmed Bey*), *Middle Eastern Studies* 14 (1): 127–30.

1978c. 'Nationalism, or the New Confessions of a Justified Edinburgh Sinner' (review of Tom Nairn, *The Break Up of Britain*), *The Political Quarterly* 49 (1): 103–11; in Portuguese in *Raiz e Utopia* 5/6: 155–59.

1979e. Review of Hugh Seton-Watson, *Nations and States*, in *Political Studies* vol. 27 (2): 312–13.

1980a. *Spectacles and Predicaments, Essays in Social Theory*, Cambridge: Cambridge University Press. Contains: 1980b, 1976e, 1975p, 1975e, 1975m, 1977i, 1978m, 1974c, 1978g, 1976h, 1975o, 1975h, 1981e, 1978c, 1975d, 1979h, 1976g, 1979a, 1977d, 1975l.

1980s. 'As raizes sociais de nacionalismo e a diversidede de suas formas', in *Alternativas politicas, economicas, e sociais at o final do secuto*. Brazilia: Editore Universided do Brazilien.

1981c. *Muslim Society*. Cambridge: Cambridge University Press. Contains: 1981d, 1975b, 1973a, 1972g, 1963d, 1974h, 1978a, 1976b, 1962e, 1976c, 1977f, 1979b; paperback edn, 1983.

1981*j*. 'Nationalism', *Theory and Society* 10: 753–76.

1981*k*. *Nacionalismo e Democracia*. Brasilia: Editore Universede de Brasilia.

1982*f*. 'The Individual Division of Labour and National Cultures', *Government and Opposition* 17(3): 268–78.

1983*c*. 'Nationalism and the Two Forms of Cohesion in Complex Societies', The Radcliffe-Brown Memorial Lecture, *Proceedings of the British Academy* 58: 165–87.

1983*e*. *Nations and Nationalism*. Oxford: Basil Blackwell.

1983*j*. 'Personal communication' about nationalism, quoted and discussed in Anthony D. Smith, *Theories of Nationalism*, 2nd edn, London: Duckworth, Appendix C, pp. 265–7.

1984*i*. Foreword to Eva Schmidt-Hartmann, *Thomas G. Masaryk's Realism: Origins of a Czech Political Concept*, Munich: R. Oldenbourg Verlag, pp. 7–8.

1985*c*. *Nazioni e Nazionalismo*. Rome: Editore Rinniti. (Italian translation of 1983*e*.) New edn 1992.

1987*j*. 'Nationalism', in Vernon Bogdanor (ed.), *Encyclopaedia of Political Institutions*. Oxford: Blackwell, pp. 382–3.

1987*r*. 'Il Nazionalismo, la Democrazia e la Storia', *Quaderni Storici* (n.s.) 66 (3): 945–59. (Italian translation by Maria Luisa Pesante.)

1988*j*. *Naciones y nacionalismo* (Spanish translation by Javier Setó of 1983*e*). Madrid: Alianza Editorial.

1988*p*. *Plough, Sword and Book*. London: Collins Harvill. Paperback edns, University of Chicago and Paladin Grafton Books, London, 1990.

1989*g*. 'Natsii i Natsionalism', *Voprosy Filosofi* 7: 119–31. (Translation of the opening passages of 1983*e*.)

1989*l*. *Nations et nationalisme*, Paris: Bibliothèque [historique] Parpot. (French translation of 1983*e*.)

1989*m*. 'The Sacred and the National', essay review of Conor Cruise O'Brien, *Godland: Reflections on Religion and Nationalism*, *LSE Quarterly* 3 (4): 357–69.

1989*o*. 'Nationalism Today: Its Origins and Nature', transcript of a discussion with Igor Kon, *Social Sciences* [USSR] 20 (4): 183–95.

1989*p*. 'Etnicitè, sentimento nazionale e industrialismo' in *Identitè culturali*, special issue of *Problemi di Socialismo* 3, Rome: Franco Agnelli.

1989*r*. 'Natsionalizm vozvrashchaietsa' (Nationalism returns) in *Novaia i novieishiya Istoria* (Modern and Recent History) 5:55–62.

1990*c*. 'The Dramatis Personae of History', review of Roman Szporluk, *Communism and Nationalism: Karl Marx versus Friedrich List*, *East European Politics and Societies* 4 (1): 116–33.

1990*o*. Interview with V. Borshchev, 'O Prirode Natsionalisma' ('About the Nature of Nationalism'), *Znanie Sila* (Moscow) 7 (7:757): 0–5.

1990*u*. 'Nationen Imperium und Ubernationale Gemeinschaft' ('Nations, Empire and the Trans National Community), in *Transit, Europaeische Revue* 1: 143–5.

1990*ad* 'Etnicita sentimento nazionale e industrialismo', *Problemi del socialismo* 3.

1991*b*. 'Nationalisme et politique en Europe de l'Est', *Le débat* 63 (January-February): 78–84.

1991c. 'An interview with Ernest Gellner by John Davis', *Current Anthropology* 32 (1): 63–71.

1991d. 'Two Escapes from History or the Hapsburg Impact on British Thought', in Alfred Bohnen and Alan Musgrave (eds.). *Wege der Vernunft, Festschrift zum siebzigsten Geburtstag von Hans Albert*, Tübingen: J. C. B. Mohr (Paul Siebeck), pp. 227–44.

1991i. *Nationalismus und Moderne*, Berlin: Rotbuch. (German translation of 1983e.)

1991j. *Narodny i Nacjonalizm*, Warsaw: Paustwowy Institut Wydawniczy. (Polish translation of 1983e.)

1991v. 'Le nationalisme en apesanteur', *terrain* 17 (October): 7–16. (French version of 1992i.)

1991w. 'Nationalism in Eastern Europe', *New Left Review* 189 (September/October): 127–36.

1991ab 'Nationalism in the New Central Europe', in Working Papers of the Institute of Sociology of the Czechoslovak Academy of Sciences, 'Prague in the New Central Europe', transcript of an international conference, 2–4 June 1990, pp. 24–27. Gellner also contributes to the discussion of his own and other papers.

1991af 'Nacionalizem', in Rudi Rizman (ed.), *O Etnonacionalizmn*. Ljubljana (Slovenia): Zbornik Studije, Kujiznica revolucionaruc teorije, pp. 239–66. (Slovenian translation of 1981j.)

1992a. 'Alle Radici delle nazioni. Tre etnie e Fondamentalismi', interview with Nicole Janigro, *Il Manifesto*, 3 March.

1992c. 'Nationalismus und rassenwahn' (Nationalism and Racial Madness), *Süddeutsche Zeitung* 6 (7 February): 26–27.

1992i. 'Nationalism in the Vacuum', in Alexander J. Motyl (ed.), *Thinking Theoretically About Soviet Nationalities*. New York: Columbia University Press, pp. 243–54.

1992n. 'Prishestvie Natsionalisma: Mify Natsii i Klassa' (The Coming of Nationalism: Myths of Nation and Class.), *Put'* (The Way) 1: 9–61.

1992s. *Uluslar ve Ulusculuk*, trans. by B. E. Behar and G. F. Özdogan. Istanbul: Insan Yazinlari. (Turkish translation of 1983e.)

1992v. 'Nationalismus und Politik in Osteuropa', *Prokla 87* 22 (2), Berlin: Rotbuch Verlag, pp. 242–52. (German translation of 1991w.)

1992x. 'Beyond Nationalism?' (in German as 'Jenseits des Nationalismus?'), *IKUS Lectures*, Nr. 3+4, Wien: Institut fur Kulturstudien 1992, pp. 31–44, discussion pp. 45–52.

1992aa 'Nationalism Reconsidered and E. H. Carr', *Review of International Studies* 18: 285–93.

1992ae 'Cé' il nazionalismo non le nazioni', interview with Annamaria Guadefni, *L'Unità* (Roma), 20 September.

1992ai Articles 'Linguistic Philosophy' (pp. 339–40), 'Nation' (pp. 402–03), 'Nationalism' (pp. 409–11), 'Psychoanalysis' (pp. 524–27), 'Unconscious' (pp. 682–83) in William Outhwaite, Tom Bottomore, E. Gellner, R. Nisbet and A. Touraine (eds.). *The Blackwell Dictionary of Twentieth-Century Social Thought*. Oxford: Blackwell.

1993b. *Národy a Nacionalismus* (Nations and Nationalism), trans. Jirí Markus, with a new preface by the author, written in Czech, Praha: Hríbal. (Czech translation of 1983*e*.)

1993*f. Nacoes e Nacionalismo*, trans. Inez vaz Pinto, Lisbon: Gradiva. (Portuguese translation of 1983*e*.)

1993*i*. 'Reborn from Below: The Forgotten Beginnings of the Czech National Revival', review of Jan Patocka, *Co Jsou Cesi? Was Sind die Tschechen?*, *The Times Literary Supplement* 4702 (14 May): 3–5.

1993*j*. 'Nationalism in a Post-Marxist World: Contemporary Reflections', in Mario Buttino (ed.), *In a Collapsing Empire*. Milan: Feltinelli, pp. 83–8.

1993*k. Natsii i Natsionalism*, trans. T. V. Berdikova, M. K. Tynnkine, post-word by I. I. Krupnik, Moscow: Progress [dated 1991]. (Russian translation of 1983*e* with a new preface by the author.)

1993*l*. 'Nationalizem in politika v Vzhodni Europi', *Teorije in Praksa* 30 (3–4): 191–8. (Slovenian translation of 1991*w*.)

1993*o*. 'Nationalisms and the New World Order', in L. W. Reed and C. Keyser (eds.). *Emerging Norms of Justified Intervention*. Cambridge, MA: Committee on International Security Studies, American Academy of Arts and Sciences, pp. 151–5.

1993*s*. 'Il mito della nazione e quello delle classe', in P. Anderson, M. Aymard, P. Bairoch, W. Barberis, C. Ginzburg and G. Einaudi (eds.). *Stori d'Europa*, vol. 1, *L'Europa Oggi*, Torino: Editore Guilio Einaudi, pp. 638–89. (Italian translation of 1992*n*. See also 1996*i*)

1993*v*. 'Natsionalism v postmarksistskaia Sinat', *Kultura* 15 (October 1993): 5. (Bulgarian translation of 1991*w*.)

1993*x*. 'Nationalism and Politics in Eastern Europe', *European Review* 1 (4): 341–5.

1993*y*. 'Nationalism in Europe', in A. Clesse and A. Kortunov (eds.). *The Political and Strategic Implications of the State Crises in Central and Eastern Europe*. Luxembourg: Institute for European and International Studies, pp. 29–32 and discussion 299–335.

1993*ae* Review of Peter Buck, *Folk Cultures and Little Peoples: Aspects of National Awakening in East Central Europe*, *Ethnos* 58 (3–4): 406.

1994*a*. 'Nationalisms and the New World Order', *Bulletin of the American Academy of Arts and Sciences* 47 (5): 29–36.

1994*e. Naties en Nationelisme*. Amsterdam: Wereldbibliotek. (Dutch translation, by Magna van Soest, of 1983*e*.)

1994*f*. 'Nacionelizmus a politike ve vychochni Europe' (Nationalism and politics in East Europe), in *Mezineroshni vztahy* (International Relations)4 (19): 20–9. (Czech translation of 1991*w*.)

1994*h*. Interview, 'Natsii i Nationalizm' (Nations and Nationalism), with L. Anninskii and I. Mamaladze, *Obshchaia Gazeta*, Moscow, 10/35, March, pp. 11–17.

1994*i. Conditions of Liberty: Civil Society and Its Rivals*. London: Hamish Hamilton. Pp. x + 225.

1994*n*. 'Lawrence of Moravia, Alois Musil, Monotheism and the Hapsburg Empire', *The Times Literary Supplement* 4768 (19 August): 12–14.

1994*p*. 'Nationalism and Modernization' and 'Nationalism and High Cultures', in John Hutchinson and Anthony D. Smith (eds.). *Nationalism*. Oxford

Readers, Oxford: Oxford University Press, pp. 55–62 and 63–69. (Extracts from 1965*a* and 1983*e*.)

1994*s*. *Encounters with Nationalism*, Oxford: Blackwell. Contains: 1990*c*, 1992*aa*, 1989*r*, 1990*q*, 1989*m*, 1987*n*, 1990*l*, 1992*al*, 1993*i*, 1993*u*, 1993*a*, 1992*d*, 1993*s*. Also contains, as chapter 7, 'Kemalism', pp. 81–91, not previously published.

1994*w*. 'Rahvused ja rahvuslus' (Nations and Nationalism), *Akadeemia* 10: 2207–38 and 11: 2429–62. (Estonian translation by Anneti Andresson of 1983*e*.)

1994*z*. *Leumin uLeumit*. Tel Aviv: Open University Press. New preface, pp. 7–12. (Hebrew translation of 1983*e*.)

1994*aa* 'Mitul natiunnii si mitul claselor' (Myth of Nations and Myth of Classes), *Polis* 2. (Romanian version of 1993*s*.)

1994*ad* 'Rahvused ja rahvuslus' (Nations and Nationalism), *Akadeemia* 12. (Third Instalment of Estonian Translation of 1983*e*; see 1994*w*.)

1995*b*. 'Rahuvused ja rahvuskus' (Nations and Nationalism), *Akadeemia* 7. Aastekëik, no. 1, pp. 197–222. (Fourth installment of Estonian translation of 1983*e*; see also 1994*w* and 1994*ad*.)

1995*g*. 'Rahrusel ja rahruslus', *Akademia* 7 (2): 420–446. (Fifth installment of Estonian translation of 1983*e*.)

1995*h*. 'Rahrusel ja rahruslus', *Akademia* 7 (3): 643–63. (Sixth and final installment of Estonian translation of 1983*e*, with a biographical note at pp. 665–70 by Eero Loone.)

1995*w*. 'Introduction' to Sukumar Periwal (ed.), *Notions of Nationalism*. Budapest: CEU Press, pp. 1–7.

1995*x*. *Anthropology and Politics: Revolutions in the Sacred Grove*. Oxford: Blackwell. Contains: 1992*k*, 1988*b*, 1988*v*, 1989*i*, 1996*a*, 1985*h*, 1994*l*, 1990*v*, 1987*k*, 1993*af*, 1991*z*, 1991*k*, 1991*c*, 1994*n*, 1992*q*, 1995*p*.

1995*y*. 'Introduction: Nationalism and Xenophobia', to Bernd Baumgartl and Adrian Favell (eds.). *New Xenophobia in Europe*. London: Kluwer Law International, pp. 6–9.

1996*g*. 'Reply to Critics', in John A. Hall and Ian C. Jarvie (eds.). *The Social Philosophy of Ernest Gellner*. Amsterdam: Rodopi, pp. 623–86.

1996*i*. 'The Coming of Nationalism and Its Interpretation: The Myths of Nation and Class', in G. Balakrishnan (ed.), *Mapping the Nation*. London: Verso, pp. 98–145. (English version of 1993*s*.)

1997 *Nationalism*. London: Weidenfeld; New York: New York University Press.

Index

aesthetics 88, 99
al-Ghazzali 21, 184
anthropology 113–22, 125, 129, 141, 156
  in America 113, 175
  in Britain 113, 120–2, 140–1
  in Central and Eastern Europe 10, 13,
    113, 115, 120, 125, 130–2, 134, 136,
    140
  see also Frazer
antisemitism 11, 33, 45, 83, 100–5, 108–9
Associationism 5, 48–9, 116–18
atomism 4–10, 60, 181, 190
  exemplified by *Tractatus* 46, 61, 66, 88,
    93, 105, 108, 190
  ironised 17, 108–9
  leads to solitary confinement 43, 45, 61,
    93–7, 139
  problems with 17–18, 48–57, 88, 182–4,
    188
  of Frazer 115, 133
  see also ethic of cognition, Hume,
    individualism, Kant
Austin, J. L. 172
Avenarius, R. H. L. 127
'Awakeners', national 13, 32, 83, 130

Beller, S. 36
Bohemia *see* Czechs
Bolzano, B. 11
Boltzmann, L. 87
Boswell, J. L. 92
Britain 9–10, 113, 129, 141, 165, 168–9, 184
British Empire 113, 142, 168, 175
bureaucracy 9, 11, 12, 17, 29, 31–2, 78,
  124, 131
Burke, E. 9, 10, 135
Burkhardt, J. 107

Cambridge 160, 165–6
Carnap, R. 184, 190
Cartesian ego 43–5, 60–1, 63, 80–1, 92–7,
  105, 107, 139, 159

Coleridge, S. 9
colonialism 120–2, 135, 141–4, 175, 176
communalism *see* organicism
cosmic exile *see* Cartesian ego
cosmopolitanism 13, 18–19, 32, 38–9, 72,
  75, 77, 82, 83, 95, 103, 138–9
Counter-Reformation 11, 30
Cracow 123, 125, 127, 136, 138, 143
Croats 104
Crusoe, Robinson 3, 17, 47, 182, 184, 186,
  187, 190
culture(s) 190
  absence in *Tractatus* 68–70, 79, 90, 93,
    105, 159
  basis of nationalist order 11, 22, 24, 28,
    37, 76, 139, 144
  defined 5
  diversity of 118
  and language 6, 30, 147–8
  and life 186, 190
  key to *Philosophical Investigations* 72,
    77–8, 98, 105, 145, 160–1, 166,
    171–2, 187
  'low' v. 'high' 22, 24, 28, 32, 103, 131,
    136, 185
  opposed by atomists 5–6, 43, 96, 139
  and relativism 186–8, 191
  of science 186, 191
  in social anthropology 121, 131, 133,
    135
Czechs/Czech lands 10, 31, 34, 104, 131

Darwin, C./Darwinism 19, 24–5, 103,
  114–16, 128–9
death 62–4, 70, 80, 98, 109
Descartes, R. 72, 77, 96, 161
  hostile to culture 43, 96
  source of atomist tradition 7, 15, 43, 96,
    176, 182–4
  and substance 52, 96
  see also Cartesian ego
Durkheim, E. 66, 118

education 22, 27–8, 131, 144, 169
1848, revolutions of 10, 31, 35, 127
Eliot, T. S. 108, 119
Ellen, R. 123
empiricism
  Durkheim's critique of 118
  and experiments 153
  and functionalism 133–4
  Hume exemplifies 47
  and language 167
  Malinowski's use of 135, 139–40
  part of atomist tradition 15, 17, 139,
    169, 189–90
  and perception 4, 44, 51, 55, 62–3, 98,
    116
  stress on observation 128, 131, 133
  of the *Tractatus* 59–61, 94–5
Enlightenment, the 17, 21, 23–4, 32, 66,
  76, 102
ethic of cognition 15, 48, 183–4, 188
ethnography 10, 13, 114, 120, 130–2,
  135–6, 140, 149
Evans-Pritchard, E. E. 175
evolutionism 114–17, 119, 120

fact/value separation 87–8, 91–2, 94–5, 190
fieldwork *see* ethnography
First World War 63, 79, 114
Firth, R. 123, 155
Flis, A. 128
Franklin, B. 184
Frazer, J. 66, 113–21, 127, 130, 135, 137,
  156
Freud, S. 20, 25, 82, 91, 103
functionalism 120–1, 127, 128, 133–5,
  140, 150–1; *see also* language

Galicia 136, 138, 143
Gallie, B. 129
Geertz, C. 175
German 12, 138
German-speakers 11, 31, 34, 104
Gibbon, E. 118
Goethe, J. W. von 104, 152, 176
Golden Bough, The 115, 127
Górale 132, 160
Greece 116
Green, T. H. 141
Gumplowicz, L. 138

Habsburg Empire 59, 168
  dilemma of 13, 34, 37–9, 74–5, 79, 85,
    86, 105, 145, 182, 188
  ends up supported only by liberals
    11–12, 32–4, 138, 143
  Janik and Toulman on 90–3

Malinowski's appreciation of 136, 143–4
  nationalists in 12, 30–4, 38–9, 71–2,
    104, 143
  position of Jews 11, 33, 36
  transformation of 10–12, 30–8
  see also Kakania
Hayek, F. A. von 12
Hegelianism 16, 60, 124–5, 129, 131,
  134–5, 141, 169, 184
Heidegger, M. 154
Herder, J. G. von 24, 34, 77, 125
Hertz, H. 87
Hitler, A. 101
Hobbes, T. 9
Hoggart, R. 9–10
holism *see* communalism
Hroch, M. 13
Hume, D. 63, 77–8
  contrasted with Wittgenstein 44, 47–50,
    55, 107
  ethics of 17, 47–8, 97
  and fact/value separation 91–2
  and induction 44, 49, 72, 128; cf. 50, 55
  links to Frazer 116–18, 156
  paradigmatic atomist 8, 15–16, 47,
    182–4, 190
  and the self 44, 96–7
Husserl, E. 154

Indirect Rule 142–3
individualism 13, 86
  as an English tradition 9
  of assimilated Jews 35
  of knowledge 3–4, 7–8, 15–16, 181
  problems with 15, 181–3
  as social trend 26–7
  as theory of science 15
  of Wittgenstein 65–7, 75, 79, 93, 105
  Wittgenstein opposes 145
  see also atomism
industrialisation 22–3, 26–7, 32

Jagiellonian University 125
James, W. 59–60, 129
Janik, A. 85–95, 97, 105
Jews 11, 33–6, 45, 82–4, 100–5, 108, 125,
  138
Jung, C. G. 119

Kafka, F. 81, 107
Kakania 29–31, 94–5, 98, 105–6, 165, 182,
  188
Kant, I. 45, 69, 77–8, 107
  as embodiment of Protestant ethic 184
  and fact/value separation 91
  and ethics 17, 66

paradigmatic atomist 15–16, 47, 49, 182–4, 190
and the self 96–7
and structure 49–50, 128
Kedourie, E. 166
Keynes, J. M. 168–9
Kierkegaard, S. 87, 89
Kipling, R. 176
Kraus, K. 87, 91, 105

language
functional theory of 145–8, 151–2, 155, 160
Malinowski on 145–56
as model for *structuralisme* 122
and nationalism 11–13, 24, 28, 31, 83, 131–2, 155
in *Tractatus* 54, 59–62, 65, 68–9, 80, 83, 86, 88, 98
in *Philosophical Investigations* 72, 83–4, 86, 94–5, 98, 145, 166, 156, 162
Latin 12, 31
Lawrence, D. H. 9–10, 19, 76
Lawrence, T. E. 166
Leach, E. 129
League of Nations 143
Leibniz, G. W. 52, 64
Lemberg 127
Lévi-Strauss, C. 122
liberalism
classic works of 12, 35
defeated in 1848 35, 127
ends by supporting Empire 11–12, 32–4, 138, 143
espoused by Jews 33–6, 138
failed to foresee nationalism 22
in 1848 makes common cause with nationalism 10, 31, 127
Malinowski's 141
opposed to nationalism 18, 20, 38, 45, 79, 104, 138, 139, 145
shares common roots with nationalism 27
Wittgenstein's 66, 75
linguistic philosophy 72, 160–73
logic
difficulty of 169
and phenomenalism 171
rejected by 'later' Wittgenstein 61, 76, 145, 170
reveals structure of language 57, 59, 64, 75
status in *Tractatus* 98
underlies ontology of *Tractatus* 46, 48, 53–4, 57, 61, 63–4, 65, 87, 108
LSE 120–1

Lueger, K. 75

Macfarlane, A. 9
Mach, E. 16, 93, 97, 124,, 127–9, 133–4, 139, 190
Magyars 34, 104
Malinowski, B.
achievement of 120, 137
compared to Wittgenstein 125–6, 138–9, 151–2, 154–5, 177, 187
and Frazer 113–14, 119, 133, 135, 137
and history 120–1, 133–6, 139
intellectual influences 127–37
on language 145–56
originality of 120, 133, 135, 137, 140
uses of in Poland 174
politics of 136, 139–44, 187–8
and science 120, 127, 140, 148–50, 152
Maine, H. 14
de Maistre, J. 21
Malcolm, N. 74, 86
Marxism 22, 74, 76, 122
Mauriac, F. 50
Mauthner, F. 105
melting pot thesis 22
Metternich, Prince C. W. L. 30
Monk, K. 63, 156
Moravia 131
Morocco 129–30
Morris, W. 9
Mucha, J. 142
Musil, R. 29

Namier, L. 138
nationalism/-ists 10, 27–8, 37, 72, 79, 127, 129
creates nations 23–4, 29, 32, 37, 82, 130
cultural versus political 79, 136–7, 139, 143–4
and ethnography 115, 120, 130–2, 136
'false consciousness' of 22, 24, 32, 37, 76, 104, 185
'genuine' 11
hostile to Jews 33, 35–9, 83, 102
ironised 72–3, 131–2
philosophical basis of 18–19, 21–5, 37–8, 102–6
Nietzsche, F. 20, 24–5, 82, 103, 107

Oakeshott, M. 9–10
Ogden, C. K. 146–7, 155, 174
organicism
and the Jews 100–106
as found in Britain 9–10
failed to produce masterpieces 34

organicism (*cont.*)
  as one of two basic options 5–6, 8, 10,
    12, 13, 85–6, 94, 181–2
  problems with 184–8
  see also nationalism, romanticism,
    traditionalism
Oxford 121, 149, 160–1, 165–6, 168–70

Paluch, A. 125
Pascal, B. 56
Patočka, J. 11
Pausanias 116
Philosophical Investigations 71, 98, 149; *see
  also* language
philosophy
  as anguish 91, 107
  as attempt to understand emergence of
    science 91–2, 95, 182–4, 189–90
  as disease of language 72, 77, 149, 162,
    162, 166–8, 191
  as doubt 44
  as elegant reassurance 60
  leaves everything as it is 145, 161–3,
    171–3
  mainstream of 15, 43, 63, 92, 107, 183
  as mystical 91
  remodels the world 183–4
  of science 15, 77, 87, 89, 127, 147, 171
  as specifying substances 52, 96
  as therapy 145, 164, 167
  see also atomism, empiricism
Platonists 149, 167
pluralism 11, 12, 74, 82, 187
Poland 124–5, 135–6, 138–9, 143, 174
Popper, K. 12, 138
propositional calculus *see* logic
positivism 86, 88, 123–4, 127–8, 135, 140,
    153, 175, 183
pragmatism 129
propositional calculus *see* logic

Quine, W. van O. 43, 96

Radcliffe-Brown, A. R. 121–2, 175
rationalism 19, 32, 67; cf. 162
relativism 161, 171–3, 177, 185; cf. 56
Richards, I. A. 146–7
romanticism
  basis of nationalism 18, 21–4, 38, 75, 104
  definition of 185
  disliked by Westermarck 129–30
  flaws in 184–5
  in anthropology 175–6
  in Britain 9–10
  philosophy of 17–20, 102–3, 185
  in Poland 123–5, 127

transcended by Malinowski 141
used by Malinowski 130, 135, 140
of Wittgenstein 63, 75–6
  see also communalism
roots *see* nationalism
Rousseau, J.-J. 97
Rumanians 34
Russell, B. 9, 16, 63, 76–7, 87, 93, 107,
    133, 169, 190
Russia 115, 127, 130, 136

Schiller, F. 17
Schopenhauer, A. 16, 58, 62, 99, 103
Schorske, C. 35–6
Schnitzler, A. 91, 138
science
  atomism as mythic charter of 15, 48,
    182–4, 190
  in British education 169
  centrality of 188–9
  conflicts with common sense 161, 171
  defined 92
  and Frazer 117
  and language 146–50, 152
  limits of 191
  and Malinowski 120, 127, 140, 148–50,
    152
  origins of 151–3, 183
  philosophy of 15, 77, 87, 89, 127, 147,
    171
  social effects of 189
  in the *Tractatus* 105
  v. pre-scientific though 52, 142–3,
    148–50
Scott, W. 9
Scruton, R. 9
Second World War 141–2, 160
set theory *see* logic
Slavs 34, 104
social anthropology *see* anthropology
solipsism *see* Cartesian ego
Soviet Union 101, 127
Spinoza, B. 52
Sraffa, P. 156
status 14, 26, 28, 38, 44–5, 76
Strawson, P. 172

Tawney, R. H. 9
Tolstoy, L. B. 77, 87, 89
Toulmin, S. 85–95, 97, 105
Tractatus 46–71, 74, 97–8, 139, 146, 149,
    151
  absence of culture in 68–70, 79, 105,
    159
  as exemplar of atomist tradition 46, 61,
    66, 85, 88, 105, 107–8, 184, 190

genesis of 87–8, 93–5, 105
ironised 108–9
masochistic pessimism of 39, 51, 56–64,
    80–1, 93, 107, 159–60
mysticism in 65–7, 70, 89–90, 98
traditionalism 7, 9, 21, 162, 184–5
Transcendental Ego *see* Cartesian ego
Trobriand Islands 132
Turks 30

Versailles, Peace of 143, 146
Vienna 11, 34–6, 63, 75, 79, 86–8, 108,
    145
  Congress of 11, 143
  contrasted with Cracow 123–4, 127–8,
    138–9
Vienna Circle 169

Webb, S. and B. 9
Weber, M. 26, 30, 184, 187
Weininger, O. 97
Werther, The Sorrows of the Young 63, 122,
    176
Westermarck, E. 129–31
Whitehead, A. 63, 87
Williams, R. 9–10
Winch, P. 171
Witkiewicz, S. I. 136
Wittgenstein, L.
  in Cambridge 160, 165–6

compared to Malinowski 125–6, 138–9,
    151–2, 154–6, 177, 187
  and ethics 87–8, 90–1, 98–9, 163
  influence of 159, 164–8, 177
  later philosophy of 71–8, 86, 94–5, 98,
    106, 145, 147, 159–64
  lived history in reverse 47, 174, 187,
    191
  masochistic pessimism of 39, 51, 56–64,
    80–1, 93, 107, 159–60
  and mysticism 65–7, 75, 87–91, 93, 98,
    105, 177
  originality of 46, 67, 72, 75–8, 107, 147,
    187
  possible influence of Malinowski on 146,
    155–6
  romanticism of 63, 75–6
  as schoolmaster 85, 95, 160
  style of 46–8, 50–1, 57, 59, 65, 68, 75,
    80, 90, 107, 167
  unawareness of culture or politics 68–72,
    74, 76, 85–7, 90–1, 98, 145, 188
  in World War I 63, 79, 95
Wordsworth, W. 9

Yugoslavia 130, 144

Zakopane 123, 125, 132, 124
Zionism 104